REGULATING FINANCE

Regulating Finance

Balancing Freedom and Risk

TOMMASO PADOA-SCHIOPPA

OXFORD
UNIVERSITY PRESS

OXFORD

UNIVERSITY PRESS

Great Clarendon Street, Oxford OX2 6DP

Oxford University Press is a department of the University of Oxford.
It furthers the University's objective of excellence in research, scholarship,
and education by publishing worldwide in

Oxford New York

Auckland Bangkok Buenos Aires Cape Town Chennai
Dar es Salaam Delhi Hong Kong Istanbul Karachi Kolkata
Kuala Lumpur Madrid Melbourne Mexico City Mumbai Nairobi
São Paulo Shanghai Taipei Tokyo Toronto

Oxford is a registered trade mark of Oxford University Press
in the UK and in certain other countries

Published in the United States
by Oxford University Press Inc., New York

© Tommaso Padoa-Schioppa 2004

The moral rights of the authors have been asserted

Database right Oxford University Press (maker)

First published 2004

British Library Cataloguing in Publication Data

Data available

Library of Congress Cataloging in Publication Data

Data available

ISBN 0-19-927056-2

1 3 5 7 9 10 8 6 4 2

Typeset by Newgen Imaging Systems (P) Ltd., Chennai, India
Printed in Great Britain
on acid-free paper by
Biddles Ltd., King's Lynn, Norfolk

Contents

Preface

After decades of neglect, financial regulation and supervision have moved to the forefront of policy making. Practitioners, academics, officials and politicians have engaged in a public debate much in the same way as they did for monetary policy since the 1950s.

Several factors have contributed to the rise in interest in public policy aspects of financial activity. The first is the reappearance of financial *instability*. After many decades of tranquillity, a series of banking and financial crises have hit—from the 1980s onwards—a number of industrial and emerging economies as well as the global financial system. This called for extensive use of taxpayers' money and raised questions about the adequacy of the regulatory framework that had been designed in the aftermath of the financial crises of the 1930s.

A second factor is the phenomenal *expansion* of finance relative to the real economy, an expansion due to the rise in wealth, the widening split between savings and investment, the institutionalisation of saving, and the swelling of public sector deficits. The financial sector, which has traditionally been among those where public intervention was most pervasive, grew to such an extent that its regulation climbed to the top of political priorities.

A third factor were the advancements in *technology*, which made it possible to circumvent many regulatory barriers and segmentations erected to safeguard financial stability and reduce competition. Real time, remote, or intra-day finance and the development of trading outside formally organised markets have rapidly subverted the basis on which traditional regulatory instruments rested.

Financial *innovation*, partly driven by new technologies in the processing and transmission of information, was a fourth factor. A wave of new products, new market infrastructures, new trading and settlement systems, and new risk management practices completely transformed the financial industry. Regulation and supervision could not ignore the progressive blurring of the segmentation between the three traditional fields of finance: banking, securities, and insurance.

A fifth factor was the *globalisation* of finance, whereby financial transactions were less and less conducted in the closed world of nation states and increasingly implicated more than one country, one currency, one regulatory and legal system, and one supervisor.

A sixth and final factor was the change in the mission and institutional profile of *central banks*. Less than fifteen years ago, most central banks were still agencies charged with the defence of all public interests associated with the currency and the financial system, under rather strict dependence on the executive branch of the government. Since then, they have turned into independent institutions, strongly focused on the pursuit of price stability, and often deprived of the function of supervising and regulating banks.

While none of the factors above is exclusively, or even predominantly, European, two further specific developments made the aforementioned factors particularly relevant for Europe. Such developments were the creation of a single market for banking and financial services in 1986-93 and the adoption of a single currency for most EU countries in 1999. The EU became an exceptionally fertile ground to nurture a debate on fundamental issues of financial regulation. An entirely new legislation had to be drafted and negotiated. Definitions for basic components of the financial system (such as a bank, a market, settlement, etc.) had to be formulated. The charter of a new central bank had to written, in which all the aspects of central banking, including the involvement in financial stability, had to be reconsidered.

The essays collected in this book result from my involvement in the developments summarised above. With one exception, they were all written after the start the euro, when I was serving in the European Central Bank. Only some of them are devoted to issues specifically arising from the adoption of the euro. Most address issues which are not specifically European. Yet, the reflections they present owe a great deal to the intellectual stimulus provided by the adoption of a single currency in Europe. Indeed, the unprecedented event of creating a Monetary Union out of a set of still largely independent states, which—among other things—retain ample regulatory and supervisory powers in the field of finance, requires by itself considerable thought about regulatory and supervisory issues in new and consistent terms.

Whatever merits this book may have, credit for them goes to Charles Goodhart in the first place. Charles encouraged me to organise my thoughts and to present them in three lectures at the London School of Economics. He has been a most stimulating partner in a number of discussions, seminars, and conferences in which commonality of interests, similarities in intellectual approach and fruitful occasional disagreement enriched and filtered my thoughts. He then invited me to collect the lectures and other essays in a book, advised me on the selection and wrote the introduction. I owe a great deal to his intellectual finesse, solid judgement, and generosity.

In the preparation of the book, but also very much in relation to some of the essays (notably Chapters 2, 4, 5, 7 and 8), Jukka Vesala has been a skilful, competent and very efficient assistant. The same is true for Andrea Enria with respect to Chapters 1 and 2. The two of them and Mauro Grande have been stimulating partners in innumerable discussions about the issues treated in this book. Ariana Mongelli has carefully reviewed the drafts to ensure consistency in the language and to remove the traces of non-native English. Claudia Ferrari has patiently and skilfully managed the manuscript. To all of them, as well as to many staff members of the European Central Bank, who have actively joined internal discussions at various occasions, I express my gratitude. Opinions and errors are only mine. Finally, I would also like to express my appreciation to the Oxford University Press, for again being interested in publishing my output.

Foreword

By C. A. E. Goodhart

Three of the essays in this book by Tommaso Padoa-Schioppa were originally given as lectures at the London School of Economics. I was involved in the organisation of each of these occasions, (and also had the privilege of acting as one of the discussants on the occasion of the presentation and discussion of the paper that forms the concluding essay of this book). After Tommaso had given his third LSE lecture in May 2002, I suggested to him that I would like to assist him in publishing a selection of his recent papers (one given in 1996, two in 1999, two in 2000, and three in 2002) on financial regulation. A salient reason for my suggestion is that Tommaso (perhaps alongside Alexandre Lamfalussy), has been the most prominent official practitioner of financial regulation in Europe, at a time when such regulation has been subject to major upheavals of focus and structure. Such changes are so profound that it will be important to report a snapshot of how the evolving scene of financial regulation, especially within the context of the evolution of the European Union and the euro-zone, looked at the turn of the twenty-first century.

First, let me record something about the man. Tommaso comes from the heart of European civilisation, northern Italy, where he was born in Belluno in 1940. He studied at Bocconi University, and then, like so many leading young Italian economists, was attracted to MIT by the influence of Franco Modigliani. After his graduation from Bocconi he worked for a small investment house (C&A Brenninkmeyer) for some two and a half years in Italy, Germany, and elsewhere, before joining the Banca d'Italia in 1968. His manifold qualities as an economist, an administrator, a linguist, and a diplomat (to name but a few) were soon recognised; he was promoted rapidly to a position of Head of the Money Market Division of the Research Department.

From there he was appointed in 1979 to be Director-General for Economic and Financial Affairs in the European Commission in Brussels. This, in effect, meant that he had burst from the Italian stage onto the world scene, also becoming a Member of the European Monetary Committee in 1979, a participant in the Committee of Governors and the Group of Ten, and a Member of the informal but prestigious Group of Thirty. He returned to the Banca d'Italia in 1983 to become, initially, Central Director for Economic Research, and then, a year later, Deputy Director General (1984–97). During the earlier part of that period, he served as one of the joint Secretaries to the Delors Committee for the study of European Economic and Monetary Union (EMU) from 1988 to 1989.

During his period of office as Deputy Director of the Banca d'Italia, his responsibilities increasingly were inclined towards financial regulation, not only in Italy, but also internationally. In 1988 he became Chairman of the Banking Advisory Committee of the European Commission (1988–91), and later Chairman of the Working Group on Payment Systems of the Central Banks of the European Community (1991–95), a role that led him onto the European Monetary Institute, where he was an Alternate Member of the Council (1995–97).

On an even wider stage, he became Chairman of the Basel Committee on Banking Supervision (1993–97), where he led the Committee towards the milestone of adopting a market-friendly use of models for the calculation of capital requirements against market risk. This was hailed, both at the time and subsequently, as a great step forward from prescriptive requirements to building on current best practices in the banking field.

In 1997, his career took a step sideways, from bank regulator to securities regulator, when he became Chairman of Consob (Commissione Nazionale per le Società e la Borsa), roughly the Italian equivalent of the SEC in the United States of America. He has remained fascinated by the connections and divisions between the securities industry and the banking system ever since, as two of his essays, notably Essays 5 and 8, testify.

His international prestige was such that, shortly after taking over as Chairman of Consob, he was appointed as both Chairman of the European Regional Committee of IOSCO and also Chairman of Forum of the European Securities Commissions (FESCO). But these positions were not to be held for long. On 1 June 1998, the six-man Board of the European Central Bank was appointed for the first time, and Tommaso became one of the founding fathers of the European Central Bank (ECB).

With his background, it was both inevitable and appropriate that Tommaso has taken the main responsibility at the ECB for regulatory issues, though he himself is reluctant to accept such attribution (within a collegiate Board), and moreover his responsibilities have extended to other issues as well, including relationships with the Accession Countries. Be that as it may, when one thinks about the ECB's approach to financial regulation, one's thoughts naturally turn to Tommaso.

Besides his main role at the ECB, he has continued to be a major player on the larger world scene, a member of both the G7 Deputies (since 1998) and the G20 Deputies (since 1999), and Chairman of the G10 Committee on Payments and Settlement Systems (since 2000). But his heart lies with the development of the European (financial) system as indicated by his three main (English language) books, to wit:

(1) *Efficiency, Stability and Equity: A Strategy for the Evolution of the Economic System of the European Community* (Oxford University Press, 1987);
(2) *Europe: The Impossible Status Quo* (Macmillan, 1997); and
(3) *The Road to Monetary Union in Europe: The Emperor, the Kings and the Genies* (Oxford University Press, 2000).

It was in the latter two publications that Tommaso devised his impossibility theorem that: (*a*) free movement of goods, (*b*) free movement of capital, (*c*) pegged (or fixed) exchange rates, and (*d*) national control of domestic monetary policy could not all exist side-by-side. At least one of these objectives had to go. As a keen European, Tommaso had absolutely no doubts that the correct choice was to abandon national control over domestic monetary policy in favour of a European (federal) monetary policy.

Tommaso has been both influential, and fortunate, to play a leading role in the establishment of his main professional objective, the establishment of a European currency, and of a European System of Central Banks (ESCB) to run the euro-zone. But, as with so much elsewhere in Europe, advances in constitutional and institutional design have taken place at an uneven pace. In particular, the centralisation of macro-monetary policy at the federal level has preceded any equivalent centralisation of fiscal policy competences or of banking and financial supervision. I shall myself comment further on the former of these disjunctions later in this Forward. It is the latter disjunction between the continuing national control of banking (and more broadly financial) supervision and the federal (euro-zone) control of monetary policy that forms a major subject of several of Tommaso's recent papers, and is highlighted here in Essays 7 and 8.

This is a convenient point to turn from Tommaso's own career to a brief description of the context, both within Europe and within the ongoing evolution of international financial regulation, which forms the background to this book. But before I do so, I would like to record several of Tommaso's qualities, which make him such a pleasure to work with and have been so appreciated by his vast range of personal friends. These include grace, courtesy, and kindness (behind which lurks a fierce determination), a deep and formidable intelligence, and an ability to give a calm and unhurried appreciation of the problems of others; in short the epitome of European and northern Italian civilisation.

As Tommaso notes, especially in the opening more historical essays, the trend of the last few decades has been from segmentation, both by financial function and geographically between separate nation states, to a financial system which has become more competitive across functions—leading to universal banks undertaking banking, securities business, and insurance—and across nations. These trends have been primarily driven by technology, but have also owed much to a resurgence of confidence in market capitalism (as contrasted with socialist or communist central direction). Direct controls of all kinds, notably credit controls over banks and exchange controls, have been removed in pursuit of efficiency, innovation, and growth.

Such earlier direct controls had turned banks into safe but boring public utilities lending primarily to the public sector and to large private sector manufacturing companies. Deregulation allowed banks greater freedom to experiment and to choose their own risk/return combinations. This entailed a greater danger of bank failure, a failure which could cause wider systemic losses to the economy as a whole than would fall on the individual manager, shareholder or depositor (especially after the extension of deposit insurance amongst a wider range of countries) of the individual bank at risk.

The enhanced competition, after segmentation was abandoned, led to greater competition, declining profit margins and capitalisation, falling capital ratios and worsening problems of bank failures, (in some cases systemic, for example, the

LDC crisis in 1982, Scandinavia in the early 1990s; in some cases not so, for example, Credit Lyonnais and Barings). That meant that deregulation, in the guise of the end of direct controls, had to be followed by re-regulation. But what new form of regulation?

Given the abolition of direct controls and the dominance of the ethos of market capitalism, it needed to be market-friendly regulation. But this involves something of a contradiction. Regulation is only necessary if it causes the regulated, or a subset of the regulated, to behave in a way that they would not already voluntarily do. So the balance between prescriptive requirements and enhancing existing procedures and current forms of market discipline is difficult to get just right.

Moreover, in the increasingly international context, financial regulation has to be equivalently imposed in all the major financial centres. Otherwise financial intermediation will simply migrate offshore. The way in which the developed countries handled this problem, in the absence of a world government or of international law in this field, was ad hoc and pragmatic, via the Basel Committee of Banking Supervision, of which Tommaso was Chairman from 1994 to 1997. But it has also been broadly successful, thanks to the hard work and sense of officials like Tommaso.

Because the Basel Committee has had no formal or legal status the various agreements ironed out in this Committee had to be translated into legally binding (or at least generally accepted) formulations in all the applicable countries. This raised a set of specifically European problems with which Tommaso has had to wrestle over the last decade or two. These involve institutional problems with the adoption of euro-wide legislation. The first of these is that the European Union is typically very slow moving in the adoption of primary legislation, that is, getting agreement on, and transposition of, Directives. The second is that there is insufficient ability to undertake secondary legislation, that is, to amend and adjust primary legislation in the light of changing circumstances. Given the rapidly evolving structure of the financial system, this latter is of particular importance. There are various reasons for such problems, and various proposals for improvement, which lie outside the scope both of this Introduction and of Tommaso's essays. It has been, however, a source of frustration and of difficulty with which he has had to cope.

For most of those involved in the regulatory process, there have been two main focuses, international (especially, but not only, via Basel) and domestic. For Tommaso there are three such considerations: international, European, and domestic. He has had to try to balance all three. He has had to do so in a context in which European monetary developments have been developing as, or more, rapidly than those of international financial regulation. It is the tensions between these major trends that essentially provide the substance and key themes of this book.

One of the many reasons why it is such a pleasure to work with Tommaso is that he grounds his analysis in a thorough appreciation of the historical development of financial regulation; it is difficult, perhaps impossible, to understand the current state of such regulation without an appreciation of its prior evolution.

Essay 1, on market-friendly regulation of banks, sets the scene for the book. It describes how the Basel Committee, of which Tommaso was at that time the

Chairman, both responded to, and shaped, those emerging trends. This is an essay of considerable (historical) importance because it outlines in depth what the Basel Committee saw itself doing in the middle of the last decade.

As Tommaso records, growth of confidence in market capitalism leads to growth of confidence in the inherent disciplinary functions of markets. That naturally leads on to the question of why the banking system should be subject to any specific external, officially imposed regulation at all. Indeed, there is a large body of thought, though flourishing in North America rather than in Europe, that would challenge the rationale for the whole paraphernalia of official regulation.

Tommaso seeks to respond to the question, 'why regulate?' also in the next essay, and the replies to that question also help to shape the answers to the associated question, 'how to regulate?' In Essay 2, on licensing banks, he addresses an American audience on the continuing need to authorise and to regulate banks. In this he develops some analytical ideas that are, I believe, an important and original contribution to the intellectual debate in this field. In my view this is a key essay, perhaps the best in the book. Precisely because he was aware that he was speaking to a somewhat sceptical, even possibly hostile, audience, Tommaso took a special care to marshal his arguments with particular logic, force, and brilliance.

In this essay, Tommaso emphasises a pyramidical formation of liquidity provision within the financial system. The central bank, at the apex, is the ultimate supplier of liquidity, with 'licensed banks—as lenders of "next-to-last" resort—on the second level and various non-bank financial institutions on the third level', (see Section 2.1). A bank is defined by its function of providing instantaneous liquidity both on its liability side, via sight and demand deposits, and on its asset side, via loans to the non-bank private sector. Interlinkages between banks, in the payments system, through the money markets, and via macroeconomic developments, make the collection of individual banks into a banking system, in a way in which we would never think of an automobile or steel-producing industry system, or, say, a restaurant system. In banking, as in other industries, there is a need to reinforce competition, and, because of asymmetric information, to protect poorly informed customers. But what is special about banks is the potentiality for systemic risk, a particular form of externality. Tommaso goes on to assert that there is unlikely to be a contagious crisis unless it does involve the banking system (see Section 2.3).[1] So, the need both to license, and then to regulate banks, follows from the interaction of their key role as liquidity providers and their (associated) exposure to systemic risk.

Essay 3, on competition in banking, succinctly describes the trends in financial regulation that have dominated over the last forty or so years, effectively our own

---

[1] I have some small reservations here. Any set of financial intermediaries with liabilities which can be withdrawn on fixed nominal (or real) terms held against assets of variable market value can suffer runs. The decline in (equity) asset prices in 2002 in the UK caused large numbers of life insurance policy-holders to try to switch policies from supposedly less to more solvent companies. A full academic analysis has yet to be done, but it may well have been the ability of such life insurance companies to impose quite severe penalties on such early withdrawals that prevented any major and systemically damaging runs from developing here.

working life. It complements the picture of the special nature of banking from the competition cum financial stability angle.

Having set out the 'why' of banking regulation in Essays 2 and 3, he next turns naturally to the question of 'how' such regulation should be done in Essay 4, on self- vs. public discipline in the financial field. Here he focuses on two key dimensions. These are, first, the use of financial standards, rather than law-based prescriptions; and second, the development of 'process-oriented' regulation, drawing on financial institutions' internal control mechanisms, rather than the traditional simple and easily verifiable 'rules' (see Section 4.2). There will, I feel, be little dispute about the first such trend. Given that financial intermediation is now international in ambit and scope, and that there is no international legal structure in this field, there is, I believe, little alternative to going down the road of international agreements on codes and standards, a form of 'soft law'.

The second question, whether the regulators should aim to build on banks' own internal control processes is probably more debatable, especially now in the light of the criticisms that have been made, by myself as well as others, on Basel II. It is natural that Tommaso would support this approach because it was the one applied, with much success and acclaim, to the calibration of capital requirements to market risks when he was Chairman of the Basel Committee on Banking Supervision in 1997 (see Section 4.4). The attempt, however, to extend that same approach to the treatment of credit risk has not gone forward so smoothly; the outcome has been dauntingly complex. Questions have also been raised whether it is the proper role for the regulator to encourage all banks to mimic the behaviour pattern of current 'best practice'; may that not reinforce 'herd-like' behaviour? All this remains a difficult and contentious area.

In Essay 5, Tommaso returns to a theme, of which his background and career in Consob as well as the Basel Banking Committee, gives him unrivalled mastery—that is, the relationship between securities activities and banking. Here, he documents the growth of the European securities markets in recent years. He explains how dependent the successful functioning of such securities' markets is upon the continuous and close involvement of the banks. The process of securitisation may, indeed, have changed the risk profile of commercial banks, raising market risks relative to credit risk. This means that (systemic) risks to the banking system may nowadays be more likely to arise out of disturbances to the non-bank financial system, (LTCM may have been an example). Banks, however, are still special, as systemic crises only occur when banks get into trouble (see Section 5.3). That '... justifies the differences between the regulatory and supervisory framework relating to banking and that relating to securities' (see Section 5.4).

Up to this point Tommaso has been primarily covering general international issues concerning financial regulation, rather than specifically European issues, and indeed many of the main examples, for example, LTCM and Enron, come from outside of Europe. In the last three essays of the book he turns to issues specifically connected with EU developments. First, in Essay 6 he reviews some challenges for regulation in the European Union. This is an excellent brief introduction to current issues, including three main questions: 'one supervisor or many?', should these be 'inside or outside the central banks?', and finally 'National or European?' He concludes that 'there are clear signs that a single European financial industry is emerging'. While I would agree with that, it does not necessarily follow that a single Euroland financial regulator/supervisor is feasible or optimal in the current conjuncture. Nor does Tommaso make that jump, though he does claim that in the context of a euro-wide financial system, 'the burden of proof that competences can remain purely national lies on those who want to preserve them' (see Section 6.6).

The final two essays of the book, (along with Essay 2) are, in my view, the most important, addressing the issues with most immediate substance. Essay 7, on banking supervision in Euroland, deals with the problems of maintaining financial stability within a system where there is no longer a 'coincidence between the area of jurisdiction of monetary policy and the area of jurisdiction of banking supervision'. This is an 'important novelty of the new Euroland constitution . . .' (see Section 7.2).

In Section 7.5, dealing with crisis management, Tommaso describes three solutions: 'private money solutions', 'taxpayers' money solutions', and 'central bank money solutions'. He argues, I believe correctly, that the ESCB is as capable of handling the latter, as were national central banks on their own previously. The former two solutions, private market-based or taxpayer funding, remain, however, primarily national in character, especially the latter where Tommaso recognises that 'the introduction of the euro leaves crisis management actions involving taxpayers' money practically unaffected'. While he hardly remarks further on that point, it represents, as I shall discuss further, the Achilles heel which is likely for the foreseeable future to prevent the achievement of his own preferred objective, which I reproduce below in its entirety.

'In my view, we should move as rapidly as possible to a model in which the present division of the geographical and functional jurisdiction between monetary policy and banking supervision plays no significant role. I do not mean necessarily a single authority or a single set of prudential rules. Rather, the system of national supervisors needs to operate as effectively as a single authority when needed. Whereas the causes of banking problems are often local or national, the propagation of problems may be area-wide. The banking industry is much more of a system than other financial institutions.'

The final essay is rather longer than the others. The earlier essays were given initially as lectures, which set an effective limit on their length. Instead Essay 8, on central banking and financial stability, was prepared as a background paper for a session at the ECB's second Central Banking Conference held at Frankfurt in October 2002. Tommaso spoke, quite briefly, about the paper before it was discussed by a group of discussants, rather than reading it virtually in full, as was the case with the other Essays.

Several central banks are no longer responsible for banking supervision, including the Bank of England, the Bank of Canada, and the Bank of Japan. Nevertheless, their position means that they cannot avoid (not that they would wish to do so) a responsibility for financial stability. The central bank's responsibility for the payments' system and its unique ability to inject additional liquidity into the system, notably via the lender-of-last-resort function, ensures that conclusion. Nevertheless, the relationships between the central bank and the other players in the system, notably the separate financial/banking supervisor(s), and national Treasury remain delicate. Both the definition of, and means to achieve, financial stability are much less clear-cut, than in the case of price stability. So many of the issues are quite common internationally; Tommaso discusses several of these, for example, whether there is a conflict between price stability and financial stability (rarely) and how to handle asset price bubbles (gingerly) with customary care and sense.

In the case of Euroland, however, the scale of the problem is further aggravated by the split of jurisdiction between national supervisor and euro-wide monetary policy, an issue already discussed in Essay 7. This forms the subject matter of Section 8.8. Given that 'the euro-area is a single financial system ... the stability of the financial system ... has in effect become a euro-area-wide concern. Then he continues: 'The current approach is to fundamentally stick to the framework based on European regulation with national supervision, while trying to improve its functioning. To be effective, supervision must "see" the whole system, which is impossible without close cooperation and information sharing between central banks and supervisory authorities. Hence, to address financial stability concerns from an area-wide perspective, bilateral and especially multilateral cooperation needs to be further enhanced in the EU committee structures. The Banking Supervision Committee of the ESCB provides a platform for EU central banks and banking supervisory authorities which is being used for further deepening of cooperation and information exchange.'

I hope that I am not being unfair, or too forward, in interpreting Tommaso as wishing for a more centrally integrated structure for banking supervision within the euro-area, closely associated with the ECB. If that is a correct interpretation, then I have to state that I see a major problem with that line of approach, which relates to the different jurisdictions of a federal monetary policy and national fiscal policies in the euro-area.

This disjunction has worried me ever since I worked on the Report on Community public finance in the perspective of EMU, entitled 'Stable Money—Sound Finances', *European Economy*, no. 53, (1993). I was an outside academic expert. The report sought to assess the minimum fiscal changes that were needed to supplement a euro-wide monetary policy. Our report advocated a shift of additional competences to the federal centre, amounting to about 1 per cent of EU GDP. The funds were primarily to be targeted at the stabilisation of asymmetric shocks. The report was not accepted by the member states, and was largely ignored and even pigeon-holed.

As Tommaso recognises, any taxpayer-money solution to a financial crisis has to be carried by the separate nation states. How a country could do so, if it was near to its limits under the Stability and Growth Pact, has not been resolved, or even seriously discussed in public. History shows that severe financial crises during recent decades have invariably been met in some large part by taxpayers' funds. But if the national Treasury is going to have to face this contingent commitment, it will want to be in a position to minimise it by close monitoring and control both of its own national supervisory authority, and of the process of EU-wide consultation, cooperation, and crisis handling.

As earlier noted, I was one of the discussants in October 2002 to Tommaso's paper (Essay 8), and I shall also take the opportunity to reproduce a shortened version of my own remarks then, as follows: a central bank can create liquidity, but it cannot provide for new injections of equity capital. Only the fiscal authority can do that. As Tommaso Padoa-Schioppa stated: 'The pattern of crisis resolution in different countries was also rather similar, not least in that the role of central banks was relatively limited in comparison with the role of the government and its agencies. Whereas in most cases some initial liquidity support or bridging loans was provided by central banks, it was often clear from the outset that the problem was insolvency rather than illiquidity' (see Section 8.4). In response to these comments at ECB Conference, Tommaso added a short section in this essay (see Section 8.10) noting that it is the smooth winding-down of large failed institutions and handling the market repercussions, which constitutes the major challenge for international cooperation, rather than the resolution of solvency crises.

The problem that I foresee is that most financial crises, in future as in the past, will involve some concern about solvency and the need to repair capital adequacy. This is obviously not to say that all potentially insolvent banks should be rescued at the taxpayers' expense. But there will be cases where rescue may seem the optimal approach, and this has to be decided jointly between the central bank and relevant fiscal authority. Moreover, by the time commercial banks come to the central bank they may have already used up their better collateral in getting market loans, so any Lender of Last Resort (LOLR) actions will tend to involve some risk to public sector, that is, taxpayers' funds.

This need for the central bank to interact with its fiscal counterpart in the assessment, prevention and resolution of financial crises is much harder within the Eurosystem than elsewhere. In other countries the national central bank can enter discussions with the national Treasury, which has the ability to use taxpayers' funds, if need be, to resolve national financial crises. The ongoing difficulties in Japan, however, reveal how difficult this may be even within the context of a single nation state. Within the euro-area the ECB operates at the level of the Eurosystem, but it has no fiscal counterpart. There is no competence for the budget to extend funding for the resolution of financial crises. Hence the relevant fiscal authorities have, perforce, to be at the national level.

This causes a disjunction. For the time being it, perhaps, does not matter greatly since so much of retail financial intermediation remains national, rather than trans-European. Thus, any financial crisis, for the time being, is likely to remain primarily concentrated in one country rather than spread over the whole euro-zone. Indeed in a crisis today the main spillover effect may well be felt in the wholesale financial centre in London, rather than in neighbouring countries within the euro-zone. If so, the question of who should bear the burden, and take the decisions, can remain reasonably enough at the level of the national authorities. But this condition, of national separation of retail financial intermediation, is beginning to go, has already largely disappeared in Scandinavia, where the commercial bank Nordea spans all the countries, (and also perhaps in Benelux), and should be replaced by more pan-European institutions. If so, the question of burden sharing between national authorities in the process of financial resolution may become much more difficult.

Padoa-Schioppa argues, in both Essays 7 and 8, that the stability of the financial system has in effect become a euro-area-wide concern. But so long as the relevant fiscal authorities remain at the national rather than at the federal euro-wide level, then euro-wide issues will continue to be decided by Lamfalussy-type committees of national authorities, as we are currently seeing, in which the euro-wide agencies, both the ECB and EC will, most likely, play a supporting rather than a central role.

Now I rather doubt the capacity of committees of national authorities to be very good at problems of burden sharing, as this will increasingly arise in future as the European financial systems become more integrated across borders. Such problems of burden sharing may be both particularly acute and particularly difficult to handle in fast-breaking financial crises. But getting the show back onto a euro-wide basis must involve, crucially involves, the need to face and to resolve such issues of fiscal structure and governance. Unless the Eurosystem is prepared to face this fiscal issue squarely, I see no alternative to the present trend towards euro financial stability control via committees consisting of national authorities.

That ends the excerpt from my discussant comments on Essay 8 at the October 2002 Frankfurt Conference. So, while I understand Tommaso's wish for greater centralisation of supervision and crisis management within the euro-area, I rather doubt whether this can be achieved, until or unless proper reconsideration is given of the necessary extent of fiscal federalism that would, in my view, be appropriate to give proper support to the single euro-area monetary policy.

But I do not want to finish on a slightly discordant note. Tommaso Padoa-Schioppa's work on financial regulation has been, and remains, a beacon of illumination to us all. His work not only provides a key record of the thoughts and analysis of the central players in this field during the last eventful decade, but has in many respects extended and pushed forward the debate.

I feel proud and privileged to be able to contribute to the publication of his essays.

C. A. E. Goodhart
Financial Markets Group
London School of Economics

Sources of the Essays

1. Originally: 'Market-friendly Regulation of Banks: an International Perspective', speech held at the 27th Tagung des Ausschusses für Geldtheorie und Geldpolitik im Verein für Socialpolitik in Frankfurt on 24 February 1996. Published in Szenarien der Europäischen Währungsunion und der Bankenregulierung, Duncker & Humbolt, Berlin, 1997.

2. Originally: 'Licensing Banks: Still Necessary?', William Taylor Memorial lecture no. 5 delivered in Washington on 24 September 1999. Published by the Group of Thirty, Washington DC, 2000. Available on the ECB website.

3. Originally: 'Bank Competition: A Changing Paradigm', dinner speech held at the Centre for Financial Studies in Frankfurt on 7 April 2000. Published in the European Finance Review, vol. 5 nos. 1–2, 2001, Special Issue, 'Competition among Banks: Good or Bad', selected papers from the conference, pp. 13–20. Available on the ECB website.

4. Originally: 'Self vs. Public Discipline in the Financial Field', lecture delivered at the London School of Economics, Financial Markets Group, on 20 May 2002. Available on the ECB website.

5. Originally: 'Securities and Banking: Bridges and Walls', lecture delivered at the London School of Economics, Financial Markets Group, on 21 January 2002. Published in the LSE Special Paper Series, March 2002. Available on the ECB website.

6. Originally: 'Challenges for Regulators in the European Union', panel discussion at the joint Deutsche Bundesbank/BIS Conference in Frankfurt on 28–29 September 2000, 'Recent Developments in Financial Systems and the Challenges for Economic Policy'.

7. Originally: 'EMU and Banking Supervision', lecture delivered at the London School of Economics, Financial Markets Group, on 20 May 2002. Published in LSE Special Paper series, March 1999. Also published in International Finance, vol. 2, no. 2 (1999), pp. 295–308 and in 'Which Lender of Last Resort for Europe?', Central Banking Publications, C. A. E. Goodhart (ed.), 2000. Available on the ECB website.

8. Originally: 'Central Banks and Financial Stability; Exploring a Land in Between', paper presented at the Second ECB Central Banking Conference on 25 October 2002, 'The Transformation of the European Financial System'. Available on the ECB website.

List of Abbreviations

BCBS	Basel Committee on Banking Supervision
BCCI	Bank of Credit and Commerce International
BIS	Bank for International Settlements
CPSS	Committee on Payment and Settlement Systems
CHIPS	Clearing House Inter bank Payments System
CLS	Continuous Linked Settlement
CONSOB	Commissione Nazionale per la Società e la Borsa
EC	European Commission
ECB	European Central Bank
ECOFIN Council	Council of the EU Ministers of Finance and Economic Affairs
ELA	Emergency Liquidity Assistance
EMU	Economic and Monetary Union
ESCB	European System of Central Banks
EU	European Union
EUR	Euro
FATF	Financial Action Task Force
FDIC	Federal Deposit Insurance Corporation
Fed	Federal Reserve System
FESCO	Forum of European Securities Commissions
FSA	Financial Service Authority
FSAB	Financial Accounting Standards Board
FSF	Financial Stability Forum
FX	Foreign Exchange
G7	Group of Seven (includes United States, Japan, Germany, France, Italy, United Kingdom, and Canada)
G10	Group of Ten (includes G7, Belgium, the Netherlands, Sweden, and Switzerland)
G20	Group of Twenty (includes G7, Argentina, Australia, Brazil, China, India, Indonesia, Mexico, Republic of Korea, Russia, Saudi Arabia, South Africa, Turkey, and the EU)
GDP	Gross Domestic Product
IAS	International Accounting Standards
IASB	International Accounting Standards Board
IAIS	International Association of Insurance Supervisors
ICT	Information and Communication Technologies
IMF	International Monetary Fund
IOSCO	International Organisation of Securities Commissions
JPY	Japanese Yen
LDC	Less Developed Countries

LTCM	Long Term Capital Management
LOLR	Lender of Last Resort
MoU	Memorandum of Understanding
NCB	National Central Bank
OECD	Organisation for Economic Cooperation and Development
OTC	Over The Counter
P/E	Price/Earnings
RTGS	Real-Time Gross-Settlement
SEC	Securities and Exchanges Commission
SSS	Securities Settlement System
TARGET	Trans-European Automated Real-Time Gross Settlement Express Transfer
UK	United Kingdom
US	United States
USD	US Dollar
US-GAAP	US Generally Accepted Accounting Principles

1

Market-friendly Regulation[1]

1.1 Bank Crises and Regulatory Failures

In recent times general confidence in financial regulation has been shaken by crises involving major international banks, such as Barings, Credit Lyonnais, and Daiwa, or large segments of national financial industries, such as the crises that swept the thrift institutions in the United States, the Scandinavian banks, and segments of the Japanese system. Scepticism about the ability of supervisors to prevent bank failures has spread. The reaction to episodes of fragility in the financial system used to be a call for more stringent controls and new rules; now many observers question the very need for supervision and advocate a new era of free banking. Such observers argue that the benefits of pervasive regulation in terms of the safety and soundness of the system are outweighed by the costs to economic agents, savers, and taxpayers.

Recent economic theory has contributed to this change of attitude by tracing disruptions in financial markets back to errors, slowness, or inaction by supervisors or to inadequacies in the regulatory framework. The argument for public intervention in the field of financial regulation—that is, market failures resulting from imperfect information and systemic risk—is more and more commonly turned around. A part of the economic profession now holds that regulatory failures, though less frequent, are likely to be more significant and costlier than market failures. The purpose of this essay is to examine the response of bank and financial regulators to this recent wave of criticism.[2]

A discussion of regulatory failures can be fruitful only once a widespread misconception has been cleared up. The task of supervision is not to prevent each and every bankruptcy; the mere fact that some banks go under is not in itself evidence of a regulatory failure. On the contrary, public coverage on a scale that precluded any exit from the market would severely damage efficiency by sheltering shareholders and top managers from market discipline.

The task of regulation is to correct two basic weaknesses of the market: first, the inability of depositors and investors to monitor how intermediaries use their money, which may result in excessive risk-taking and fraudulent conduct, and, second, the danger of a chain reaction, with the insolvency of a sick institution spreading to healthy ones and imposing high social costs. Hence, supervisory authorities have the narrow function of designing and enforcing rules of prudent behaviour on the part of financial intermediaries and, in a crisis, of limiting the damage.

Regulation may, nonetheless, fail to achieve its goals; under certain circumstances, it may generate new distortions in market mechanisms and impose excessive costs on participants or even on the economy as a whole. Historically, there have been cases of public regulations encouraging, instead of discouraging, risky or inefficient behaviour. For example, the US thrift crisis was partly due to laws that promoted real estate investment by providing easier access to long-term credit. Once interest rates rose in the late 1970s and early 1980s, the maturity mismatch of thrift institutions resulted in sharply rising funding costs and diminishing profits. The resulting financial problems caused many institutions to take on extra risks (moral hazard), resulting in subsequent failures. In other countries, widespread public ownership of banks and high barriers to entry into national markets long impeded the full play of competitive forces.

This essay will show that in recent years, largely as a result of the internationalisation of financial markets, authorities have become increasingly aware of the risk of perverse incentives and excessive costs of intrusive regulation. It is useful to start by explaining the concept of market-friendly regulation, that is, an approach designed more to enhance markets' ability to produce satisfactory equilibria than to prevent undesirable behaviour through coercive measures. Under this approach, public authorities may even promote the creation of new markets. The discussion will then show that international cooperation offers the best environment for the development of the market-friendly approach. A review of the work of the Basel Committee on Banking Supervision follows, as a good example of a regulatory response respectful of spontaneous changes on the market's side. Finally, it is shown that a market-friendly response to the globalisation of financial markets calls for closer cooperation between banking, insurance, and securities supervisors.

1.2 Market-friendly Control

A questionnaire prepared for the Seventh International Conference of Banking Supervisors held in Vienna in September 1994 surveyed the main features of regulatory systems around the world. Some general tendencies clearly emerged. First, while state ownership of banks is still widespread in many countries, privatisation is under way or imminent almost everywhere. Second, with the notable exception of the separation between banking and commerce, rigid limitations on banks' activities are being lifted and there is a move toward the universal bank model; this requires supervisory methods to shift from the segmentation of markets to incentives to avoid excessive risk-taking. Third, the barriers to geographical expansion (through branching as well as entry into foreign markets) have been significantly lowered.

This can be seen as a response to the emerging inefficiencies of earlier regulatory arrangements. This does not mean that such arrangements have been proved wrong, only that financial innovation and internationalisation dramatically altered the functioning of the banking and financial markets to the point where many supervisory instruments became ineffective or too costly. Of course, many of the previous regulations were also very intrusive (such as bank lending limits and interest rate controls) and distorted the effective allocation of funds in the economy. Thus, the liberalisation of such regulations significantly contributed to the efficiency and growth in the economy. Supervisors have become increasingly convinced of the need to intervene only in so far as market outcomes are inefficient and to design instruments that minimise interference with entrepreneurial choices. They had to take a step back and help the market to produce more efficient outcomes instead of trying to replace it with administrative measures. This means that defences have to be developed within rather than outside the market and that regulation should minimise coercion by using devices that imitate market discipline by establishing the proper incentives, that is, incentives that make it disadvantageous for a bank to choose excessive risk or fraud.

Sometimes market discipline is lacking because the market itself is lacking: imperfections may be so serious that they actually prevent the emergence of a market. In these cases, the regulator could act as a market creator. It is true that the absence of markets is not necessarily a source of financial instability, and the development of new financial markets may actually introduce elements of fragility: for instance, the Mexican crisis in 1994 and the danger of its spreading to other countries has cast shadows on the huge growth of emerging capital markets. Yet, the lack of certain markets or their limited development may make it more difficult for the system to overcome a temporary crisis: for example, the lack of an inter-bank market could exacerbate the consequences of a bank's liquidity crisis. In general, the creation of new markets yields efficiency gains that are beneficial for the economy as a whole.

In order to operate properly, markets need infrastructures, such as computer networks and physical exchange floors. They also require agreements on such matters as trading rules, participation limits, and settlement procedures. Since every participant has free access once the initial costs have been sustained, potential participants may not be willing to bear the cost of setting up the market.

A market will be created by private initiative only if economic agents coordinate their actions and share the expectation that a large number of transactions will cover the fixed costs incurred. This makes the process leading to market creation very fragile and vulnerable to the collapse of cooperation. Because of these difficulties the market may not emerge at all. Furthermore, when private forces fail to generate efficient market structures, public authorities can usefully step in, designing suitable solutions and enforcing them through appropriate incentives for participants to cooperate.

Examples of successful action by public authorities in market creation are widespread. In France, Matif, the highly computerised market for new financial products was promoted by the Government. The same can be said for the earlier big bang in the United Kingdom and for the restructuring of Germany's stock exchanges. In Italy, although the inter-bank deposit market (MID) is based entirely on private agreements, it received a decisive impulse from the central bank in the setup phase. In a different way, the CHIPS payment system in the United States was powerfully influenced by public recommendations, especially those of the Committee on Payment and Settlement Systems, which were taken up in a private market agreement.

The authorities can play their role of market creators in different ways, ranging from the issue of a formal act establishing a market as a public institution similar to a branch of the administrative system, to the adoption of an approach that conceives the market as a private firm, albeit a regulated one. While at the beginning of this century legislators often followed the first approach, the EC Directive on investment services leans towards the second. It defines a 'regulated market' as one for which public authorities either issue regulations on specific matters or approve rules promulgated by private self-regulatory bodies, not as an institution which is public in itself. This confirms the general tendency towards less pervasive public intervention.

1.3   The Basel Committee

The need for international action in the field of banking supervision arose in the early 1970s. The watershed was the collapse of the Bretton Woods regime, marking the definitive shift from official institutions to market forces (international banks) in the determination of exchange rates and the financing of external imbalances.

The growth of an international financial market based on the transactions of profit-driven private agents called for the extension from the national to the international sphere of the traditional policy functions of banking supervision. As a matter of fact, by the early 1970s the international capital market had already grown to a considerable size. The oil price rise in 1973 caused a further enormous expansion of cross-border claims as the international banking system, with the blessing of the authorities, took on the task of redeploying the oil exporters' financial surpluses. The growth of international banking was not without risks as was demonstrated in the following year by the failure of Herstatt Bank, the substantial foreign exchange losses of Lloyds Bank in Lugano, and the collapse of Franklin National Bank.

The easiest response to difficulties arising from the rapid expansion of banks' cross-border activities would have been the non-cooperative one, that is, the erection of barriers to international banking. This would have been a backward step in the process of opening national economies and in the evolution towards more competitive financial markets. This was the response given in the 1930s and 1940s. In the late 1960s and mid-1970s the path of segmenting national markets through foreign exchange controls and other restrictions on financial activity was also followed intensively by countries such as the United Kingdom, France, and Italy. Meanwhile, however, at least in the field of banking supervision, the decision to step up international cooperation, close loopholes in the international network of prudential controls, and keep regulatory arbitrage from triggering 'competition in laxity' among national authorities had also been taken. In the twenty years that followed, remarkable progress was to be achieved in this field at the same time as geographical restrictions on banking business lost their force and governments gradually removed exchange controls and liberalised capital movements. The Committee took the internationalisation of banking as given and made considerable efforts to encourage sound supervisory standards on a worldwide basis.

The Basel Committee was designed as the international forum for the promotion of a safe and fair supervisory environment in which minimal prudential standards would be respected by all. To accomplish this, the Committee had to accept the existence of different regulations, while trying to raise safety standards and level the playing field. The natural way was to 'skim off' the cream from the banking industry itself, by adopting the best practices in risk control and providing proper incentives. Suitable solutions for intermediaries operating in different markets had to be found.

For the reasons just explained, a market-friendly approach was thus embodied in the very construction of the Committee. The harmonisation between different supervisory schemes could only be minimal and was, therefore, consistent with the residual role of regulation. A feature of this attitude has been the involvement of the regulated industry in the decision-making process. Many of the proposals formulated by the Committee over the years came from working groups with close links to the banking industry. Formal consultation with market participants and other interested parties, originally practised by only a few countries, gradually has become a common procedure, thus making an important contribution to achieving effective solutions without burdening agents with unnecessary regulations. Rather than the 'capture' of the authorities by the regulated institutions, this consultative process can be seen as 'going with the grain of the market' in the search for pragmatic solutions consistent with market discipline and best practices in the industry.

As in any other field, international cooperation in bank supervision can also be influenced either through voluntary agreements or by establishing a supranational power endowed with legal authority. Voluntary agreements have been pursued through the Basel Committee on Banking Supervision and of many other regional groups of supervisors created outside the G10. However, the European Union chose the latter solution of legal authority. Although the two methods work differently, in banking supervision they have been mutually reinforcing: EC directives have been the main instrument for transposing the Basel Committee's ideas and proposals into European regulations, by contributing to the creation of the single market for financial services.

In what follows, the Basel Committee's regulatory responses to the growth of the international financial markets will be reviewed. References to the work of the European Union will be made only to highlight differences compared with the Committee's results. The work of the Committee can be described by referring to the three fundamental pillars on which it is built:

- ensuring that no banks escape effective supervision;
- ensuring that banks have adequate capital; and
- enhancing market discipline.

For reference, a list of the Basel Committee's main decisions and actions can be found after Essay 4.

1.4 Catching all Banks

To avoid gaps in regulatory coverage as well as competitive distortions, all banks have to be subjected to effective supervision. Cooperative efforts are necessary to prevent contagion by intermediaries operating in poorly regulated environments. As a number of bank crises have shown, one way of circumventing supervision is to do business through branches or subsidiaries located in countries where controls are lax: the shuffling of assets between several jurisdictions can defer the detection of difficulties, while the propagation of the crisis is facilitated by international banking linkages.

For the last twenty years, the 'Magna Charta' of international cooperation between banking supervisors has been the 'Basel Concordat'. The Concordat, through a series of documents identifies two separate supervisory bodies for international banking groups, that is, banks that operate in more than one country through branches or subsidiaries. The first is the host-country authority, which licenses and supervises the individual unit. The second is the home-country authority, which, as the supervisor responsible for the parent bank or head office, supervises the group as a whole. Crucial importance is attributed to the exchange of information between the two authorities.

When international banking started to grow on a significant scale and offshore centres developed, the risk of contagion by unregulated subsidiaries increased. The Banco Ambrosiano case (1982) revealed gaps in the international agreements specifying who was responsible for the supervision of banks' subsidiaries, especially when the international activities of a banking group were coordinated by a holding company. The Concordat was accordingly amended to incorporate the concept of consolidated supervision.

Consolidated supervision treats a banking group as a single entity. Besides extending the coverage of effective supervision, it prevents banks from 'double-leveraging' their capital through tiers of subsidiaries. In an international environment, consolidated supervision is the instrument for harmonising the treatment of intermediaries that, by choice or by law, adopt different organisational structures. This instrument was created at the international level, but has since been introduced in domestic legislation as well. When a bank wants to enter a non-traditional line of business perceived as potentially risky, regulators usually choose between two alternatives: either they allow the bank to perform the new activity directly and design supervisory instruments to prevent excessive risk, or they require it to carry out the new activity through subsidiaries and oblige it to create organisational barriers (firewalls, Chinese walls, etc.). In so far as it crosses firewalls, consolidated supervision may prompt regulators to reconsider the usefulness of administrative segmentation of financial activity, as is happening in the US debate on the Glass–Steagall Act.

The Basel Committee has always seen the authorisation process as critical, as the moment in which the competent supervisors need to devote careful attention to the viability of operations and agree on joint arrangements. The BCCI collapse showed that the existing Concordat was not adequate when the structure of the banking group was opaque and specially designed to evade supervisory controls. It led to the Committee issuing its so-called minimum standards, which establish the basic principles for the supervision of international banking groups. The minimum standards state that the home-country authority must be in a position to perform effective consolidated supervision, and must therefore be empowered to obtain all relevant information and prohibit corporate structures that impede supervision. They also state that cross-border banking establishments should be approved by the host-country authority and that the latter can deny authorisation or impose restrictive measures if it is not satisfied with the existing controls.

At present the minimum standards represent the foundations for the safe growth of international banking and their widespread implementation will permit the further opening of national frontiers to the cross-border supply of banking services. Following the issuance of the minimum standards, the Committee has decided to work with the authorities of the leading offshore centres to design implementation arrangements permitting home-country authorities to exercise effective consolidated supervision.

1.5 Capital Adequacy

Banks can operate with very little capital, thanks to the scope for leverage inherent in deposits. But capital is fundamental to their safety and soundness and to systemic stability, because it provides a buffer against losses and serves to protect depositors.

Well-established economic theory states that in the absence of regulatory requirements banks would tend to combine a low capital ratio with a strategy of excessive risk-taking. As argued by Michael Keeley (1990), banks that have been weakened for any reason (i.e. have a low 'charter value' and weak economic solvency) have much to gain from increased risk-taking. These incentives are due to the asymmetry in the risk–return combination for banks' shareholders. If risky behaviour produces losses and the bank fails, the most shareholders can lose is the capital they have invested, while the remaining costs are borne by depositors (or deposit insurance). If, instead, the gamble succeeds, all the extra return accrues to shareholders whereas depositors are paid only the stipulated interest rate. As noted by Mathias Dewatripont and Jean Tirole (1993), scattered and uninformed depositors cannot induce more prudent management behaviour. Thus, economic theory suggests that regulation is necessary to ensure adequate minimum capital and to threaten managers with greater supervisory intrusion if the bank's capital position deteriorates.

In the aftermath of the Latin American debt crisis, bank supervisors in several countries became increasingly concerned about the deterioration in the capital base of the main international banks relative to the risks they faced, notably in their lending to heavily indebted countries. Several industrialised countries had no specific solvency ratio and there were substantial disparities between the ratios in place. The resulting differences in conditions also fuelled domestic pressures to restrict the entry of foreign banks or to lower capital requirements in response to the perception that banks in some countries enjoyed unfair competitive advantages, thanks to lax capital standards.

This is the background to the Basel Committee's increasing involvement, starting in the early 1980s, in the issue of raising capital standards for international banks. When this work started, capital was measured in a variety of ways, making meaningful international comparisons very difficult. Some simple measures, such as the ratio of capital to assets, ignored the increasing importance of off-balance-sheet operations and treated all assets as equally risky. Once the definitional discrepancies had been reconciled, the Committee's empirical work in measuring average bank capitalisation in different countries revealed a wide range of practices and regulations. It also confirmed the concern about the ability of capital to support growing levels of risk.

The Capital Accord adopted by the Basel Committee in 1988 constitutes a milestone in the field of banking supervision and a major success of international economic cooperation in general. The Accord introduced a minimum capital requirement for the international banks of the G10 countries set in relation to their credit risks. To this end it provided a common definition of capital elements and a weighted approach to the measurement of both on and off-balance-sheet credit risks. The substance of the Accord was subsequently embodied in the EC directives on banks' own funds and solvency ratios, and thus made a fundamental contribution to the opening of previously segmented national banking markets and to the harmonisation of member countries' regulations.

Since the implementation of the Accord, actual capital ratios have risen significantly, and most internationally active G10 banks now meet the minimum standards. The Accord formally applied only to international banks, but was extended in practice to all the banks of the G10 countries. Moreover, thanks to the Accord, both financial markets and supervisory authorities outside the Group of Ten paid increased attention to capital adequacy.

The generalised move of the regulatory apparatus towards solvency ratios at the end of the 1980s not only meant that major steps were taken towards the two objectives of strengthening the banking industry and improving international cooperation, but also represented a significant shift towards a market-friendly regulation. Up until the mid-1980s it had been common practice for bank supervisors in many countries to control banks' risk exposure through the direct authorisation of individual loans, credit ceilings and restrictions of various kinds on the types of assets banks could acquire, as well as the geographical areas or economic sectors in which they could operate. Since it was introduced, the Basel capital ratio has been the object of intense debate and occasional criticism. But no one can deny that it has brought much greater neutrality, transparency, consistency, and flexibility in the relationship between banking and regulation. Compared with previous arrangements, banks have gained considerable freedom in their business decisions.

The Capital Accord specifically addresses credit risk. In fact that associated with counterparty insolvency is still the principal cause of banking losses and the chief concern of most supervisors. Credit risk is, of course, likely to be exacerbated by excessive exposure to single borrowers or connected groups.

However, in the last decades banks have also become increasingly subject to country risk, which arises because a government's decisions may prevent debtors in that country from honouring their foreign currency liabilities. The Capital Accord considers country risk by adopting different weights for different debtor countries.

Since the recent evolution of international banking has seen very substantial growth in banks' trading activities, the supervisors of the G10 countries became increasingly concerned about their exposure to market risk. For example, concerns stemmed from the risk of losses arising from on and off-balance-sheet positions as a result of movements in prices, including interest rates, exchange rates, and equity prices.

After several years of technical and diplomatic preparation, at the end of last year the Committee adopted an amendment to the 1988 Accord introducing specific capital requirements to reflect market risk. From the standpoint of this analysis of market-oriented approaches to bank regulation, the most significant feature of the amendment is that banks are permitted to use their own internal models to measure market risk as an alternative to the standard method. This is a major innovation and demonstrates the Committee's willingness to recognise that market participants are sometimes in a position to provide the best solutions to the problem of limiting exposure to risks. Of course, such flexibility must not lead to inadequate prudential standards nor distort competition, for instance, by producing widely different capital charges for identical risk positions. This is why the use of in-house models must be authorised by the competent supervisory authority and is subject to compliance with a set of quantitative technical standards as well as with a number of qualitative requirements designed to ensure that management has adequate risk control systems at its disposal. Essay 4, Section 4.4, will refer to the latest developments in the Basel Committee's activity in expanding the use of internal systems for regulatory purposes to credit and operational risk areas as well.

1.6 Market Discipline

Minimum capital requirements are essential, but they cannot be considered the sole safeguard against insolvency. They provide an incentive to avoid excessive risk, but they cannot eliminate the possibility of substantial losses, and hence of bankruptcy. This is why many of the Basel Committee's initiatives seek to spur the market to produce, at the level of both the firm and the market, measures against excessive risk; this is done by disseminating the use of effective internal controls and enforcing market discipline through more extensive disclosure of relevant information. Having said this, one should recall that internal models are increasingly used for direct regulatory purposes as well, as discussed above.

Over many years, the Basel Committee has worked with its own members and with industry participants to review and shape the most advanced risk management techniques. It has also sought to identify best practices for the management of various risks. Recent bank crises, such as the collapse of Barings, show how damaging poor internal controls coupled with the granting of significant discretionary powers to individual traders can be. The Committee attributes crucial importance to formalised procedures, clearly identified responsibilities, centralised monitoring of positions, and effective management information systems as means of removing or minimising the risk of similar breakdowns occurring again.

Disclosure to counterparties and market participants, in general, of relevant information about firms' situations, risk positions, organisational structures, and risk management systems is another essential means of stimulating the market's self-defences, and hence reducing the need for more intrusive forms of intervention by the public authorities. Experience suggests that private incentives may prove inadequate to produce a satisfactory level of information; market transparency is not necessarily produced by market forces, because no individual player is likely to have an interest in starting the game. Regulatory intervention can be useful, at least to set in motion a process whereby the market penalises opaqueness. To this end, in 1995 the Basel Committee, working in cooperation with its counterpart in the securities field (the Technical Committee of IOSCO), developed a set of recommendations for 'Public Disclosure of the Trading and Derivatives. Activities of Banks and Securities Firms' and surveyed actual practices by a number of market players in a public document that it is hoped will stimulate 'demonstration effects' and help break the stalemate of inadequate disclosure. In the same vein, the Basel Committee is interested in the possibility of minimum harmonisation of disclosure practices across countries and institutions.

Some radical advocates of pure market mechanisms in the academic world claim that public disclosure could be extended to the point that traditional supervisory instruments become unnecessary. One country, New Zealand, seems to have been enticed by this view into placing increasing reliance on the disclosure of information to discipline bank behaviour. However, the banking industry in New Zealand is rather peculiar because it is dominated by branches or subsidiaries of foreign banks, which are, of course, subject to the more traditional supervision of their respective home-country authorities.

Disclosure and internal controls cannot entirely substitute regulation, no matter how effective they are. In the first place it is doubtful whether they would be truly effective without public intervention. More importantly, there is no conclusive analytical argument showing that optimal internal controls and maximum transparency would make it possible to avoid the market failures that constitute the rationale for traditional supervisory instruments. Hence, internal and market disciplines and regulatory discipline need to be seen as complements (rather than substitutes), and they might even help minimise regulatory failures.

The work of the Basel Committee in the field of risk management techniques, as well as in that of disclosure, has mainly relied on a rather original regulatory and cooperative technique developed within the Committee itself: that is the issuance of 'best practices'. Such documents, while lacking the regulatory force of uniform rules such as those embodied in the Capital accord, present a broad range of the best practices found in leading banks and recommend supervisors and market players to make every effort to adopt them. This method allows each country's supervisors and intermediaries to converge at their own speed towards higher levels of safety and soundness, in a self-reinforcing process. This is another form of regulation that is respectful of market forces, in so far as it facilitates the circulation of knowledge among intermediaries, helping to overcome the coordination problems that private agents face.

1.7   Responding to Globalisation

During the last twenty years the enormous advances made in telecommunications and data processing, together with market operators' search for flexible and effective instruments for the transformation of savings, have powered the globalisation of financial markets in three ways. First, geographic restrictions have been lifted. Second, functional frontiers have been pushed back as technology permitted the creation of more complex contractual instruments combining the characteristics of the three basic contractual forms that traditionally have been reflected in the three branches of the financial industry: debt, equity, and insurance. Meanwhile techniques have been developed to allow the unbundling of risk into separate financial products and increased the marketability of financial contracts. Third, institutional partitions are coming down as the distinctions between financial institutions are eroded. A variety of products tend to be distributed through a single sales network, with banks offering insurance policies and pension plans, securities firms offering payment services as an adjunct to portfolio management, and insurance companies distributing mutual fund units.

While the freedom enjoyed by markets leads to a more efficient allocation of capital and faster economic growth, it brings new challenges for the traditional structure of regulation and supervision, historically based on the clear-cut segmentation of financial markets between the banking, securities, and insurance industries.

Removing unjustified disparities between the rules that govern different institutions offering similar services is, first of all, a question of fairness, or a level playing field. But the search for consistency in the overall regulatory approach to the financial system also stems from the danger that differing treatment of the same risk profiles may drive business towards areas—whether geographical, functional, or institutional—where prudential standards are less demanding and transparency is lacking. This does not mean, of course, that complete harmonisation is necessary, since applying the same standards to institutions that are intrinsically different in the composition of their assets or liabilities might be even more unfair than maintaining present arrangements. But a joint effort is required to assure that major disparities between regulatory approaches are justified and do not distort entrepreneurial choices or increase risk within the financial system. To a certain extent, competition among regulators can be seen as a disciplinary tool to get supervisors to remove unnecessary regulations; but in the absence of coordinated action, such competition may result in greater systemic risk. In some countries, the search for regulatory consistency between banking and securities regulation has led to the merger of the banking and securities authorities into a single body.

Contacts between the Basel Committee and securities regulators date back to the end of the 1980s. The result of the first joint meetings was the recommendation for information 'gateways' at both the national and the international level, following the positive experience of information exchanges among bank supervisors.

As regards the capital requirements for market risks, the contacts between the Basel Committee and IOSCO aimed at establishing common approaches for banks and securities firms did not lead to a successful outcome. However, the technical work carved out jointly by the two Committees provided the intellectual basis for the so-called standardised method of calculating the capital requirements for market risks. This method was adopted first by the Basel Committee and then by the European Union in the Capital Adequacy Directive (CAD). In Europe the construction of the single market for financial services has brought equal treatment of banks and securities firms, which should facilitate further harmonisation worldwide. The CAD includes a mechanism, which will allow the Committee's final agreement on internal models to be implemented. This possibility also means that regulated institutions will not have to bear the costs of implementing measurement systems that might be replaced in the near future.

Consolidated supervision is another area in which a convergence of banking and securities supervisory approaches is desirable. The Basel Committee has always seen consolidated supervision as the most effective means of preventing banks from circumventing restrictions on their activity via unregulated subsidiaries. In a number of countries, however, securities supervisors still tend to concentrate supervision on the regulated firm, while leaving some affiliates completely uncontrolled.

Finally, the coordinated efforts concerning the disclosure of banks' and securities firms' trading and derivatives business should be recalled. Collaboration in this field led to a report being issued jointly by the Committee and IOSCO in November 1995, as mentioned above. This document reviews the disclosure in annual reports of the trading and derivatives business of a sample of large internationally active banks and securities firms in the G10 countries. The report is intended to provide intermediaries with a picture of the sort of information currently disclosed by their peers and induces less transparent players to disclose more information. The adoption of higher standards of public disclosure will make for greater comparability of activities and facilitate markets' perception of the risks involved.

A major challenge that market integration poses for bank, securities, and insurance regulators stems from the rise of financial conglomerates supplying a range of financial services in the three traditional fields of finance and sometimes engaged in non-financial business as well. Conglomerates are hard to supervise because some of their activities may not be regulated at all, and those that are regulated usually involve a number of different authorities. Their business is often structured so as to take advantage of the least onerous regulatory regime and, in some cases, may be so complex that effective supervision is almost impossible. At the same time conglomerates are likely to be especially vulnerable to the risk of contagion between their components, because if one firm gets into trouble it will probably draw capital from the connected businesses, possibly undermining market confidence in the solvency of the whole group.

With the aim of bringing these concerns into focus and finding adequate answers, an informal Tripartite Group of supervisors was established in 1993 at the initiative of the Basel Committee. In July 1995 the group issued a report analysing the problems posed by financial conglomerates and putting forward recommendations to improve their supervision. The thrust of the report can be summarised as follows. In the first place it states that capital adequacy must be assessed in a group-wide perspective; this can be done either through consolidated supervision or by using a 'solo-plus' approach, in which the supervision of individual entities is complemented by an overall qualitative and quantitative assessment of the solvency of the group. Second, the report stresses the need for an extensive exchange of information between the supervisors responsible for the different entities within a conglomerate; in order to facilitate the gathering of information and the assessment of the group as a whole, it suggests that it would be helpful to have a lead supervisor. Third, the report indicates that supervisors should be given adequate powers to obtain information on the management and legal structure of the conglomerate and, if necessary, to prohibit group structures that prevent adequate supervision.

Following the publication of the Report, the Basel Committee, IOSCO and IAIS have established a 'Joint Forum' to build on the Tripartite Group's work. This has contributed to the awareness of the need to enhance consolidated supervision. In the European Union this process has led to the adoption of respective Community legislation (the Directive on consolidated supervision).

1.8   Still Open Debate

Recent financial crises have stimulated debate on the adequacy of current regulatory arrangements. On the one hand, there are those who argue that more pervasive rules are needed to prevent banks and other financial intermediaries from taking on excessive risk in innovative instruments and volatile emerging markets. On the other hand, and perhaps more commonly, regulation is accused especially in academic circles of having perverse effects, by giving rise to moral hazard and encouraging risk-prone behaviour, and hence of imposing excessive costs on the financial system and in the worst cases on taxpayers as well. This argument refers, in particular, to the existence of deposit insurance and other safety nets for banks.

In many countries, the period of liberalisation has been followed by banking crises as regulation and supervision were not yet in tune with the new environment. Notwithstanding this and considering the enormous changes that have occurred all over the world, there are good grounds for claiming that regulators have succeeded in keeping abreast, shown increasing respect for market mechanisms and prevented systemic fragility from becoming pandemic.

International cooperation has been a privileged ground for market-friendly regulation: the need to reconcile different approaches, financial structures, and regulatory and legal traditions, together with the absence of strong legal powers of enforcement, have obliged the international bodies responsible for banking supervision to be much more flexible and market-minded than several national agencies. In the field of banking supervision international cooperation has delivered very positive results. Looking ahead, it may be that the experience and general approach of the Basel Committee will prove useful outside the field of banking supervision, and perhaps outside the world of finance as well.

Notes

1. I acknowledge the assistance of Andrea Enria and Paola Sapienza in the preparation of this speech.
2. See also Essay 2, Sections 2.3 and 2.4 for a closer review of these arguments.

2

Licensing Banks[1]

2.1 Two Mottos

Financial and technological innovation is fostering competition in the supply of services once provided only by banks. Both facts and ideas are moving towards erosion, if not abandonment, of the principle of licensing banks. The entry of new players in the business of supplying bank-like products and the increasing reliance on electronic channels for their distribution is challenging the belief that strict controls over entry into the banking business are really needed.

Two different mottos are currently creeping into the debate. The first, 'no regulation', views technological developments as depriving banks of their special features. It implies that no specific dividing line should be drawn between banks and other corporations, so that any entrepreneur would be left free to enter the market without any public regulation and/or safety net influencing his/her behaviour and ability to innovate. The Cato Institute, together with George Benston and George Kaufman (e.g. 1995), can be taken as champions of this line of thought. The second motto, 'let things happen', can perhaps be inferred from the words of no less influential a person than Alan Greenspan (1997): 'Government action can retard progress but almost certainly cannot ensure it' and '... our regulatory roles are being driven increasingly toward reliance on self-regulation similar to what emerged in more primitive forms in the 1850s in the US'. According to this view, the rationale for bank regulation should not prevent the private, non-banking sector from trying out new solutions, with a greater role to be played by self-regulation. Both mottos suggest that a new free banking era seems to lie ahead of us.

This essay will argue that the licensing principle should be both restated and strengthened. It has to be restated in order to limit, as much as possible, public interference in the process of financial and technological innovation, and to ensure that end users will enjoy the full potential benefit of the process. However, it has also to be strengthened and implemented on a global scale in order to preserve the ability of our financial architecture to deal with systemic tensions and to ensure competitive equality among market participants.

More specifically, I am convinced that bank licensing needs to be maintained in order to uphold the pyramidal organisation of the financial system, with the central bank at the top as the ultimate supplier of liquidity, licensed banks—as lenders of 'next-to-last' resort—on the second level and various non-bank financial institutions on the third level. Banks have a special position because of their function of providing liquidity on demand to the other sectors of the economy, allowing for both credit and debit positions. This function is also a durable one, since the demand for liquidity is not affected by financial or technological innovation. Indeed, I perceive this as the most appropriate definition of the essence of banking. Finally, and almost tautologically, non-bank financial institutions can be defined as institutions that, for their liquidity needs, have to rely on support from a bank.

This construction also reflects the different objectives of regulation and supervision as related to the two layers of financial institutions. Owing to the 'fragility' of the function of providing liquidity, systemic regulation, and supervision, including measures to maintain public confidence in the banking system, need to be extended to banks. Banks, as other intermediaries, also need to be subject to prudential regulation and supervision, thus reducing the risk of a single institution failing and mitigating the moral hazard effects created by the safety net. Conduct of business and consumer protection regulations, in addition to requirements related to the disclosure of information, apply to banks as well, although here the approach is largely shared with other financial institutions, and even with non-financial firms. The third layer institutions do not need to be subject to the full range of measures; however, the reasons for licensing and regulating them are beyond the scope of this lecture.

Summarising my conclusion how best to maintain viable licensing, a regulatory approach mindful of the public interest at stake and friendly to market calls for a combination of two elements. First, reserving the core banking activity, that is, the provision of liquidity on demand, for licensed and supervised institutions. Second, refraining from placing any binding constraint on the range of financial activities that these institutions are allowed to perform. As will be shown, this approach would best accommodate any new forms of de facto banking.

The essay will begin by examining events and conceptual developments relating to increased non-bank involvement in the activities traditionally dominated by banks. It will then discuss the arguments that support the special role of bank licensing. After that, it will go on to explore the problem of maintaining the licensing principle in practice. This calls for an examination of the two issues of the essence of banking, which should remain licensed, and the appropriate scope of other permissible activities for licensed banks.

2.2 'Non-Bank' Banking

Traditionally, banking has been seen as a cluster of products and services, whose joint supply implied taking a set of different, but tightly bundled, risks. Deposit taking and the provision of payment services generally have been considered as fundamental elements of banking activity. Moreover, the ability to meet the financing needs of a wide variety of customers, through day-by-day contacts enabled by a network of branches, has long been interpreted as a special feature of banking organisation. Nowadays, financial innovation and technological change are driving towards a world in which such long-standing pillars no longer seem to hold.

Looking at the assets side first, new financial contracts (such as derivatives) or modifications of traditional contracts (such as securitised loans) have allowed financial intermediaries to unbundle products and risk profiles previously included on the bank balance sheet; bank loans can be embodied in securities and credit and market risks can be traded separately from their underlying assets. The traditionally strict correspondence between the types of financial contract, of risk, and of the institution managing it has become more and more blurred. Relevant portions of what was previously considered core banking business have now become disentangled from banking and are handled by a much larger set of institutions. The evolution of credit derivatives and asset-backed securities, particularly in the United States, provides examples of new ways to disentangle and trade credit risks. As another example, the French 'fonds communs de créances' sell units of a composite portfolio of bank loans, thus separating illiquid assets from sight or very short-term forms of funding, such as deposits.

Turning to liabilities, we see that deposit-like products are increasingly supplied by non-banks, which in many cases also provide payment services. Money market mutual funds are just one example. In many countries they offer an explicit or implicit par value clause, so that the subscriber is sheltered from adverse market movements. Furthermore, even if the fund needs to rely on a bank to provide cheque writing and payment services, its products are increasingly perceived as strict substitutes for banking services. These institutions cannot open credit lines or supply funding facilities to customers. It is possible, however, to use complex financial contracts, incorporated in negotiable securities that would provide the same service. While money market mutual funds are generally subject to detailed regulations, listing precisely the type of securities in which they can invest, there is nothing preventing a de facto supply of banking services. I, therefore, tend to agree with Ernest Patrikis' view that they should be viewed as 'over-regulated, under-supervised banks with no capital'.

Another development pointing in the same direction is that of non-financial companies, such as supermarkets or department stores, supplying accessory financial services to increase the attractiveness of their basic business. The cards and the credit facilities offered by such companies are one example of how it has become possible to move into areas of deposit-like products together with payments services and overdraft facilities.

In some countries the flourishing of finance companies also seems to be contributing to the blurring of the distinction between banks and non-banks. On the assets side, finance companies act as a sort of specialised credit institution, often supplying short-term funding to the corporate sector. As for the liabilities side, while this used to consist mainly of own funds, bank loans, and commercial paper, more recently ever-newer funding instruments have been developed. The survey of finance companies conducted by the Federal Reserve shows, for instance, that by 1996 traditional liabilities only accounted for 33.7 per cent of the total (49.5 per cent in 1990), while 'debts not elsewhere classified' amounted to 39.3 per cent (32.3 per cent in 1990). The growth of new sources of financing is, of course, a positive sign of innovative capabilities, and probably most of these liabilities comprise medium-term notes and asset-backed securities. However, once again, these developments seem to foreshadow a scenario in which finance companies come very close to carrying out full-blown banking activity.

The event that poses the greatest challenge to the licensing principle is perhaps the diffusion of non-bank means of payment and settlement. Even though payment instruments and the service of settling transactions by transferring assets are still predominantly supplied by banks, no major technical obstacle prevents the future entry of non-banks into this market. Electronic money, used for either face-to-face or Internet transactions, has materialised in the two forms of closed and open circulation. Whereas with closed circulation the (electronic) money always returns to the issuer after use, with open circulation holders use it to settle an indefinite array of transactions, which is very much what happens with banknotes and coins. The main difference between the two arrangements concerns the frequency and value of settlement, which is greatly reduced in the case of open circulation. However, in both cases the issue of electronic money by non-banks challenges the role that banks traditionally have played in providing payment instruments and final settlement of transactions. In some EU Member States (the United Kingdom, Finland, and Luxembourg) and in the United States, electronic money is currently also issued outside the banking system. Closed circulation is adopted in many national electronic money schemes, while the Mondex e(lectronic)-money scheme is a paramount example of open circulation, one that could suddenly spread if it finds favour with the public.

Last but not least, consider the revolution in the delivery network. The traditional branch is no longer the only place where the bank meets its clients. Customers are increasingly able to access financial services electronically, via computers, mobile telephones, and the television. For the bank, the geographical location of the premises is gradually becoming irrelevant, and economies of scale are increasing dramatically owing to the size of capital investments required to keep pace with technology and to provide adequate security.

Today, banks outsource some of their activities to technology companies, in order to exploit fully the opportunities offered by electronic access. Such companies are gradually developing the infrastructures and the skills that could be used to offer banking services autonomously. At the end of this path, it is quite possible that the master is supplanted by the servant, as the latter has superior technological skills, control of the means of electronic access, and is not burdened by the cost of maintaining both a branch and an electronic infrastructure. Firms that supply and control access to the Internet (such as Yahoo, Excite, and Microsoft) can significantly drive future market developments.

In addition, the so-called customer relationship, that is, the special assistance that can be given to customers, thanks to the intimate knowledge developed through repeated contact, can no longer be considered a distinctive feature of traditional banking. There are already fields of electronic commerce in which sophisticated data-processing capabilities have been developed to the point of allowing the service supplied via the Internet to be personalised. The customer is recognised, and is offered a menu of choices based on his/her preferences.

Do these developments point at a gradual disappearance of the traditional notion and organisation of the core banking activity, namely the provision of liquidity on demand, allowing for both credit and debit positions? I would argue that this is indeed the case. The very term 'non-bank banks' currently used in the debate indicates that full coincidence of the set of activities performed and the licence granted already has been disrupted.

There are already non-bank institutions that actually or potentially provide core banking services or their close substitutes. Of course, for the time being, the function of providing liquidity is still dominated by banks; non-banks rely largely on the provision of liquidity by a licensed bank, because this entity has access to central bank liquidity. However, the crucial point is that this licensed entity can be very small in comparison with the activity performed by the whole group or conglomerate, because the 'laws of large numbers and netting' mean that the final settlement is usually only a small fraction of the entire customer credit and debit positions. Hence, this small entity can support a wide range of non-licensed, de facto banking services. This practice is already quite significant, and the public perception is that core banking services are produced by non-bank entities. I will return to the implications of this issue later on.

Not only facts, but also ideas are challenging firm adherence to the licensing principle. The conviction that we are heading towards an unregulated industry for banking services, where every individual or company can freely enter the market and supply any type of financial contract without undergoing special supervision, is starting to spread. Since Bill Gates identified branch banking with dinosaurs, many have foreseen a future in which banks, especially the smaller local and traditional ones, are driven out of business by unfettered competition from companies, which fully exploit the new technological opportunities for efficient collection, management, and transmission of information. Two types of liberal attitudes are developing. They are briefly examined below.

The extreme supporters of the 'no regulation' motto think that there is no longer any special feature that distinguishes banks from other financial companies or, for that matter, from any commercial firm. Hence, they suggest that the licensing principle should be abandoned, together with extensive public regulation and the safety net.

This new generation of 'free bankers' often refers to the experiences of the nineteenth century as a model for the future evolution of the banking system. In doing so they seem to overlook the fact that in the actual experiences of free banking the special nature of banking had always been recognised. Even though no specific licensing requirements were in place, specific rules concerning the responsibility of owners in the event of insolvency, the need to deposit securities with a state agency, and sometimes, even capital and reserve requirements were adopted.

A less extreme version of the 'no regulation' motto is adopted by those who advocate a re-evaluation of some successful free-banking experiences, such as those of Scotland and within the United States. From this standpoint, historic free banking can help to provide an understanding of what may happen when financial and technological innovation erases the exclusive role of central banks as suppliers of high-powered money. Mervyn King has recently argued that owing to developments in computing power and electronic transfers of wealth 'there is no reason... why final settlement could not be carried out by the private sector without the need for clearing through the central bank'. In a world of competing private payment instruments, very much resembling a pure exchange economy, there would be no room for a monopolist, that is, the central bank, to decide who should be allowed to have access to the business.

A more pragmatic approach follows the 'let things happen' motto. This approach focuses on the risks of regulatory interference in the innovation process. Followers of this approach seem to be enjoying growing support for the ideas of letting new products and distribution channels develop freely and of relying as much as possible on the ability of market participants to adopt self-regulation. In order not to distort private incentives, so they say, public regulation should be seen as an *ex post* intervention, to be activated only if and when systemic problems arise. In Alan Greenspan's view, 'the private sector will need the flexibility to experiment, without broad interference by the government'. Therefore, non-banks should be allowed to devise new solutions and to compete with banks as far as possible, without strict implementation of the licensing principle.

2.3 Why a Licence?

At the end of the path foreshadowed by these facts and ideas, bank licensing would vanish. It is somewhat surprising, to my mind, that public debate, in both academic and political circles, has so far devoted only limited attention to a careful appraisal of the advantages and disadvantages of this ultimate implication. In order to determine whether it is desirable to advance further towards such a situation, this section will turn from the facts and ideas working towards an erosion of the licensing principle to the arguments in favour of firmly preserving it.

First, it will deal with the arguments put forward by the supporters of free banking, since devices for screening the institutions accessing the market also naturally emerge if there is no public regulation. Actually, once licensing by public authorities is not used as a rationing device, it is likely to be more respectful of market outcomes than the typical 'club' rules prevailing in a free banking world. Second, the section will argue that there are good reasons for licensing in so far as it allows banks to be distinguished from other financial and non-financial companies and a special role in the institutional framework to be attributed to them, aimed at safeguarding financial stability.

Ideological disputes, in which free traders and supporters of public intervention are set against each other, do not help when the issue of licensing is addressed. As a matter of fact, I am convinced that the regulatory framework that has gradually developed in the last ten to fifteen years is not so distant from the 'historic free banking' experiences. As already mentioned, in those experiences the special nature of banking activity was also widely recognised as a rationale for their specific regulation. Moreover, the key instruments then introduced to limit the effects of bank failures were not so far removed from the present ones.

In historic free banking, banks were generally required to deposit high quality bonds as collateral to redeem their liabilities at par value in case of difficulties. This constituted a sort of compulsory insurance aimed at protecting note holders, along much the same lines as present deposit insurance arrangements. Another pillar of free banking regulation was a form of unlimited, or partially limited, responsibility on the part of bank shareholders. These arrangements stemmed from the acknowledgement that bankers might be inclined to gamble with depositors' money, especially when business perspectives start to look bad, since limited responsibility would protect them from excessive losses. Modern capital requirements fulfil the same function, aligning as far as possible the incentives of bank owners and managers with those of depositors and ensuring that a sufficient buffer of own funds shelters the bank from unexpected losses.

Of course, the difference—which is certainly not irrelevant in the context of this essay, is that in historic free banking entry in the market was not regulated, and banking institutions had no access to the liquidity support of central banks.

However, if we take a closer look at the free banking experiences, we see that in many cases private arrangements have spontaneously emerged to fulfil the same function. In order to economise on liquidity needs and to cope with liquidity strains, associations (i.e. clearing houses) were frequently created to clear cheques and provide emergency liquidity assistance to members. These associations extended membership only to banks with an adequate capital and required a membership fee. They monitored the behaviour of their members through regular audits, used sanctioning powers on imprudent behaviour that was damaging to other members, and had the power to expel members. Thus a sort of procedure of 'licensing plus supervision plus liquidity support' emerged as a natural device to cope with the typical problems encountered by banks because of their special role.

The problem with these club-type arrangements was that, being collusive in nature, they artificially created a tiered system ranging from first-class banks running the clearing house, followed by other minor members, to the 'underworld' of non-members. Hence, as Fred Hirsch (1977), for example, has argued, in a system without a central bank there seems to be a tendency towards concentration and an oligopolistic structure, which can generate anticompetitive behaviour. Furthermore, the high number of cases in which the suspension of convertibility had to be declared indicates that the ability of these private arrangements to cope with major liquidity needs in times of stress was limited. Thus, the advent of public involvement in the licensing process was a way of preserving the screening function of the clearing-houses, while amending the drawbacks arising from their private nature.[2]

It is true that public control of entry also has its shortcomings. In the aftermath of the crises of the 1930s banking legislation was substantially tightened, thus establishing an oligopolistic structure in which sufficient generation of extra profits would cushion the industry against losses. Moreover, a variety of public goals were pursued, heavily influencing the allocation of credit and the structure of the financial system.

Extensive reliance on conduct regulations, such as price and interest rate controls, credit ceilings, restrictions on permitted activities, and limits set on branching, seriously affected the business opportunities of financial institutions. In most countries these controls involved an external assessment of the needs of the markets and a sort of social planning that impaired competition and artificially raised banks' charter values.

In the long run, this approach proved to be not only costly and inefficient, but also increasingly ineffective, as market participants found ways to circumvent restrictions. However, in recognising the drawbacks of past regulatory approaches and amending their inefficient components we should be very careful not to lose other components the validity of which remains intact. One should not, as the saying goes, throw the baby out with the bathwater.

As discussed in Essay 1, in recent years public regulation and supervision gradually have adopted and strengthened a market-friendly attitude. Substantial progress has been made in devising regulations that mimic market functioning and rely on incentives instead of forcing a particular market outcome. Prudential and information requirements gradually have become the pillars of the regulatory framework: the former including, for instance, capital requirements and large exposure limits, and the latter defining the types of information to be provided to market participants in order to improve market discipline.

Regulation and supervision also have been geared towards ensuring efficient risk management by the banks themselves. The complexity of the risk profile of each institution and the high speed at which the positions of financial markets and banks change make uniform and simple regulatory formulae increasingly ineffective and even distortionary. The 'internal models' approach, adopted for market risks by the Basel Committee on Banking Supervision in 1997, was a significant step away from controlling transactions and risk positions towards monitoring the way in which business activity is conducted. The further work now under way on revising the Capital Accord also with respect to credit risk is proceeding along the same route.

Strict adherence to the licensing principle is fully compatible with the promotion of competition and wide access for new entrants. Indeed, licensing does not have to be, and should not be, intended as a public rationing device. It is true that the rationing of new licences has been practised in many countries for many years. However, today, controls on entry into the banking market focus increasingly on minimum initial capital requirements and on an assessment of the quality of managers and relevant shareholders. The screening of the quality of shareholders and managers is similar to that practised in other professions, such as for architects or medical doctors, where customers are unable to assess the qualifications of the supplier. If properly exercised, these controls do not prevent any sound banker from entering the market.

Should then, public authorities take another step backwards, leaving the responsibility of controls to the industry itself? My answer is that self-regulation is necessary and desirable, but cannot be a substitute for public regulation and supervision.

Today, we can see the efforts that are being made by the industry to promote best practices for risk management among market participants. A most recent example is provided by the recommendations of the Counterparty Risk Management Policy Group, concerning the management of market, credit, and liquidity risk. I am firmly convinced that these initiatives are useful when they anticipate and complement public policy measures. Indeed, regulators should rely as much as possible on the self-defence mechanisms, which can be devised by market participants. Self-regulation, however, does not supply sufficient protection against systemic disruptions, and its intensification, although welcome, cannot allow supervisors to relinquish their responsibilities. As a matter of fact, the recent reform of financial supervision in the United Kingdom was also a correction of the shortcomings of a fragmented world of self-regulatory bodies.

The industry cannot take into due account the negative externalities of a crisis which can extend well beyond the boundaries of the set of 'member' institutions. Moreover, the knowledge that public authorities are not in a position to stick to a 'no involvement' stance if confronted with a major breakdown might lower the incentives to take, in a timely fashion, all the measures needed to curb risk prone behaviour. Furthermore, even more important in the field of licensing practices, self-regulation is likely to impose even stricter access requirements, since incumbent players have a collective interest in limiting competitive pressures from new entrants.

Ultimately, public regulation and supervision are rendered necessary by the fact that simple, voluntary coordination among market participants is unlikely to correct a market failure.

The second set of arguments, discussed below, relate to the need to preserve the special position occupied by banks in our financial architecture.

As shown in the short overview on the free banking era, the licensing principle emerged historically as a fundamental tool to identify the institutions that were granted access to the liquidity support of central banks. This evolution gradually produced a layered financial architecture, a sort of pyramid with the central bank at the top, licensed banks subject to specific regulation on the next level down, and other financial, non-supervised institutions one further level down. Thanks to this organisation, the financial system proved increasingly able to take a greater amount of risks, while limiting the scope of systemic disruptions.

Even in very different institutional frameworks, the licensing procedure always plays a central role in identifying the institutions responsible for providing liquidity to other intermediaries and to the economy as a whole. It is aimed at screening high-quality initiatives, which will then be subjected to extensive prudential monitoring. This special regime is warranted since these 'elect' institutions enjoy the insurance supplied by the safety net. The possibility of having access to central bank liquidity if the need arises and the explicit or implicit public coverage of their liquid liabilities helps to foster the confidence of the general public in their viability, thus favouring an easier funding of their activities.

When the central bank is entrusted with supervisory responsibilities, the selection of counterparties for monetary policy purposes and the set of licensed banks tend to coincide. When this is not the case, the central bank itself has to choose its counter-parts carefully, relying on criteria that allow safe and prudent institutions to be singled out. This 'quasi-licensing' by central banks is often accompanied by some sort of monitoring of the counterparties, which in some institutional settings goes so far as to include on-site inspections. In screening the eligible institutions, the central bank has therefore another 'key to the door', which might prove valuable in amending the shortcomings of an increasingly relaxed attitude by supervisors. However, this might be insufficient if much of the de facto banking activity is in the non-bank components of the group, with the licensed entity deprived of any real function apart from accessing central bank liquidity. In any case, the procedures proposed by supervisors and central banks should largely contribute to the same goal: the design of an institutional framework capable of limiting the likelihood of systemic crises.

Very recent experiences show that, notwithstanding the impressive progress that we have recorded in financial practice, systemic crises are still a real threat. The development of new instruments, such as OTC derivatives and structured notes, has greatly increased the ability of financial institutions to leverage capital positions. The episodes involving highly leveraged institutions, like LTCM, and more generally the disturbances that took place in 1998 after the Russian crisis, show that high leverage may well exacerbate the adverse impact of a shock.

In the aftermath of the most recent crisis, many observers have advocated an extension of regulation and supervision and a specific licensing procedure for highly leveraged non-bank institutions. Others have taken the view that banks, as licensed and regulated 'core' intermediaries, can deal with the problems posed by highly leveraged institutions, supplying liquidity when needed and carefully monitoring their non-bank counterparts. Without going into the details of this debate, it has clearly confirmed the need for a regulated and supervised set of institutions.

Numerous examples show that adverse movements of financial market prices have caused stress at non-bank financial institutions, with the banks acting as 'lenders of next-to-last resort' to channel liquidity where it was most needed. This is exactly what gives banks a special position in the financial structure and explains why bank stability is so relevant.

Systemic crises may well originate outside the banking system (and do so with increasing frequency); regulation and supervision of financial institutions are, thus, now extended well beyond the boundaries of licensed banks, and are sometimes also coupled with some form of public insurance. However, if we look back at the episodes of turbulence of the last decade, a striking regularity is that difficulties assumed systemic relevance only when and where the banking system was fragile. When turbulence occurred outside the banking system it could be managed if banks were in a position to support the liquidity needs of other intermediaries, letting those that were insolvent face their own destiny and mitigating the risk of the whole market collapsing. Crises not involving banks or a disruption of the monetary process—what Anna Schwartz (1986) has called 'pseudo crises'—have had few systemic implications. The collapse of the junk bond market or the standstill in the commercial paper market, to give just two examples, did not jeopardise the overall functioning of the financial system. When, however, the banking system itself comes under pressure, we are still confronted with a marked need for public intervention.

Strict enforcement of the licensing principle in banking is essential for the survival of the present organisation of the financial system in which institutions are seen as being on different levels, with the central bank providing ultimate insurance against the risk of meltdown. If the principle were abandoned or seriously eroded, one of the very foundations on which market economies have prospered for about a century would be undermined and the resilience of such economies to serious financial stress would again become doubtful.

In fact, if non-licensed and non-supervised entities assume a relevant role in providing full-blown banking services, the ability of the central bank to cope with systemic disturbances may well be jeopardised. Moreover, a central bank liquidity guarantee, and hence a public safety net, would be unduly broadened beyond the scope of supervised and regulated intermediaries. The well-known moral hazard arguments, calling for an adequate regulation and supervision whenever a safety net is provided, would be disregarded, with adverse consequences for the overall amount of risk-taking in the financial system.

Eventually, it all boils down to a question of confidence. If the licensing principle were significantly relaxed, public regulation and supervision would not survive. The coherence between the activities performed, the controls exercised by public authorities and the insurance coverage would be broken.

The general public would clearly perceive that banking activities are carried out by entities that are not licensed or supervised as banks. This could lead to a loss of confidence in the financial system and in the ability of the institutional framework to deal with threats to stability.

To sum up, licensing is an essential prerequisite of public regulation and supervision. It represents a building block of an institutional framework aimed at containing the scope of systemic risk, organised in different tiers of institutions and attributing to banks a special role in providing liquidity support. It is consistent with a policy aimed at enforcing good market practice and limiting moral hazard related to the safety net. Finally, as the experience of the last decade shows, it is not an impediment to financial innovation.

I do not advocate defensive regulation, erecting insurmountable barriers to entry for new players in an attempt to save banks from extinction; my point is simply that, when such players conduct banking business, they need to be licensed as banks.

2.4   Are Banks Special?

Up to this point, the essay has spoken about licensing banks as if there were no controversy about what a bank is, while this is naturally not the case. Of course, it would be impossible to be strict on licensing if there were no clear and enforceable definition of a bank. Thus, before discussing the options available to ensure appropriate licensing, we obviously need to be more precise in defining the activity that needs a bank licence. In this context, two questions need to be distinguished. First, what is the essence of banking, that is, what is necessary and sufficient for a business to be considered a bank and, therefore, to be subject to a licensing procedure? Second, what is the appropriate scope of banking, that is, what other activities should a bank be allowed to carry out?

First, is the essence of banking. The academic state of the art has evolved strongly over time on this question. Anyone who has examined this topic has probably noticed that the individual pieces of literature often deal with only a part of the issue, and that the whole picture appears so complex and changing that it does not distil a clear-cut definition. Yet, what I see emerging from the academic debate is an agreement that the joint supply of deposits and loans puts banks in a unique position to provide liquidity on demand. This feature strikes me as a durable one.

It was first recognised in the early 1970s that banks are not like intermediaries in other industries which just buy goods—in this case money—from those with excess supply and sell them to those with excess demand, saving on the transaction costs in between. If banks did only that, they would probably face extinction because the progress in the fields of telecommunications and computer technology is greatly reducing the costs of exchanging information between lenders and borrowers. Applying the progress in the economics of information, it was acknowledged that banks transform financial contracts and securities in such a way that overcomes informational asymmetries between lenders and borrowers, which are of a fundamental nature and exist despite technological advances.

There are three basic conclusions from this literature. First, as originally pointed out by Douglas Diamond (1984), banks supply the basic economic services of processing information about borrowers and monitoring their actions, but end up with opaque assets due to the non-marketability of the loan contracts. Second, as shown by Douglas Diamond and Philip Dybvig (1983), banks provide liquidity insurance to depositors, but the maturity mismatch between deposits and loans makes them vulnerable to runs. Third, the possession of private information by banks generates a logical link, strongly connecting the assets and liabilities sides of bank activity, which puts banks in a unique position to supply liquidity on demand. This function, however, entails systemic risk, since instability at a single bank can spread via contagion, which in turn is the basic justification for the safety net (deposit insurance and lending of last resort), regulation, and supervision.

It may be interesting to note that the theoretical discussion is broadly in line with a common factor of the existing legal definitions of banking activity. Indeed, any legislation in the world would define an institution granting loans on its own account and collecting deposits from the public as a bank. This may not be a necessary condition in the existing legal definitions, but it is certainly a sufficient one. In addition, the First Banking Co-ordination Directive of 1977 adopted this definition and prescribed objective criteria for the granting of a bank licence. This Directive started the long process of harmonising the key prudential provisions in the European Union; the fact that harmonising licensing was the starting point demonstrates the central role of this regulation.

Can we expect institutions supplying liquidity on demand to remain in place in the foreseeable future? Or, as the 'no regulation' motto suggests, will innovation on both sides of banks' balance sheets, non-bank settlement through electronic means and competing payment instruments annihilate the special role of banks, and, with it, the need for regulation and supervision, not to mention central banks' monetary control?

My clear answer is that no annihilation is in sight. To explain why, it is instructive to refer to the fundamental step forward in the history of financial markets which John Hicks (1974) calls the passage from an 'auto-economy' to an 'overdraft economy'. By this was meant the passage from an economy in which agents' financing needs can be satisfied only if savings have been previously accumulated to one in which access to liquidity is granted on demand at pre-set conditions through debt instruments. The flaw in the reasoning underlying the 'no regulation' motto consists, in my view, of overlooking the fact that such passage was economic in nature, rather than technical. New technologies may modify the modus operandi of the overdraft economy, but would not represent effective progress if they were to drive us back to a situation in which overdraft facilities were no longer possible and no institution could offer liquidity on demand to those in need of it. Hence, the demand for liquidity provision in an economy is independent of the financial and technological innovation process.

For example, the impressive growth of bond markets and the spread of securitisation in the United States, even of small-business loans, have supplemented, rather than replaced, the demand for checkable deposits and credit lines by banks. Even in Fischer Black's (1970) thought-provoking world without money, where all transactions are settled, perhaps electronically, on privately held accounts, banks are identified as institutions allowing their customers to switch freely from credit to debit positions. This is the essence of liquidity provision. The economic need for it will not be swept away by computers.

To conclude, providing liquidity on demand will remain indispensable for the functioning of a market economy; it is the core activity of institutions that we should continue to call 'banks'; it continues to entail systemic risk. Because it is not possible to supervise an activity without referring to an economic agent that carries it out, the essential step is to identify such an agent via a licensing procedure and to supervise it carefully. Finally, the whole scope of the activity should be regulated and supervised as a bank; regulation and supervision should not be limited merely to the 'tip of the iceberg', namely, the ultimate settlement with central bank money.

Turn now from the essence to the scope of banking. Somewhat surprisingly, this second issue has not been as actively researched as the first. For a long while, the debate focused on the possible conflicts of interest arising from the joint supply of banking, securities, and insurance services; some literature also addressed the issue of separation of banking and commerce. The starting point was the debate on the factors determining the disruptions of the banking and financial systems experienced during the Great Depression. Some theoretical and empirical contributions have challenged the relevance of these factors, arguing that excessively narrow definitions of the permissible activities for each category of intermediaries was preventing competition and hindering the efficiency of the market for corporate control.

However, while a degree of consensus was being reached on the need for broadening the scope of banking activity, Robert Merton and Zvi Bodie (1993) recently have argued that in order to eliminate the systemic risks involved in banking, we should impose a narrow bank model. This solution would oblige banks to hold their assets in liquid, safe, and marketable assets only, thus breaking up the maturity transformation and, hence, the two-sided function of providing liquidity carried out by banks. In so doing, they follow the suggestion of a '100 per cent reserve' banking, put forward by James Tobin and Milton Friedman years before. The 'narrow bank' would be closely supervised, while the remainder of banking and financial activity should be completely free of any licensing and supervision arrangement, as well as excluded from any access to the safety net.

It is difficult to argue against a proposal supported by three, and perhaps more, Nobel Prize winners. Yet, on the basis of actual experience and the function of supervising banks, I would advise against following the narrow bank model. Such a restriction would damage the basic economic rationale of banks and break up the present synergies, leading to efficiency losses. This view also has academic support. For instance, Anil Kashyap, Raghuram Rajan, and Jeremy Stein (1999) demonstrate that, and deposit-taking and providing credit lines can be regarded as manifestations of the same liquidity provision function, there are synergies between the two; the need for liquid reserves and other resources would be greater if the two services were produced separately. Moreover, the way in which financial activity is now structured in complex organisations of financial groups or conglomerates would make it attractive and easy for firms to circumvent this regulation. Finally, in the presence of deposit insurance, narrow banking is also advocated by its supporters as a means of reducing the moral hazard problem of excessive risk-taking by the insured institutions by restricting the investment options available for them. However, by artificially restricting the margins earned by banks, one could actually increase the incentives to gamble in order to earn higher return on investment. Hence, a narrow banking model would need to be coupled with very strict supervision of compliance with the investment restrictions and the monitoring of any circumventing behaviour.

Paradoxically, adoption of the narrow bank model could lead to a financial environment in which non-bank banks develop even further and uncontrolled and unsupervised risks spread even more. This is so because, although the core function of banks can be clearly identified, a definite dividing line between traditional banking and other activities cannot be easily drawn. The defence of this frontier would not withstand the endless, and in some respects even socially useful, attempts to bypass regulatory restrictions. In an ideal regulatory arrangement we would indeed offer intermediaries a wide menu of choices, ranging from an all-encompassing banking licence to more limited charters, with supervisory requirements graduated according to the systemic concerns raised by each item on the menu. However, this ideal arrangement would be very difficult to attain.

2.5 How to License?

The facts reviewed at the beginning of this essay show that some toothpaste has already gone out of the tube, or is in the process of doing so. While the ability of non-bank financial institutions to compete with banks on specific product lines is a positive development, allowing the core banking service to be supplied by non-licensed, non-supervised entities would seriously impair the resilience of the financial system. To avoid this undesirable development, an effort is called for to focus on the essence of the banking business, and not on the practical instruments, organisation, or technology used in carrying it out. The sooner the supervisory community acts, the lower the costs of the transition will be, and the smaller the probability of having to revert to a heavily regulated environment in order to restore public confidence.

Can a strategy be identified to tackle this problem? Even though there is no single, simple 'silver bullet' definition of banking activity, common principles can and should be identified and the options narrowed down. Hence, let me now move from the theoretical discussion to a more pragmatic review of the options available with respect to defining (*a*) the essence of banking and (*b*) the scope for allowed other activities. Three options can be identified, representing different combinations of the possible answers to the two questions concerning the essence of banking and the scope of activities. They are labelled here the 'narrow–narrow', 'broad–broad', and 'narrow–broad' options, respectively.

The 'narrow–narrow' option identifies banks as providing liquidity on demand and lists a limited range of other activities that they can undertake. According to this approach the licence is seen as a great competitive advantage for banks, which is balanced by restrictions on the scope of business. Banking legislation implemented in the United States in the 1930s, and relaxed only in recent years, is the major example of this approach.

In the 'broad–broad' option, no specific attention is devoted to confining the essence of banking to deposit taking or to the joint provision of more than one service, and the scope of banking activity includes a wide range of financial services. In the extreme case, all providers of financial services have to be licensed and supervised as banks, irrespective of their liability structure. French banking law and German legislation before the recent amendments are the best examples of this approach, although they do not extend so far as to include securities dealing among the set of services that only banks can perform.

The 'narrow–broad' option entails a definition of banks as institutions which couple deposit-taking with the supply of loans, but it places no restriction on the possibility of offering the whole range of financial services. By contrast with the first option, attention is focused on identifying the activities that can be performed by banks only, rather than on the business barred to banks. Banks coexist and compete with non-banks in a number of markets, but the joint supply of deposits and loans is reserved for them. They remain the only providers of liquidity for the financial system and the economy at large. The prominent example of this option is the legislation of the European Union. The combination of a narrow essence with a broad scope is achieved by separating the definition of bank (Article 1 of the First Banking Co-ordination Directive) from the indication of a list of activities (an Annex to the Second Banking Co-ordination Directive) that different national legislators can allow (narrowly defined banks) to conduct. The list of activities covers a broad range of financial services and it can be updated under a flexible procedure, in order to adapt to changes in the nature and scope of banking services. Mutual recognition by each Member State of the others' licensing processes is coupled with harmonised minimum standards so that the host supervisors can rely on the controls exercised by the responsible home country's authority on the banks operating in their jurisdictions. Although it is referred to as following a universal banking model, this approach accommodates differences in national definitions, which can range from narrow–narrow to broad–broad.

The three options can be evaluated on two main grounds: impact on the innovation process and docility to public control. It can be argued that the narrow–narrow model is strongest on the former and the weakest on the latter, the broad–broad model representing the opposite case. The narrow–broad option would be an intermediate one on both grounds.

The broad–broad model would be the least conducive to innovation: if every company introducing new ways of doing old things already had to fear the scrutiny of public authorities and forced absorption into the banking system, it would have weaker incentives to innovate. As an all-encompassing solution, the broad–broad model would naturally be the most forceful approach with regard to the maintenance of public control.

As argued before, regulations and supervisory tools can be devised to be 'market-friendly' (as indeed they have been recently), interfering little with the innovation process. However, the US-type narrow–narrow approach is more exposed to the risk of relaxing the public control of banking activity, since it constrains banks' activities, but does not prevent non-banks from providing banking services and actually provides the highest incentives to do so. The EU-type narrow–broad approach is more effective in attributing to banks their specific role in the architecture of the financial system. Whichever approach is taken, the appropriate response to the supply of banking services by non-banks that rely on methods not contemplated in the current legislation is to update the definition of banking so as to include these new methods. The proposal of a EU Directive specifying that the issuance of electronic money should be subject to bank-like licensing and prudential controls is an example of the inclusion, in the realm of supervised business, of all the new tools for delivering de facto banking services. In the United States this has been regarded as falling outside the area that requires a bank licence.

My inclination toward the composite, EU-type, may not surprise you, as I took an active part in the work which led to the adoption of this model for the European Union. The model has enough flexibility to deal with the new forms of banking, but also has the advantage of supporting the level playing field and is less prone to circumvention than the narrow–narrow model. The problem with the broad–broad approach is that it does the job of guaranteeing public control too effectively. It can expand the supervisory responsibilities and the scope of the safety net too far, amplifying the moral hazard problem and endangering the effective monitoring of all licensed institutions.

A legislative definition of banking activity is of no help if customers can freely access the services of non-chartered banks incorporated in countries in which the licensing principle is not rigorously followed. This is why a degree of international cooperation is clearly called for. Otherwise the industry would be open to breaches in the licensing requirements and the general public would have no assurance that those offering banking services in the narrow, 'essence', definition are actually chartered—and regulated and supervised—as banks.

The risk of an international route of circumvention is growing as new technologies progressively allow bank customers to look throughout the world for the best source of services, including retail banking services. The 'Core Principles' issued by the Basel Committee on Banking Supervision are the first step in the direction of attributing global reach to the basic principles of the licensing procedure. However, we must go further on this route, agreeing on the essential elements of banking activity, continuously updating the definition of the contractual and technical means of fulfilling this function, and, above all, sharpening the instruments used to enforce a strict implementation of the licensing principle.

Of course, reaching international agreement about the scope of banking activities would be a much more difficult task. In fact, I do not think we really need a monolithic notion of the list of financial services in which banks can be involved. Not even the European Union felt that this was necessary for its highly integrated Single Market. Actually, regulatory competition can be fruitful in adapting the scope of activities as financial innovation and technological progress open new frontiers in market practices. In any case, what recent experience shows is that if regulators have a restrictive attitude towards the scope of permissible activities, banks can easily circumvent national provisions by opening subsidiaries in other jurisdictions.

To stress a final point, one needs to be strict when enforcing any adopted licensing principle. More precisely, there needs to be adequate imposition of sanctions in the case of abusive banking. Whenever licence is abused or there is apparent circumventing behaviour, strict sanctions should be imposed.

2.6 Still Necessary

This essay has shown that two possible attitudes can be adopted in the face of the challenges posed by technological change and financial innovation. The first is to step back and limit the scope of the safety net to a narrowly defined set of institutions with strict restrictions on the composition of assets and liabilities. The second is to adopt a definition of banking that would allow the licensing and supervisory framework to recognise as a bank every firm performing—with whatever technical means, organisation, and contracts—what in economic terms is a banking function.

All the arguments that are put forward in this essay suggest that the second solution is preferable. The fundamental strengths of the present financial architecture should be preserved, while moving towards regulation that does not prevent us from reaping the benefits of financial innovation.

For some, my argumentation may have a strong continental European flavour, allowing economic activity to take place only after explicit permission from the public authorities. In the United States, the approach has been to intervene only when public interest is clearly injured. I am an admirer of the US system, which is in many senses a superior system in terms of promoting freedom of enterprise. Nevertheless, in such a systemically delicate area as banking, one cannot afford to adopt the attitude of 'letting things happen'.

The task of regulators is not, of course, to prevent Darwinian selection in the financial system. Dinosaur banking should not be protected from extinction, but rules have to be laid down to avoid ruthless experiments of genetic manipulation leading us into a world in which no certainty exists about the quality of the product delivered and the reliability of the firm supplying it.

Notes

1. I acknowledge the assistance of Andrea Enria and Jukka Vesala in the preparation of this lecture. Useful comments on an earlier draft were provided by Chester Feldberg, Curzio Giannini, Mauro Grande, Mervyn King, and Danièle Nouy.
2. Essay 8 continues on a related discussion of the emerging roles of central banks in financial stability and prudential supervision.

3

Competition in Banking[1]

3.1 Who Likes Competition?

The question 'Competition among banks: good or bad?' is highly stimulating, and the answer—despite a long debate—is not at all obvious. The attitudes towards the market economy are not unambiguous.

As a matter of fact, no market participant really likes competition. Businessmen tend to praise the competition they practise vis-à-vis other firms, but they usually blame competition when they suffer as a result of it. The ethical attitude of a businessman, like that of a shopkeeper, is very often not to compete, and not to make life difficult for other people in the same profession.

Competition ranks even lower in the financial businessmen's favourites. This is so because banking activity is closely related to a sense of security, especially security concerning the future. Also, according to many people, the instability that, at least at the level of the individual firm, is inevitably brought about by a competitive system is really not congenial to banking. The Governor of the Bank of Italy in the 1950s—a person who is still held in high regard, years after his death—maintained the view that competition among banks was something to be feared as a potential source of serious disruptions. I belong to a generation which has seen a complete change of attitudes.

This essay will refer to this change, touching on four points. First, it will elaborate on the journey that can be called from the old to the new approach, namely from the approach prevailing when I was a student and during my early years as a central banker to that which has been developing subsequently and towards which I, to some extent, have contributed. Second, the essay will discuss how far this new approach can go. Third, it will bring into the picture aspects relating to the international dimension. Finally, it will address the specific aspects of the euro-area dimension.

3.2 A Policy Shift

The journey from the old to the new approach constitutes a move from a negative attitude towards a positive one with respect to banking competition. The old approach—'competition is bad'—can be analysed by looking at several fields of public policy which have a bearing on banking activity. This discussion will focus in sequence on prudential supervision, monetary policy, competition policy, and securities market supervision.

First, is prudential supervision. The legislative reforms adopted in most countries as a response to the banking and financial crises of the 1930s shared one basic idea: in order to preserve the stability of the banking and financial industry, competition had to be constrained. This fundamental proposition was at the root of the reforms introduced at that time in the United States, Italy, and most other countries.

It was widely believed that in an oligopolistic environment banks could enjoy extra profits, which would foster the stability of individual banks and the banking system as a whole. In such a situation, individual banks could absorb losses more easily and the banking industry would always have sufficient funds to rescue an ailing institution, in the rare cases in which difficulties occurred. Under these circumstances, the usual technique for dealing with a banking crisis was to call upon other institutions to persuade them to take over the 'problem institution'. This is what I have experienced several times during my professional life. However, also more recently an orchestrated solution was used for dealing with the LTCM crisis, even though in this case the rescuing institutions were involved in the crisis and had an inherent interest in contributing to its solution.

Until relatively recently, there was no embarrassment in pursuing and supporting explicit limitations of competition. Policy-makers limited banking competition in different ways. These included, for instance, the rationing of banking licences and regulatory segmentation between financial activities (e.g. between commercial and investment banking), as in the United States until quite recently, and in many other countries which did not adopt a universal banking system. Another type of widely used restriction was the geographic segmentation of the markets. This was pursued through the prohibition of interstate banking and branching in the United States. In other countries, banks were frequently restricted to lending only limited amounts of money outside the area where they had their headquarters, while the establishment of new branches was often limited through special authorisation procedures. In many cases, the supervisor was entitled to screen a very large range of bank operations and each transaction of this kind had to be explicitly authorised.

Second, is monetary policy. Monetary policy was, for a long period, also consistent with the old approach, according to which competition was bad. Chief instruments of monetary control were credit ceilings, defining a maximum permissible rate of growth for credit aggregates. The transmission mechanism of monetary policy was largely administrative in nature. When the central bank moved the official rates, commercial banks responded almost automatically, not by means of a market mechanism relating to the availability of liquidity, but simply through a public announcement. In fact, very often the latter measures were taken by bankers' associations, and not by individual institutions. Furthermore, the exchange rate was fixed not only in the sense that there was a fixed central rate; as a matter of fact, its level was decided by the central bank on a day-to-day basis. Since the market was so thin this was a feasible option.

Third, is competition policy. Probably the only country with an antitrust legislation during the 1930s was the United States. In many European countries, competition policy laws were issued only in the two decades following the Second World War, while in Italy the first antitrust authority was established in 1990. Also, where there was legislation and authority in place to protect competition, very often their jurisdiction was not extended, either formally or practically, to the banking industry. Where there was an authority with responsibilities for competition policy in the banking industry, that authority was very often the supervisory authority itself. Even in the United States the Federal Reserve System has some competencies in the field of competition policy for the banks it supervises. The same applies to Italy and the Netherlands, where the central banks are entrusted with widely ranging tasks in the field of competition policy. Even where there was a very strongly based competition authority, as has been the case in the European Union ever since 1958, its extensive powers were usually not applied to banks. Only in the 1980s did the European Court of Justice establish that banking activity should not be excluded from an application of the Articles of the Treaty concerning competition policy. In the mid-1980s, I witnessed this change whereby a specific line of activity referred to banks was opened in the Directorate General of the European Commission in charge of competition. The Commission has more and more frequently challenged the cases of state aid to the banking sector on grounds of competitive fairness, most recently also in Germany.

Finally, securities market supervision. For a long while, in many countries a large part of the banking system was virtually unaffected by securities regulations. First, banks were often not incorporated as limited companies, so that their shares were not traded on regulated markets. Second, most of a bank's activities vis-à-vis their depositors and other creditors were not subject to the various disclosure requirements and rules of conduct aimed at protecting the investors.

In all four of the policy fields, a positive view of competition has gradually overcome the old approach. While the intention is not to go through all the peculiarities of the new approach in all the four fields, the following will highlight the major differences in today's policies in respect of the old approach.

Supervision is, as we are now in the habit of saying, 'market-friendly'. It relies very much on the idea that if banks were strengthened by the gymnastics of competition, the banking system would be stronger and more resilient to shocks. Of course, competition means selection. Hence, such an attitude also implies that authorities must be ready to let the weakest banks leave the market.

Freeing competition in the banking sector by liberalising intrusive regulations (such as credit and interest rate controls) was even more fundamentally related to the desire to improve the allocation of financial resources in the economy. However, to the extent that competition is not enough to enhance the robustness of the banking system, supervisors need to retain their control—not by the old type of intrusive controls, but by instruments that are themselves 'market-friendly'. Such instruments do not force a particular market outcome and allow for free competition, but keep a check on banks' risk-taking. Modern capital requirements, for example, are more respectful of entrepreneurial choices than procedures for directly allowing or forbidding the extension of particular loans, which are too risky or not sound according to the supervisors' judgement.

Monetary policy now relies on a transmission mechanism, which is based on profit-driven decisions made by the economic and financial agents operating between the central bank and the real economy, in the first place by the banks.

Competition policy is actively applied to the banking industry and the security supervisors treat banks just like any other listed or limited company. After I moved from my country's central bank—which is also a banking supervisor—to the securities commission, I found myself in a decision-making body in charge of approving public offerings by banks which required new capital. From the point of view of the rules of the security supervisors, you are looking for the maximum degree of transparency and so the objective is a prospectus, which provides a detailed picture of the situation of the bank issuing the new shares. On the other hand, the tradition of the banking supervisor is that if a bank has a weak point it may be better not to let the market know. Hence, there is a natural dialectic, even tension between these two kinds of supervisors.[2] As long as the security supervisor has no jurisdiction over the banks, either because the banks are public institutions or because the tradition is that they deserve different treatment from that applied to other listed companies, this tension does not increase.

What has been described so far is a real '180-degree' change. It is rather easy to locate the emergence of the old view—which, by the way, was very new in those years, following a period of lightly regulated markets and even free banking—in the aftermath of the Great Depression. It is much more difficult, however, to identify a precise period in which the new approach developed. Roughly speaking, it developed rather slowly between the mid-1970s and the mid-1980s, when most countries underwent this change.

If one asked what caused the change from the old to the new approach, and if one were allowed to mention only a single factor, I would say that technology was the key element. Certainly changes in ideas and policy recommendations played an important role, but technology played a leading role by making it possible to circumvent the type of regulatory impediments that were set up in the 1930s.

3.3   How Far to Go?

The new approach has not yet produced all its consequences. First, the liberalisation is still incomplete in many respects. Second, it takes time for the effects of liberalisation to emerge. In a sense, we may currently be living in the best phase, still enjoying the positive aspects of the old approach and some of the benefits of the new one. Banks are still regarded as crucial for financial stability and economic performance, and thus enjoy the kind of public protection—and rightfully so—which is not extended to other industries.[3] At the same time, increasing competition in financial services has brought significant benefits to banks' customers, and has thus promoted economic growth.

It is not obvious, whether the present trend is a reliable indicator of what the new approach will bring about in the long run. As the pendulum changed direction in the 1930s, it could change direction once again, at some point.

Moreover and perhaps more importantly, competition is not the only mode in which the banking industry works, and this is a major difference with other industries. A very important mode of interaction between firms within the banking industry is— and has to be—cooperation. We frequently refer to the banking 'system', but never to the automobile 'system'.

This different attitude is largely due to the fact that in the banking industry there are certain services, which do call for cooperation, while this is not the case in other industries. The most important ones are payment services, but others can also be identified. To an extent these limits to the 'text book' model of free competition can be a stabilising factor for the banking sector, as they allow for a sound inter-bank payment mechanism and liquidity redistribution, for instance. At the same time, banks' cooperation in payment networks does not need to limit free competition over customers using competition parameters such as interest rates and service charges. This can be naturally safeguarded through active competition policy.

A third reason why a new approach may not go as far as one could imagine has to do, somewhat paradoxically, with its success. Very often a 'market-friendly' approach to legislation and regulation of banks is also sympathetic to self-regulation. However, self-regulation is a cooperative exercise, and may even degenerate into a collusive exercise. Thus, if a competitive banking system develops naturally via injections of elements which are precisely of the opposite nature, one may wonder whether the competitive approach can go all the way. The pendulum has swung back in the United Kingdom, which was the fatherland of self-regulation, with the creation of the Financial Services Authority that took over most of the responsibilities previously assigned to an array of self-regulatory agencies.

All in all, how far can the new approach go? My tentative answer to this question is that a competition-oriented policy towards the banking industry may face certain limitations, which today are still not as clearly perceived as they might be in a few years' time.

3.4 The International Dimension

What has been said so far is applicable to any single 'national economy'. How does the internationalisation of banking contribute to the general picture? I think it contributes in at least three ways.

First, it represents an additional stimulus to competition, simply because it enlarges the set of competitors and generates a wider market, in which competition may develop more openly. This leads to the further selection of market participants and new stimuli to the surviving participants.

Second, the international dimension introduces competition among rules, prudential systems, and supervisory structures. In a way, it also puts the policy functions in a 'competitive game', which is unusual in a closed economy. Perhaps the only example prior to the Eurosystem was the structure of insurance supervision in the United States, which still lies in the States' competence. Normally, the jurisdiction of the States constitutes the jurisdiction of the supervisory authority, so there is no competition among supervisors. This form of competition is brought about by internationalisation.

Third, the internationalisation of banking generates a need for enhanced cooperation in the policy functions. Even if that degree of cooperation is pushed to its limits, it does not eliminate a certain competitive element among policy-makers or policy agencies. To some extent, this is a healthy element. For instance, when it is not entirely clear which regulatory instrument is the best, it may be beneficial to have the possibility of experimentation and competition among different approaches and selecting the most effective one.

3.5 The European Union and Euroland

It has to be noted at the outset that the European Union and the euro-area are to be kept distinct, simply because the single market and the single currency are not the same thing.

The single market is at this stage far more similar to a domestic system than it is to an international arrangement. But, as such, it is even more competition-oriented than national systems normally are. It provides almost in full the freedom that can be enjoyed in a domestic system. At the same time, some disciplinary functions typically exercised in a national system, such as supervision and prudential regulation, are provided to a much lesser extent. Furthermore, the single market entails an active competition policy.

Banks enjoy total freedom of establishment and provision of banking services, far more so than in the United States. The prohibition of interstate banking was fully abolished earlier in Europe. In addition, the rapid creation of the single market, through minimum harmonisation of banking legislation, did not wipe out competition among rules, which still works for the non-harmonised rules and practices. There is no single supervisor for the single market, while a single authority, the European Commission, has the task of stimulating competition, also in the banking industry. It is a unique blend, biased towards competition more than any other previously experimented solution.

However, the single market has always remained segmented by the multiplicity of currencies. Thus, in the area where the single currency has been introduced alongside the single market, the features just described have been enhanced even further.

The Eurosystem (the 'Federal Reserve System of the euro', namely, the system which includes the national central banks of the euro-area and the ECB) presents an additional peculiarity which needs to be addressed. Essay 7 discusses the unique situation in which the jurisdiction for monetary policy—the euro-area—does not coincide geographically with the jurisdiction for prudential supervision—the nationally chartered institutions. As noted, a similar phenomenon occurs in the field of insurance supervision in the United States, where the competence remains at the State level, but this separation of jurisdictions has never been experienced before in the banking field.

An additional complication is that the national central banks are very often entrusted with the responsibility of supervising banks, but as supervisors they are a national authority. I have worked for a national authority for thirty years now, and I know that these bodies are expected to look after their own national interests. National interests very often involve promoting the strength and competitiveness of the national banking system, or of the national financial centre.

Hence, the Eurosystem is facing the complex challenge of reconciling a notion of public interest in monetary policy, which refers to the euro-area, with a different notion of public interest in banking supervision, which, in some cases, is assigned to the same components of the system which share responsibility for the monetary policy function. In this case, the national central banks are also the responsible supervisory authorities. This peculiarity implies that the Eurosystem, in order to function properly, needs a degree of cooperation among national banking supervisors in order to cope with a banking industry quickly becoming area-wide. If that cooperation did not take place smoothly, an additional element of competition would be added to those already discussed, namely competition among some of the very components of the Eurosystem itself. Moreover, cooperation between national authorities needs to be stepped up in order to ensure effective banking supervision.

3.6 Good, But . . .

As this essay has tried to illustrate, the public policy response to the question of whether competition among banks is good or bad has changed profoundly into viewing competition as predominantly positive since the mid-1970s or so. This has not only been limited to revitalising competition policy, but also has involved a profound change in the attitudes towards the regulation and supervision of banks, ranging from close controls to 'market-friendly' minimum prudential standards and the enforcement of good internal risk management practices. Banks have also been forced to a significant extent to follow the same disclosure standards as other firms when they wish to tap capital markets. Finally, monetary policy has been reformed so as to function in a market-based financial system and the old instruments directly interfering with the credit aggregates have been abandoned.

The banking industry has become significantly more competitive than in the past, and competition is likely to increase further. New competitive pressures are emerging from abroad, owing to the liberalisation of international banking and capital flows, and as a result of the adoption of new banking technologies. However, there are some limits to regarding banking as moving towards the 'text book' ideal of perfect competition. These limits are a result of the peculiar characteristics of the banking system.

The word 'system' is the key; there is a natural element of cooperation among banks, which form the core of the monetary system, channelling liquidity to the other participants of the financial system and managing the payments traffic in the economy. These core transactions can only take place within a set of stable and respected institutions. Indeed, the creation of such a system for the euro-area via the common currency, large value payment systems and the inter-bank market calls for effective cooperation between the competent authorities in order to maintain the integrity of the euro-area banking system.[4]

Notes

1. I acknowledge the assistance of Simone Manganelli in the preparation of this speech.
2. This issue is further discussed in Essay 5, Section 5.4.
3. See discussion in Essay 5, Section 5.4.
4. See Essay 7 for further discussion.

4

Self vs. Public Discipline[1]

4.1 The Mode of Regulation

In the debate about financial regulation, the questions 'who should regulate?' and 'what should be regulated?' have been raised very frequently in recent times.[2] It seems, instead, that the 'how' issue, that is, the mode of regulation—and its consequences for achieving the underlying public policy objectives of systemic stability and investor protection—has not attracted all the attention it deserves.

In striving to discuss the question 'how to regulate?' this essay will address the development of the regulatory framework in the financial field along two key dimensions. First, the preference for financial self-imposed standards over law-based prescriptions and second, the preference for regulation based on financial institutions' internal control mechanisms ('process-oriented' regulation) over traditional simple and easily verifiable rules.

To be precise, this discussion will cover both regulation and supervision. Regulation refers to rule-making whereas supervision deals with the enforcement of the rules and the risk assessment conducted by supervisory authorities.

In both dimensions, the ongoing development towards standards and process oriented regulation has many desirable properties, as it is 'market-friendly' and allows the regulatory framework to adjust quickly and flexibly to financial innovation. However, one must be aware of the associated substantial outsourcing of disciplinary functions to financial institutions. Public authorities need to be alert to the potential pitfalls associated with this delegation of power and be careful not to hand over functions, which are public in nature. Authorities should, therefore, retain the possibility of 'call-backing' the outsourcing contract whenever needed to safeguard adequately the public interest. The case of Enron in 2002 was a painful, but perhaps healthy, reminder of the dangers in placing too much trust on the self-corrective features of the market mechanism.

This essay is organised as follows. It starts by setting out the conceptual road map used to explore the complex landscape of controls in the financial industry. Subsequently, it will review the evolution of the methods of financial regulation (along the two dimensions of this map) towards the use of standards and process-oriented regulation. Finally, the essay will turn to the policy issue of how to maintain effective control when significant self-regulatory powers are delegated to financial institutions.

4.2 Conceptual Map

To define the conceptual map, two pairs of opposite concepts provide the essential dimensions for analysing how the methods of financial regulation have recently evolved.

The first dimension is the contrast between self-imposed standards and law-based regulations as the basic tool for exercising discipline. Self-imposed standards constitute an informal mode of governance; they are formulated under a consensus principle by those to whom they are addressed and compliance with them is voluntary. By contrast, law-based provisions represent formal public regulations, which are stipulated in the law or issued by the competent public authorities.

While law-based provisions are binding by construction, due to their legal status, standards can also be binding, but only by practice. For instance, complying with standards can be required to be active in a specific market due to peer or market pressure. Hence, one should not always associate hardness with public rules and softness with standards; in some circumstances, standards can be even more compelling than public rules if, for instance, control is entrusted to a weak public authority. My direct experience provides a telling example. In Rome, people park their car without much inhibition in the most convenient place, even if there is a rule against it, and there is hardly a policeman, let alone anyone else, who will bring it to their attention. In Frankfurt, however, no policeman is fast enough to exercise discipline before other drivers, or the multitude of attentive pedestrians, does so in a strong and noisy way. As scholars of law know very well, and economists have learned from Hayek (1945 and 1974), habits are law. Hence, what ultimately differentiates standards from law-based provisions is that they emerge endogenously from the prevailing industry practices, while law-based provisions stem from exogenous public intervention.

In the financial field, several self-regulatory standards have been established by the industry itself, possibly with a public sector contribution. Interestingly, we also find the use of standards to be frequent in the international arena, as a tool to coordinate the regulatory policies of national authorities, because there is no formal legal structure in place at world level.

The second dimension of the conceptual map is the distinction between rules-based and process-oriented regulation. In the rules-based approach, the requirements are based on simple and often mechanical formulas, which are formulated in an objective way and applied in a uniform manner. This approach ensures consistency across financial institutions, but it disregards substantial variation in their risks and business activities. In addition, a simple rule easily becomes outdated by market developments and arbitrage opportunities. While this always has been true, technological advances and financial innovation have made it increasingly difficult to determine a single set of rules.

By contrast, the process-oriented approach rejects the idea of 'one-size-fits-all' rules, as it relies on financial institutions' own internal control processes. Process-oriented regulation does not impose a uniform framework for all institutions and hence lacks comparability across them. It is, therefore, more difficult to implement and verify in practice. However, it has the major benefit of being readily adaptable to dynamic developments in the financial industry, provided that internal procedures are kept in line with market developments. To quote Alan Greenspan, '[t]he use of new technology and instruments in rapidly changing financial markets means that the supervisor must rely on his evaluation of risk management procedures as a supplement to—and in extreme cases, a substitute for—balance sheet facts'.

Now, when locating regulatory innovations on the conceptual map, it is not a coincidence that nowadays we see the emergence of industry standards and process-oriented regulation at the same time. Both are flexible, market-friendly forms of governance. Both can emulate market developments and adjust to them more easily than law-based requirements and mechanical rules. Both place the emphasis on the self-disciplining mechanisms in the financial industry.

In going forward, I shall review both the relevance of financial standards and the evolution towards process-orientation in financial regulation. In terms of both dimensions, both a national and an international level will be referred to. Obviously, the international stage has gained much importance in recent times, as there is an ever-greater need for international coordination due to the integration of financial markets and extensive cross-border operations by financial institutions and investors.

4.3 Industry Standards

It is instructive to characterise the development of financial standards, starting from their original development in the national sphere.

Standards have existed as a source of an industry's self-discipline almost since the beginning of modern market economies. Their function was to define the terms of supply and marketability of products, thus facilitating trade in any given industry. Indeed, when thinking of standards, people probably first visualise industrial and technical standards they observe in everyday life—like the plane ticket. In some cases, standards appear as a natural (if not always fully logical) outcome of technical evolution—such as the normal computer keyboard—or they are the result of careful preparation and agreement among industry participants and associations. Of course, this aspect of facilitating trade has also applied in the financial industry—for instance, the standardisation of bank accounts and bank transfer instruments.

While removing obstacles to trade, standards can also develop into an effective form of governance, possibly serving as a substitute for public regulation. In political science, standards and public regulations are actually viewed as alternatives, and the availability and strength of the different options are used to explain the choice of one over the other. Accordingly, standards have emerged as the primary means of governance where there has been no strong central legal authority, or where the balance of power has been with the industry.

The use of standards in the function of governance is also very old. This occurred, for example, in the Middle Ages, well before a centralised state authority had taken shape. Businessmen spontaneously produced 'merchant law'—or *lex mercatoria*—whose principles and rules were managed by the merchants themselves. What kept people united under the same set of rules was the shared conviction of belonging to the same community—the key sanction being a rejection from that community. This is often still the case with modern standards.

In the financial field, standards played an important role, in the past, as a form of governance to contain risk-taking of financial intermediaries. Subsequently, they have been replaced by publicly issued prudential regulation, which mainly addresses banks, but increasingly also other financial institutions, with the objective of safeguarding financial stability. The period of free banking in the United States is a case in point. In the United States, towards the end of the nineteenth century, thousands of different bank notes were in circulation. 'Free-banking states' did not require a licence to enter the banking industry. The so-called wildcat banks, which assumed greater risk and inflated their currency to the point where it could no longer be continuously redeemed, were constrained only by private associations acting as standard-setters. The respective associations maintained a 'club-type' control over the members of the industry, but they were not successful in imposing effective restrictions on risk-taking behaviour and in preventing banking panics. On account of this negative experience, self-regulation was practically abandoned and was replaced by the public prudential regulation of banks, for the most part after the Great Depression.[3]

In contrast to the prudential banking regulation focused on financial stability, the regulation of securities market activities has traditionally aimed at protecting investors via controlling the conduct of business by banks and other financial institutions, sometimes also non-financial institutions.[4] In this field, private standards have tended to grow in importance.

Trading in stock markets has been historically governed to a large extent by self-regulatory organisations. This self-regulatory tradition has been wide-ranging in Anglo-Saxon countries. In the United States, for example, the New York Stock Exchange and the National Association of Securities Dealers and Clearing Agencies have retained important self-regulatory competencies. It was less so in continental Europe, where legal centralism, strong government authorities and public ownership have left little room for self-regulation to develop. Even in Europe, however, industry regulation has gained ground. The very recent proposal to reform the Investment Services Directive, for example, contains an express clause allowing the delegation of regulatory and supervisory responsibilities to regulated markets. In general, the importance of self-regulation in this field could increase further, as many exchanges have been transformed into private companies.

As securities markets are very important for the smooth functioning of the financial system as well as for the management of government debt, public authorities have a legitimate interest in this field. In this context, free competition is a major public concern, since the 'private club' nature of stock markets and their monopolistic dominance in national financial systems may have led to artificially high costs for firms and investors. Possibilities for international listing and cross-border investment, however, are now eroding monopolistic practices, thus making self-regulation more compatible with free competition. The official sector can play a major role in fostering effective competition; for instance, the current revision of the Investment Service Directive places much emphasis on unconstrained access to regulated markets by firms and investment service providers.

Another important area in the conduct of business in securities markets relates to accounting and disclosure requirements. The Enron case provided fresh indication of the critical importance of this area.

Traditionally, Anglo-Saxon countries and continental Europe have had different approaches to accounting: standards-based and law-based, respectively. In the United States, the predominant Accounting Principles, the US-GAAP, date from the 1930s and are now produced by the Financial Accounting Standards Board (FASB), a private sector standard-setting body staffed by professional accountants. In continental Europe, governments have controlled accounting directly by means of company law provisions. Accordingly, in the European Union, the Company Law Directives set out the basic rules, although there are still differences between countries.

Accounting and disclosure have a major importance for public confidence in financial markets, which in itself is a public interest. The Enron case and other accounting scandals have significantly weakened such confidence, as they have shown how many tricks can be used, even legitimately, to hide the truth and to prop up the stock market price until the very verge of collapse. This included the abuses of using unconsolidated special-purpose vehicles and off-balance-sheet derivatives. Even though the coverage of the US-GAAP is comprehensive, it did not cover these loopholes.

After Enron, the debate intensified on how to strengthen the accounting and auditing framework. The Enron case indeed suggests great caution when discipline in this area is exercised through private standards only. Luigi Spaventa, the Chairman of the Italian securities commission (Consob), recently argued that—thanks to the lesser reliance on industry standards and to beneficial legal provisions—such a case would be less likely in the European framework. Specifically, the seventh EU Company Law Directive requires the production of consolidated data, which limits, to a certain extent, the possibility of using special-purpose vehicles to hide losses. There are, of course, many other lessons from Enron, as will be discussed in the course of this essay.

Financial standards established by private bodies are increasingly an international phenomenon as well. This is a consequence of the fact that the state authority has been eroded by the borderless nature of financial activities. Just like at the national level, these international standards relate mainly to the area of conduct of business in securities markets.

First, market participants, organised in trade associations, have been quite active in developing standards for trading activities. For instance, the International Swaps and Derivatives Association has developed the international contractual model for swaps, while also working on best practices for derivatives markets, and the International Securities Market Association is establishing uniform best practices for securities trading and settlement.

Second, there is an ever-more compelling need to agree on international accounting standards. Financial markets are increasingly global and accounts must be comparable for investors. Take just the case of Daimler-Chrysler and Mercedes-Benz, which are now one and the same company listed both in the United States and in Germany. In spite of the fact that a distance should be the same whether it is measured in miles or kilometres, the accounts disclosed to the New York and German stock exchanges provide contrasting information. The International Accounting Standards Board began its work back in 1973 and it will play a key role in the harmonisation efforts by developing the IAS standards. These were recently recognised by the European Union as a basis for future reporting requirements. The United States, however, have not yet accepted them.

As mentioned above, standards are also used by public bodies as the tool of international cooperation. Here too, they have the general pros and cons of private standards, while they are obviously not to be regarded as an alternative to public regulation. Thus, they can be more flexible and market-friendly tools for achieving the particular public objectives, but safeguarding these public objectives can be more difficult when relying on a voluntary discipline rather than legally enforced regulation.

The most visible international financial standards are those developed by the specialist groups of supervisory authorities and central banks in the fields of financial stability or payment systems, such as the BCBS, IOSCO, IAIS, and CPSS. These standard-setters have, by-and-large, passed the initial stage of creating mutual recognition and trust among their members. It should also be noted that there are clear differences in the level of ambition of different standard-setters. The least ambitious form of international standards consists in adopting a minimum common denominator of existing national requirements. By contrast, the most advanced form may go even beyond some of the pre-existing national requirements; the main example of the latter was the first Basel Capital Accord of 1988.

The main feature of international standards is that the addressees are the standard-setters themselves. National authorities are, in principle, merely advised to implement such standards as part of national regulation and practice. This implies, in turn, that the implementation of the standards can not be taken for granted, but has to be assessed case by case. Indeed, the voluntary nature of standards—in the absence of a formal international power—is a clear weakness of this mode of international governance.

Two routes have been identified as remedies to this weakness. First, the implementation of standards may be subject to an independent assessment of compliance. The assessment may even be published in order to strengthen the incentives for the fulfilment of the agreements on a national level. In this regard, the work currently done by the IMF and the World Bank is to be acknowledged and praised. The second route is 'self-control' and peer pressure. For example, the implementation of the FATF's anti-money laundering recommendations by national authorities is verified by peer review, on the basis of which the FATF assesses compliance in individual jurisdictions.

To summarise, private industry standards play an important role as a disciplining device in the area of conduct of business in securities markets, whereas they have lost ground in the prudential field. This role is probably due to the ability, shown by the securities industry until recently, to discipline itself effectively, in line with public objectives. Most recently, this ability has been put into question by the increasing complexity of financial markets and instruments, as the Enron case shows. Indeed, in response to post-Enron concerns a tendency to reinforce public regulation relative to self-regulatory arrangements can be observed in Anglo-Saxon countries. As to the international level, an important role is played by standards developed by the multi-lateral forums where public authorities cooperate. In this context standards are set entirely on a voluntary basis and the main challenge remains of ensuring compliance across different jurisdictions.

4.4 Process-oriented Regulation

As regards the second dimension of the conceptual road map, that is, the axis between rule-based and process-oriented regulation, a shift from the former to the latter is emerging as a clear trend. This is clearly visible in many fields of financial regulation.

In the prudential field, reliance on financial institutions' formal internal models—validated and verified by supervisory authorities—was a path-breaking innovation first introduced internationally, when the Basel Committee on Banking Supervision, in 1997, established capital requirements for market risks. Subsequently, in the context of the revision of the 1988 Basel Accord, a similar approach has been proposed for credit and operational risks. While its achievements are clearly outstanding, it is not entirely appropriate to fully credit the Basel Committee with the invention of process-oriented regulation (see Annex 1). Drawing on my experience as Chairman of the Committee when the market risk amendment was launched, I can say it has been quite incidental that the development of sufficiently mature internal modelling techniques by banks has coincided with the development of international regulatory coordination.

Actually, the seeds of process-oriented regulation were sown on a national level before steps were taken on an international level. Regulation and supervision already have been geared for some time towards ensuring efficient risk management by banks themselves, rather than focusing solely on compliance with legally determined rules. The main reasons are that the complexity of the risk profile of each institution and the high speed at which risk positions can change have made uniform and simple regulatory formulas increasingly ineffective. In this way, the regulatory framework is becoming less intrusive and more market-friendly as emphasis on rules-based restrictions declines.

The principles of process-orientated regulation seem to have played a greater role in the Anglo-Saxon countries than in continental Europe. The US and the UK authorities have been the keenest supporters of the internal models-based approach in the international setting as well. Indeed, looking back, the process-orientation of the United States has taken the form of strong reliance on examinations and extended supervisors' discretionary powers. The same has applied in the United

Kingdom, as confirmed by Sir Andrew Large by stating that: 'we should not lose sight of the fact that so much in regulation has not been about structure but about attitude and management: the "how" of regulation; the way it is done'.

Over time, more and more supervisors, in more and more countries, have been moving towards process-based supervision in order to cope with the changing risk profile of credit institutions. This refers to developing risk analysis methods that allow a differentiated supervision, tailored to each individual institution's risk management needs, thus abandoning the 'one-size-fits-all' approach of rules-based regulation.

An analogous but not identical dichotomy as 'rules vs. processes' in prudential regulation can be found in the conduct of business field. This can be referred to as 'rules vs. principles'. Both pairs of concepts share the basic feature that they contrast formal and detailed requirements (i.e. 'rules') with regulations, which allow, and indeed require, substantial involvement of individual firms and ample flexibility as regards the compliance with the set requirements (i.e. 'processes' or 'principles'). Process- and principles-orientation are more robust over time than detailed rules, which can easily be made obsolete by market developments. However, while in the process-oriented approach authorities' main role consists in setting out requirements for internal procedures of financial institutions and validating their output, in the principles-based approach authorities essentially stipulate the desired outcome, but not the exact ways of delivering it. One could even say that in principles-based regulation the responsibility for delivering the appropriate outcome rests *more*, not less, strongly with the regulated entity than in the case of detailed rules. In the latter environment, meeting the letter of the regulation—rather than upholding with its spirit and objectives—could be regarded as fulfilling the responsibility of the regulated entity, and may be used as a way to circumvent the original purpose of the rule.

In the debate after the Enron case, the distinction between rules and principles has been made to characterise the two alternative approaches to accounting. This refers to relying either on specific, detailed disclosure requirements or broad principles which set out the basic objectives for disclosure, while leaving individual firms the freedom, but also the responsibility, to present their own specific activities and risks by drawing on their particular internal control systems.

Here, the positions of the United States and Europe are reversed, since the US-GAAP is based on very formal, detailed rules, while European accounting rules and the current international IAS standards rely much more on general principles. Enron clearly took advantage of the prescriptive accounting rules in the US framework, stretching them to their limit, as the rules—even though very detailed—did not cover the specific instruments used by the business to hide its losses. After the failure of Enron, a discussion has arisen concerning the relative merits of rules and principles for accounting as the appropriate basis for developing accounting standards and overcoming current deficiencies. Again, the main benefit of the principles-based approach is that its basic objectives can not be easily circumvented, and made obsolete, by financial innovation in the same manner as detailed accounting rules can be.

A similar evolution of financial regulation can be detected from explicit rules to process-orientation also on the international level. It is increasingly acknowledged that the traditional rules-based regulation does not best suit the international financial markets. This is due to the geographical constraints of state powers and—as on a national level—to the limitations of the rules-based approach in tackling financial innovation and the circumvention efforts of market participants.

As we know, the Basel II proposal is based on three pillars. Pillar I is a measurement framework that refines the 1988 Accord by drawing on banks' own risk assessment systems. It replaces the one-size-fits-all approach with more risk-sensitive options. Pillar II is the supervisory review of banks' capital adequacy and internal assessment. Finally, Pillar III is market discipline, that is, encouraging safe and sound banking practices through effective disclosure. The degree of detail of Basel II is very high. However, the workability of this framework largely rests on the self-assessments of banks and on the consistency of the supervisory review across jurisdictions.

In summary, there is a clear trend towards process-orientation, in particular, in the area of prudential controls, which are in the domain of public regulation rather than industry standards. This trend is beneficial and does not appear to be reversible in the foreseeable future. However, it necessarily requires strong public discipline to function properly and also effective market discipline to complement public action. The regulations based on firms' internal practices impose a heavy verification burden on supervisory authorities and may leave room for 'gaming incentives' by the regulated entities. In concrete terms, this means that when its financial condition deteriorates, an institution may be tempted to hide problems and manipulate results. Therefore, competent authorities have to be very strict in validating internal solutions and in asking for necessary revisions. In other words, effective supervision has to take centre stage in the overall regulatory framework, when financial institutions' internal control mechanisms are used as a basis for regulatory requirements.

4.5 Externalities and Captivity

The final part of this essay dwells further on the issue of effective public discipline. This issue becomes highly relevant when a move towards process-oriented regulation in the prudential field is combined with self-disciplinary standards in the field of conduct of business. These two developments, which were reviewed above, imply a clear shift towards market-friendly regulation, delegating increasing regulatory powers to the financial institutions themselves.

Two crucial problems need to be kept in mind when discussing the effectiveness of public control. Indeed self-disciplinary regimes can fail (and have failed) because of two main reasons. The first is that only public authorities can ultimately take due account of the possible problems caused by negative externalities. The second is that regulation may be captured for the benefit of the industry itself. The developments in the regulatory framework described earlier in this essay can exacerbate the two problems, as the influence of the industry on its own governance is enhanced. This applies both in the national and international dimensions. In addition, the international dimension has its own specific concerns.

Systemic risk is obviously the main externality requiring public control. The inability to account for the externalities it involved, ultimately led to the collapse of the historical free banking arrangements based on self-regulation and to the institution of public prudential regulation. Clearly, the financial industry alone cannot duly take into account the wide impacts of a crisis, which can extend well beyond the boundaries of a single institution or a segment of the industry. It still seems that today, as in the past, difficulties assume systemic relevance only when the banking system is hit. It is the special role of banks and the associated systemic risk which continue to provide the justification for the specific public control of the banking industry and the focus on the issue of externalities in the area of prudential regulation.[5]

Another important and often underestimated externality is the implication that the behaviour of financial institutions may have for overall economic growth. This issue is relevant, for instance, in the area of regulatory capital. One should be aware that the shift towards the use of internal risk measurement systems for regulatory capital purposes has the likely implication that the way in which risks are managed by financial institutions, with regard to changing economic conditions, will have a greater impact than before. This impact will, of course, depend crucially on the specific nature of the internal risk assessment process. It is widely recognised that the amount of capital required, as determined under the new Basel Accord, would significantly increase in a recession if banks continue to apply the currently most widespread 'point-in-time' risk measurement methodologies. This so-called pro-cyclicality could hamper banks' capability to extend credit and might, thus, produce adverse overall economic consequences.

The impact on the business cycle could be seen as an externality, which is unlikely to be taken into account by individual institutions. Banks may not internalise this feature of the 'point-in-time' risk measurement, while they appreciate its ability to adjust quickly to risk differences among borrowers. Accordingly, this type of risk measurement may lead banks to restructure their portfolios when the economic conditions change. This means, in fact, transferring the negative impact of a recession to the rest of the economy. Therefore, public authorities may need to intervene in the implementation of the Basel II proposal on a national level and to encourage the adoption of the 'through-the-cycle' approaches to capital allocation.

Turning to the second problem, regulatory capture can be defined as designing and implementing regulatory requirements for the private benefit of the firms being regulated—at worst to the detriment of the public at large. One recalls the famous sceptical attitude of George Stigler (1988) that industry associations and major firms will make sure that regulation will be designed for the industry's benefit. Other scholars, with more nuanced views (such as Jean-Jaques Laffont and Jean Tirole 1993), have suggested that public rules established by independent authorities are least likely to suffer from regulatory capture.

In this context, the case of the potentially undue influence of industry lobbies can be taken up by returning once again to the Enron case. It seems now clear that the US accounting rules were indeed captured by the powerful industrial lobby and that this hindered progress towards adequate transparency, preventing early and effective reaction to the problems which materialised in the Enron affair. In particular, the FSAB is now under heavy criticism for its very sluggish and eventually inconclusive stance on consolidation accounting. FSAB's projects on special-purpose vehicles and off-balance-sheet abuses were also apparently put on hold, under pressure from a powerful corporate lobby group, as managers had found that vehicles can usefully deliver 'flexibility'.

If future Enrons were to be avoided, greater independence in setting accounting rules is needed as well as more effective international cooperation. Under the auspices of the IASB, work has already commenced on the priority areas identified in the Enron case: off-balance-sheet derivatives and special-purpose vehicles.

These examples should be sufficient to support the view that effective public discipline is needed to address both the problem of externalities and the problem of regulatory capture.

As is increasingly recognised, public authorities could also share the burden of disciplining the industry with the equity and debt-holders of the financial institutions. A central role for this market discipline is envisaged—for the first time—in the third Pillar of the new Capital Accord.

The actual extent to which market discipline could play a role in complementing the discipline by public authorities is subject to varying views. The strongest support can be found in views based on neoclassical rational expectations, which regard markets as being in continuous equilibrium with information-efficient prices. Indeed, the prices of the securities issued by financial institutions need to reflect their risks if any market discipline is to work, because there has to be an impact on the cost of funds.

There is positive empirical evidence, gathered for European banks, that the prices of bank securities do constitute an indicator of their soundness. Similar evidence also exists for the United States. Hence, market discipline can apparently play a useful role in complementing supervisors' monitoring activities and would be further supported by enhancing the disclosure regime. However, alternative 'Neo-Austrian' theories (as e.g. recently explored by Harald Benink), and theories pointing to the impact on prices of strategic behaviour in financial markets, warn against possible over- and undershooting in market prices. Also these views have gained empirical support. This suggests, in turn, that there are hazards in basing too much explicit regulation on market prices, as would happen in a more widespread application of the Fair Value Accounting in the banking field.

Turning to the international dimension, a specific problem exists because here a strong public authority simply does not exist. On a national level, where such an authority is available, a move towards industry-standards and process-orientation can be beneficial. On an international level, the same move can be more of a mixed blessing. To be consistent, developments within the international regulatory framework would have to be on a par with the adequate international powers and control mechanisms.

Indeed, if—due to political and institutional arrangements—the only jurisdiction equipped to provide a public good is the nation state, the overall global optimum (corresponding to the now-emerging notion of global public goods) may never be achieved. National authorities are unlikely to take into account the externalities of their actions on an international level. At worst, they work for the benefit of national financial institutions when implementing and interpreting commonly agreed standards, at the expense of the objectives of safety and soundness and even a level playing field. This can be seen as another, less obvious, case of captive regulators.

Considering again the example of Basel II, a system will be put in place where the regulatory capital requirements (Pillar I) and also, to a large extent, market discipline (Pillar III) are shared on an international level. The necessary supervisory actions of checking and verifying the outcome of banks' internal processes (Pillar II) remain, however, on a national level. Unless mechanisms of substantial international cooperation in the implementation of the Basel II requirements are put in place, comparable treatment of banks within different jurisdictions, in an adequately stringent way, may not be guaranteed. Adequate safeguards, even against possible favouritism by local supervisory authorities when implementing the new requirements, need to be in place.

4.6 Friendly, not Captive

This essay has discussed the evolution of the methods of financial regulation towards using self-imposed standards and process-oriented regulatory tools as alternatives to simple, unequivocal legal rules. This evolution involves significant outsourcing of self-regulatory functions to financial institutions or industry associations. In the light of past experiences, this development is basically to be supported as market-friendly and innovation-adjustable. It can, however, involve important pitfalls. The issues of negative externalities and regulatory capture may, in particular, generate problems when such delegation of responsibility occurs.

Thus, the main message of the essay concerns the appropriate scope of entrusting regulatory functions to the industry itself. As we have seen, delegation is, in principle, favourable, but the appropriate role assigned to the market is not the same as full reliance on the 'invisible hand'. One must firmly maintain the possibility of effective public discipline whenever needed. Market-friendly regulation needs to be coupled with a strong and 'non-captive' public authority. Furthermore, we should be aware that this essential counterpart is not present on an international level; this can be a source of serious problems unless bridged by effective cooperation.

In particular, the case of Enron is a reminder that one needs to distinguish clearly between the scope of public intervention and its effectiveness. Where there is room for public action, a minimum scope of intervention should not be the same as weak intervention. With Enron, the signals provided by market authorities and policy-makers were not sufficiently strong to ensure adequate transparency and avoid conflicts of interest. While initiatives to improve the situation were proposed over a relatively long period of time prior to the incident, the prevailing pressure from the corporate sector lobbies prevented substantive achievements.

Regulators and policy-makers have much in common with teachers. A teacher should be friendly to pupils—just as regulators need to be market-friendly—but like teachers, regulators always have to remember who they are and exercise the necessary discipline when needed.

Annex 1. *Agreements by the Basel Committee on Banking Supervision*

Supervisory core principles	Harmonised regulatory standards	Supervisory cooperation within and across financial sectors	Other issues
2001 Principles for the management of credit risk Risk management principles for electronic banking **1999** Core principles methodology Risk concentration principles **1997** Core principles for effective banking supervision Principles for the management of interest rate risk **1990** Information flows between banking supervisory authorities (supplement to the Basel Concordat) **1983** Principles for the supervision of banks' foreign establishments (Basel Concordat)	**2003** The New Basel Capital Accord (third Consultative Document on reforming the Basel Accord) **1996** Amendment of the Basel Capital Accord to incorporate market risks **1995** Framework for supervisory information about the derivatives activities of banks and securities firms (jointly with IOSCO) **1992** Minimum standards for the supervision of international banking groups and their cross-border establishments **1988** International convergence of capital measurement and capital standards (Basel Accord)	**2002** Sharing of financial records between jurisdictions in connection with the fight against terrorist financing the relationship between banking supervisors and banks' external auditors **2001** Essential elements of a statement of cooperation between banking supervisors **1999** Intra-group transactions and exposures principles (jointly with IOSCO and IAIS) **1998** Supervisory cooperation on year 2000 cross-border issues **1996** Basel/IOSCO joint response to the G7 heads of government request **1990** Exchanges of information between banking and securities supervisors	**2003** Sound practices for the management and supervision of operational risk **2001** Customer due diligence for banks Sound practices for the management and supervision of operational risk **2000** Sound practices for managing Liquidity in banking organisations Best practices for credit risk disclosure Banks' interactions with highly leveraged institutions (HLIs): implementation of the sound practices paper **1999** Sound practices for loan accounting and disclosure Sound practices for banks' interactions with HLIs **1998** Sound practices for loan accounting, credit risk disclosure and related matters

Self vs. Public Discipline   53

Notes

1. I acknowledge the assistance of Pedro Gustavo Teixeira and Jukka Vesala in the preparation of this lecture.
2. See Essays 2 and 5 for discussion on the 'what' question, and Essays 6 and 7 on the 'who' question.
3. See also Essay 8, Section 8.2.
4. To be discussed at greater length in Essay 5.
5. See also Essay 5, Section 5.3.

5

Securities and Banking[1]

5.1 Ageing Walls

This essay will focus on the changing relationship between banking and securities activities. Whereas for a long time, since the 1930s, separation ('walls') has prevailed between banking and securities, more recently increasing links ('bridges') have developed between the two activities.

The increasing role of securities markets everywhere in the world and the increasing links between banking and securities activities have had relevant implications for the risk profile of individual financial institutions and the financial system as a whole. Consequently, new policy issues have arisen with regard to the regulatory and supervisory framework. In Europe, these developments have been accentuated by the advent of the euro, and policy-makers have paid special attention to it, as reflected in the work of EU related bodies such as the Economic and Financial Committee and the Committee of Wise Men.

For the sake of clarity, one should first define the notions of banking and securities. As already noted in Essay 2, only a specific legal type of financial institution—a bank—is allowed to conduct what was there called the 'essence' of banking business, that is, granting loans on their own account and collecting deposits from the general public. As regards securities firms, they include a variety of institutions, which do not conduct the core 'loan-deposit' banking business nor sell insurance products. They can be, *inter alia*, investment funds, investment banks, broker–dealers, and financial advisers.

Although the notion of the essence of banking is common to virtually all jurisdictions, differences were more pronounced, until recently, in the scope of other financial activities allowed to banks. In the United States and Japan—which for many decades had required a strict separation of banking and securities activities—a combination of the two activities was permitted by the end of the last decade. In the European Union, 'universal banking' has always allowed securities businesses to be conducted by banks.

This essay is organised as follows. It will start by examining relevant structural changes in the financial system. After that, it will turn to the issue of which risks to individual institutions and the whole financial system are generated by the recently built bridges between banking and securities activities. Finally, the main implications of the banking–securities combination for the regulatory and supervisory arrangements will be addressed.

5.2 New Bridges

Consider first the relevant developments in the financial system. Following the increased size and sophistication of securities markets, structural changes have progressively occurred on a global basis. Profound changes have also occurred in bank-dominated continental Europe, especially since the boost provided by the euro. Five changes are particularly relevant: securitisation, institutionalisation of investment, emergence of complex financial instruments, conglomeration, and consolidation.

Securitisation refers to the shift in the financial system away from the dominance of non-marketable instruments (bank loans and deposits) to marketable securities. On the demand side, this shift has been generated by the substantial increase in financial wealth held by households—itself a result of our societies becoming increasingly affluent—and the development of voluntary long-term saving to supplement public pension schemes. On the supply side, the increasing use of securities market funding by firms has been related to obtaining more competitive interest rates and diversifying debt structures.

The pace of securitisation is particularly rapid in Europe, where bank deposits and public pension schemes used to be dominant. In the euro-area, the share of direct and indirect securities holdings in households' assets is now considerably above the share of deposits. The stock market capitalisation of euro-area listed companies is now above 100 per cent of GDP, up from just 30 per cent in 1995. This figure is affected by stock price changes, but a doubling in the number of listed companies since 1995 confirms an increased use of equity market finance. As for the bond markets, the annual growth rate of issuance by euro-area non-financial firms has been well above 20 per cent over the past three to four years. The overall size of the debt market—including also previously predominant government and bank bonds—is now approaching the volume of bank credit. No doubt, the recourse to market-based finance in Europe is still significantly below that of the United States, but the gap is rapidly narrowing. This development has substantially increased the demand for investment banking services, where some major European banks now act as global investment banks, mainly competing with global players of US origin.

In the past, there was—whether *de jure* as in 'Glass Steagall countries' or de facto as in continental Europe—a kind of wall between banking and securities activities. Indeed, banks used to channel funds from low- or medium-wealth households to most firms, whereas only high-wealth households invested in securities by directly purchasing the equities or bonds only issued by the few largest firms. Securitisation means that dealing in securities is now also recurrent among lower-wealth households and smaller and higher-risk firms. For example, the share of higher-risk bond issuers with less than an A-rating has increased to 25 per cent in 2000 from ten in 1998 in the euro-area. Similarly, in the euro-area equity market, the number of listings of small growth companies increased tenfold between 1998 and 2000.

The second major trend—institutionalisation of investment—refers to the increased purchase of securities via collective investment vehicles, such as mutual funds, pension funds, and life insurance. Rather than providing funds directly via the financial market, households invest in collective vehicles to obtain diversification benefits, and thus higher expected returns, while keeping their risk levels acceptable. Wealthy households pursue the same objective also through private asset management services. The increased size and sophistication of financial markets have also made investing in collective vehicles relatively cheaper than entering into securities markets directly.

Also, this process has been very rapid in Europe. In most continental European countries, all types of collective investment have increased much faster than direct holdings of securities. The total value of mutual funds has increased at the fastest rate by 25-fold since the early 1990s.

The institutionalisation of investment has preserved, and even expanded, the role of financial intermediaries despite the increased role of securities markets. Even though there is increased competition from non-bank intermediaries, the importance of banks has not tended to decline either. This is clearly the case in Europe, where, in asset management services, European banks have been able to exploit their extensive retail distribution networks to reach ultimate investors, thus gaining a dominant position, that in many EU countries goes beyond 80 per cent of total collective investment. Major European banks actually redesigned their strategies as they saw higher profit margins and greater growth prospects in asset management and investment banking activities than in traditional banking. Such strategies were successful in boosting non-interest income and profitability, also because of the boom in securities markets until mid-2000. In 2000, non-interest income accounted for 52 per cent of EU banks' total net income, whereas it was less than 30 per cent in 1996. For major banks active in the securities field, the replacement of traditional interest income has gone much further—the share of non-interest income reaching in some cases 70 per cent of total income.

All in all, securities activities have become more important for many banks, either directly or via their subsidiaries, thereby establishing a strong bridge between banking and securities activities.

The third structural change is the rapid growth in complex financial instruments designed to unbundle, trade, and transfer risks. Although the statistics available are somewhat unsystematic, it can be said that the global markets for complex instruments—which for a considerable part consist of OTC derivatives—have doubled in size several times in ten years or so. Whereas these instruments originally developed in the market risk area, they have been progressively extended to the field of credit risk as well. This tendency is also clearly visible in Europe.

Among the instruments created to handle credit risk, the repackaging of bank loans into marketable securities represents the oldest development. In addition to traditional mortgage loans, this technique now extends to loans to small and medium-sized enterprises and consumer credits and covers instruments such as asset backed securities and collateralised debt obligations.

Another important category of instruments to transfer credit risk consists of credit derivatives. Although the market for these instruments is still relatively small in comparison with more mature derivatives, it has greatly expanded in recent years.

Using the various credit risk transfer instruments, banks can even completely shift the credit risk they accrued in their credit origination to other banks or other financial institutions such as insurance companies and investment funds. Recent market reports suggest that this risk-shifting behaviour has been significant, insurance companies taking on a bulk of the risk.

The development of complex financial instruments is in line with the notion—once put forward by Robert Merton—according to which the existence of sophisticated securities markets allows financial institutions to replicate all traditional financial products. In terms of the bridges between banking and securities activities, there are two important aspects. One is that banks are losing their monopoly position over instruments involving credit risk, as credit risk can be traded and reallocated to other financial institutions. The other is that the distinction between non-marketable loans and marketable securities tends to fade.

Conglomeration, the fourth relevant change can be defined as the conduct within one financial institution or group of at least two of the three traditionally distinct activities of banking, securities, and insurance. This general definition could lead to different legal definitions. For instance, the EU Directive on financial conglomerates requires the presence of insurance to qualify a conglomerate, since the capital regulation for banks and securities firms is already laid down under a single framework by the Capital Adequacy Directive (CAD). In the United States, on the other hand, a financial conglomerate is defined by the Gramm–Leach–Bliley Act of 1999 as a financial holding company, which can (but is not bound to) offer the full range of financial services.

Recently, the drift towards conglomeration has been quite strong in Europe. In the euro-area, mergers and acquisitions across sectors have accounted for roughly 30 per cent of all financial industry deals in terms of value over the past five years. Banks have increasingly merged with, or acquired, securities firms, to take advantage of the developing securities markets. Interestingly, new types of conglomerate structures have also emerged, such as the combination of banking activities and pension fund management. The traditional form of conglomeration, which was the setting up of bank-insurance groups, has also continued to develop, driven by reforms in national pension systems as well as by synergies in the distribution of different financial products.

The possibility of conglomeration gives financial institutions some latitude in choosing the corporate structure that suits them best. Some banks—as in the universal banking model—choose to take advantage of their banking franchise and undertake securities activities in-house, while establishing adequate Chinese walls wherever necessary. Other banks choose to conduct securities businesses via a separate subsidiary to avoid any market presumption of conflicts of interest between banking and securities businesses. Others go even further in the separation by creating a holding company and carrying out securities activities in a sister affiliate of a bank. Compared with the direct provision of securities services by banks, the latter two organisational forms might be adopted to convey the perception that a wall still exists between banking and securities activities, even though intra-group linkages bridge them.

The fifth and last trend discussed here is consolidation, which consists in the establishment of large and complex financial institutions with sizeable market positions. Consolidation is the outcome of mergers and acquisitions both within and across sectors of the financial system. The pace of consolidation has been rapid in recent years. Economies of scale related to wholesale trading, the processing of market information and the servicing of large institutional and corporate clients have increased. Therefore, both banks and other financial institutions have been forced to expand in size to be able to conduct successful business activities in securities markets. These developments have been thoroughly documented and analysed in the 2001 report of the G10 central banks, coordinated by Roger Ferguson, the Vice Chairman of the US Federal Reserve.

In Europe, the advent of the euro has triggered a particularly significant movement towards consolidation, as the segmentation of markets along the different currencies made it impossible to fully exploit the economies of scale. The fact that 70 per cent of the value of all mergers of euro-area financial institutions over the past ten years has taken place in the last three years illustrates how strong the impact of the euro has been. Although most of the deals have been domestic, their motivation often reflected the need to operate effectively in more integrated securities markets. Moreover, the share of cross-border mergers has been increasing.

The consolidation of banks and securities firms into large and complex institutions has led to an increased concentration of wholesale trading activities into single entities, yet another development that cuts across the traditional boundaries of banking and securities products. By contrast, in the retail financial sector, the market landscape is more diversified, with small banks and securities houses competing against the large financial institutions.

All five structural changes reviewed above point to major bridges between banking and securities activities. These bridges have been built in recent years in fundamental areas of financial activity. Recapitulating them briefly, securitisation has extended the recourse to markets to individuals and firms, which previously resorted predominantly to banking services. Institutionalisation of investment has shifted the focus of banks beyond the traditional loan–deposit activity. Complex risk transfer instruments have reduced the dominance of banks in the credit business. Conglomeration has led to the establishment of corporate structures, which bind together different financial services. Finally, consolidation has resulted in major market positions for large and complex financial institutions in several financial instruments.

5.3   Ensuing Risks

This essay now turns to the implications of these market developments for the risks of individual intermediaries and the financial system as a whole.

As to individual banks, their participation in securities activity stemming from the developments just reviewed changes the risks to which they are exposed, increasing the importance of market risks and income volatility risks, while reducing that of credit and interest rate risks (the traditional banking risks). Market risks can arise in particular from banks' own proprietary trading activities supporting retail asset management and investment banking businesses. As for income volatility risks, these have already demonstrated their relevance, as the recent reduction in capital market activity has caused a significant drop in investment banking volumes and income of some of the major European banks.

The potential costs of the change in the risk profile has to be balanced against the benefits from increased diversification, the gains from enhancing bank–customer relationships, and economies of scope in the production and distribution of financial services. Rather than trying to strike any balance between costs and benefits, the changes in banks' risk profiles should be assessed in the context of the regulatory and supervisory arrangements concerning the safety and soundness of banks.

The increased trading in complex financial instruments substantially changes the risk profile of the financial institutions participating in these markets. On the one hand, the rise of risk transfer instruments is a positive development, because these instruments allow the risk to be taken by the best placed institution. On the other hand, these instruments allow institutions to take large risk positions and to reallocate them rapidly to third parties. Because of these aspects, the transparency of markets and risk positions is reduced, and it may become hard for supervisors to monitor the 'true' risks run by individual institutions. Moreover, the concentration of the global activity in a few major intermediaries due to the consolidation process may lead to significant risk concentrations, which could be particularly important in OTC derivative instruments. According to some estimates, the top three intermediaries can account for almost 30 per cent of the global activity in these contracts.

The trading in complex instruments increases the importance of adequate risk management at individual institutions. It should not be forgotten that the distinction between credit and market risk is, in economic terms, one of quantity, not of quality. The magnitude of the market risk exposure of any traded security or derivative instrument converges to the credit risk exposure—that is, the full depletion of the investment. With the increased trading of credit risk the distinction between the two types of risk becomes blurred, as one can no longer clearly separate tradable and non-tradable risks from one another.

Indeed, some financial institutions have already started to develop integrated approaches to the management of credit and market risks. Quantitative tools are being expanded by many banks into the credit risk area as well—also because of the upcoming changes in bank capital regulation, which allow the use of banks' internal rating systems.

Turning to the consequences of these structural changes on financial stability,[2] the traditional doctrine is that possible disruptions to the financial system arise from banking but not from the securities field. This doctrine has inspired the basic difference in the policy approaches (both regulatory and supervisory) respectively adopted for banking and securities activities. Whereas in the case of banking policy is centred on the pursuit of financial stability, in the securities field it is centred on investor protection. This whole approach has been based on two main types of considerations.

First, financial stability concerns were not expected to arise when the securities businesses only involved small volumes. In today's highly developed financial systems, this argument has lost most of its validity.

The second and more fundamental argument is that the very nature of securities activities is such that they are not a potential source of fragility in the same way in which banking is. In view of the important structural changes described above, the validity of this argument needs to be checked. Some academics (such as Franklin Allen) have begun addressing it, but the main body of the literature has remained focused on refining the theories on banking, or looks at the issue of contagion in world securities markets.

Before exploring the stability problems raised by securities activities one should be somewhat more specific about the definition of the polyvalent notion of systemic risks. Of the various approaches to the notion, the correct definition ought not, in my view, to refer to isolated individual failures. Rather, it should refer to widespread disruptions spreading through contagion and such that the financial system is prevented from carrying out its core economic functions of channelling payments and allocating funds from savings to investment.[3]

For the purpose of a discussion, the proposition that securities activities do not threaten the stability of the financial system should be split into two parts: the risk of a run and the risk of contagion.

As regards the former, the traditional argument is that securities businesses, by dealing with liquid and marketable assets and liabilities, would be insulated from runs and liquidity losses, inherent in banking. This argument should be rejected. Analogous to bank runs, securities investors can and do run (i.e. rush to sell) in favour of higher liquidity and lower risk. Although such herding is more often associated with poorly informed retail investors, evidence suggests that it might take place also among professional investors.

Nevertheless, securities businesses operating a separate balance sheet are not necessarily at risk of failure when a rush to exit securities markets occurs. This is due to two reasons. First, investors bear the risk rather than the intermediary, when their own funds supporting the securities business are separated from the customer funds. Second, intermediaries can avoid the losses and risk of failure associated with banking—where fixed-value deposits need to be met by selling illiquid loans—if tradable assets can be downsized in step with investors' withdrawals. This difference in the vulnerability to runs constitutes an important wall between banking and securities activities.

Recent market developments, however, suggest that securities operations could be increasingly fragile vis-à-vis outflows of liquidity. Many institutions—including institutional investors, investment banks and other regulated or unregulated entities, as well as banks—engage in proprietary trading at their own risk and hold positions in complex financial instruments. In circumstances of market stress, these positions can turn out to be illiquid, to be cancelled, or to be reduced. Moreover, if leverage is extensively used to fund positions, the firms engaging in these activities can become highly vulnerable, as past incidents have shown.

The second part of the proposition, stating that contagion risk would be confined to banking, requires a somewhat elaborate answer. The reason lies in the interpretation of the expression 'confined to banking'.

It is true that, in addition to the risks stemming from their own securities activities, banks could be affected by a failure in the securities businesses of another financial institution, thus exposing the financial system to potential instability. For example, the Ferguson report on consolidation suggests that sophisticated securities markets require the participation of ever-larger financial institutions and groups. If any of these institutions encounter serious problems and there is contagion to the banking system, risks to overall financial stability may be created.

More precisely, banks could be seriously affected via their credit exposures to other financial intermediaries. The increased trading in complex financial instruments has led to a potentially important concentration of credit exposure of banks vis-à-vis securities firms. In the case of LTCM, for example, such exposures arose from OTC derivatives, prime brokerage and clearing, as well as regular lending. Moreover, the LTCM incidence brought up another, and possibly even more important channel of contagion to banks, arising from the impact on market prices and liquidity. At worst, the failure of a major securities market player—or even a disorderly winding down of its positions—could severely depress prices in illiquid markets to the point that other intermediaries are seriously affected. In the LTCM case, financial stability concerns were more related to this channel of contagion than the credit exposures of banks—as can be inferred from the statements made on the occasion by Chairman Greenspan and President McDonough.

Moreover, non-financial firms could, in principle, also be a source of fragility to banks and to the whole financial system, as they could also face important market risks and collateral values could be affected by a turmoil in securities markets. However, the risks for banks could be greater from other financial institutions than from non-financial firms because financial institutions can be highly leveraged, have very large market positions, and entertain closer links with banks.

Thus far the essay has examined the issue whether contagion can spill from the non-banking over the banking sector, that is, whether the banking system can be affected. Another issue is whether the failure of an independent securities firm could *by itself* be a source of risk to financial stability, even when banks are not affected. Here, my answer would be negative. Looking back at the episodes of turbulence over the last decade, a common observation is that difficulties have assumed systemic relevance only when the banking system and its liquidity redistribution functions were hit. Thus, it seems that the view can be maintained that crises not involving banks or a disruption of the monetary process—what Anna Schwartz (1986) called 'pseudo crises'—will have few overall financial stability implications. This notion is probably the most fundamental wall between banking and securities activities.

Contrary to the above, it is frequently argued that technological and financial innovation, enabling non-banks to mimic traditional banking products, such as loans and payment services, erodes the special position of banks. However, the reason why banks are special is not related to the non-marketability of their instruments or the uniqueness of their individual products (see also Essay 2, Section 2.3). It is related instead to the functioning of banks as critical players providing and redistributing liquidity. This function is based on the joint supply of deposits and loans—offering continuous access to liquidity—and to the maturity transformation of short-term liabilities into long-term assets. These essential functions of banks cannot easily be broken into components, because—as recent research further shows—taking deposit and providing credit lines are two manifestations of the same liquidity provision function. Moreover, banks hold a natural and unique position, lying between central banks—the ultimate sources of liquidity—and the rest of the financial system.

To conclude, it seems that market developments have four main risk implications. First, individual financial institutions are confronted with a more complex and fluid risk profile than in the past, which requires upgraded risk management. Second, potential disruptions to the financial system could well originate from securities activities, because there could be spillover effects jeopardising the soundness of major banking organisations. However, this does not amount to saying that non-bank financial institutions are becoming systemically relevant in their own right if the banking system is not affected. Indeed, the special role of banks in providing liquidity leads us to think that the extension of the public safety net to non-bank financial institutions or securities markets, in general, would not be warranted. Third, the integration of markets and the internationalisation of financial institutions facilitate the spreading of major financial disruptions across borders via credit exposures, or market price and liquidity conditions. The euro-area is a special case in this respect, given its fully integrated money market and increasingly common capital markets operating in the single currency. Finally, the potential impact of securities activities on the stability of the financial system is likely to increase, to the extent that the market trends outlined above will continue in the future.

5.4   Converging Regulation

The last topic of this essay concerns the implications of the above-discussed developments for the regulatory and supervisory framework.

Consider first the original framework. In banking, the prominent focus on stability stemmed from the dominance of traditional banking services in the financial sector and the consequent concentration of financial risks in banks. Such focus became predominant in the early decades of the last century—and particularly after the Great Depression—as the continuation of banking activity was essential to guarantee the channelling of funds to productive investments. In addition, there was a strong social concern to protect the unsophisticated depositors, who used to be called (before politically correct language rose to power) 'widows and orphans'. There was no comparable economic or social pressure to protect the securities holdings of the then relatively few affluent individuals engaged in such type of investment. Market transparency was considered adequate for them to protect their interests directly.

Indeed, securities market regulation was largely initiated to make sure that investors would be sufficiently informed to manage their own interest. Two classical examples are the disclosure and registration requirements for issuers of traded securities in the US Securities Act of 1933 and the Securities Exchange Act of 1934. The latter Act also forbade most types of manipulation of market prices, foremost insider trading. In the European Union, many important pieces of Community legislation have been enacted since the mid-1980s, when the Directive on prospectuses was adopted. It should be noted, in passing, that, in comparison with the banking regulation, the securities regulation is still scarcely developed at the Community level. This explains why the completion of the EU regulatory framework in the securities field represents one of the major objectives of the Financial Services Action Plan put forward by the European Commission.

The institutional separation between banking and securities—as, for instance, laid down in the Glass–Steagall Act of 1933—was a cornerstone of the legislation on banking and finance in countries which did not maintain the universal banking model. This separation was principally brought into force to limit the risks faced by financial institutions and to prevent possible conflicts of interest. In addition, several types of conduct-of-business regulations were imposed upon securities firms to protect investors' interests.

The distinction between the two primary objectives applied to the banking and securities regulation—respectively stability and transparency—still holds. For example, stability-oriented provisions of prudential supervision and macro-prudential surveillance are far more extensive for banks than for securities firms. Nevertheless, a bridge between the two approaches has started to be built. Prudential elements are being transplanted from the banking sector into the securities regulation, and regulations supporting market transparency and competitive equality are being transplanted from the securities field into banking. Let us briefly review these cross-sector exchanges.

Prudential requirements transplanted from the banking sector to the securities field include capital ratios and consolidated supervision to cover the overall risks of financial conglomerates. These requirements are often coupled with provisions for investor protection, for example, in the form of a dedicated compensation scheme to safeguard investors against a failure of a securities intermediary. The role of capital as a buffer to cover risks is, however, more limited in the securities than in banking sector. Whereas in banking regulatory capital is for the time being also intended to cover expected losses, expected losses of securities firms are already considered to be included in the continuous valuation of the assets of the firms, due to the application of the marked-to-market accounting. Accordingly, the regulatory capital of securities firms does not cover expected losses. It follows from this that buffers to withstand risks may not always be adequate during serious market turbulence.

The fact that banks continue to be special justifies the differences between the regulatory and supervisory frameworks relating to banking and securities respectively. Indeed, a full cross-sector harmonisation of the prudential frameworks would not be warranted. In particular, access to central bank liquidity should continue to be restricted to more tightly regulated and supervised banks. A closer control of banks is also needed to counterbalance the competitive benefits and potential moral hazard consequences, which stem from the access of banks to the public safety net.

Conversely, important elements of the original securities regulation are increasingly imported into the banking sector. This refers, in particular, to the transparency requirements, traditionally the main domain of securities regulation. In recent years, such requirements increasingly have been applied to the banking sector, since it is now widely recognised that market discipline stemming from enhanced transparency also provides banks with incentives to behave in a prudent and sound manner. This, in turn, enhances the stability of the financial system.

The role of market discipline is fully acknowledged in the New Basel Accord, with the inclusion of extended disclosure requirements for banks. The implementation of the New Accord will be an important and positive development for the European Union in particular, because in this area the frequency and content of banks' disclosure needs to be improved. Necessary as it is, however, improved disclosure is not a sufficient condition to ensure effective market discipline over banks. Many clients of banks are simply too unsophisticated to monitor banks and exercise discipline on managers. Other stakeholders might not have adequate incentives to do so, because they expect to be protected by the public safety net. In this latter respect, a decision to exclude major creditors of banks from the deposit insurance scheme would be a step forward and narrow even further the gap between the two regulatory approaches.

Some specific attempts to transplant elements from the securities field into the banking sector might be, in my view, less desirable. The recent proposal by international accounting standard-setters to replace the historical cost-based accounting by full fair value accounting in banking represents such a case. The main reason to be critical of this proposal is that a reasonably accurate fair value cannot be determined for a large part of the banking book. Secondary markets do not exist for most bank loans and current techniques to determine loan values suffer from many methodological problems. As a consequence, reliability, transparency, and comparability of financial statements would not be achieved. Even if ample market prices existed in the future, the potential volatility in prices could produce undesirable effects on banks' accounts.[4]

The process of cross-fertilisation between the two regulatory approaches contributes to upgrading both of them and helps to meet the challenges stemming from the market developments and from the newly built bridges between banking and securities. Although I do not see a need to thoroughly revise these regulatory frameworks, two issues, in my opinion, require close monitoring.

The first is the possibility of conflicts of interest arising between the provision of services to a corporate client and the investment of other customers' funds in the securities issued by that corporate client. During the recent fall of technology stocks, for example, some intermediaries have been accused of investing customer funds to keep up a favourable market price for important corporate clients, whose performance had already deteriorated. Although it applies to any institution combining the two above functions, this concern becomes particularly relevant for banks, because they have extensive 'placing power' to influence the choices of retail investors and concurrently provide lending services to firms.

Such conflict of interest might become increasingly important in Europe owing to the recent expansion of securities holdings by retail clients and the involvement of banks in such business. Actual or suspected misbehaviour also can be a serious risk for financial institutions, whose business largely relies on excellent reputation. Without questioning the strong reasons that led to its abandonment, one should not forget that the Glass–Steagall type of separation between banking and securities business was originally conceived to provide strong safeguards against the conflict of interest. Separating banking from securities activities, rather than relying on internal Chinese walls, was seen as the only way to resolve the conflict. Now, the burden to address the issue of conflict of interest falls on the various conduct-of-business regulations. The effectiveness of these regulations needs to be closely and rigorously monitored, knowing that the full implications of the removal of Glass–Steagall may not yet be visible.

The second issue relates to the existence of non-regulated securities firms, whose failure might generate major financial disruptions. Examples of these firms are leveraged private investment vehicles like hedge funds. Such firms are not even subject to disclosure and conduct of business regulations. After the LTCM case, international bodies have carefully examined the need for regulating hedge funds and other highly leveraged institutions. However, extensive debates and consultations on the subject have so far only led to indirect action, which intend to strengthen counterparty risk management by banks in order to prevent systemic contagion of hedge fund problems. Also, parallel attempts to develop market pressure towards voluntary transparency by hedge funds have not yielded significant results, mainly because the key competitive advantage of hedge funds lies with their secret trading strategy. As a matter of fact, after a pause following the LTCM incident, global hedge fund activity has resumed high growth and there is little doubt that more stringent regulation would be most unwelcome to this very dynamic segment of the financial industry. Thus, the need to monitor the problems posed by highly leveraged institutions remains in place.

The final issue that this essay briefly turns to are the implications for prudential supervision. In general terms, the development of strong bridges between banking and securities activities provides a clear justification for stepping up the monitoring of risks stemming from the securities business to individual financial institutions and the financial system as a whole.

The previous analysis suggests that particular challenges for risk monitoring arise in the area of micro-prudential supervision. They stem from changing risk profiles towards market and income volatility risks, non-transparent and complex risk positions of financial institutions, potential risk reallocation and concentration, and complex corporate structures. The effectiveness of the supervisory action requires closer cooperation at the national level between the supervision of banking and securities activities.

As for the field of the so-called macro-prudential supervision, the previous discussion of the risk to financial stability suggests that the primary need is to place adequate emphasis on the monitoring of securities activities as a possible source of major disruption. The effectiveness of the macro-prudential monitoring calls for a strengthening of cooperation between central bank functions and the micro-prudential tasks.

There are undoubtedly strong synergies between micro- and macro-prudential supervision. On the one hand, the monitoring of systemic stability benefits from information about key individual players. On the other hand, the monitoring of individual financial institutions gains from macro-prudential supervision, payment and settlement systems oversight and market surveillance.[5]

The need for close cooperation between the supervision of banking and securities (as well as insurance) also has a bearing on the structuring of supervisory agencies at country level, an issue more extensively explored in Essay 6 of this book. In principle, there are three possible approaches to strengthening the links between the supervisory functions, notably: the single agency model, the 'twin peaks' model, and a formalised cooperation via 'umbrella bodies' between specialised supervisory authorities. The balance of the different theoretical arguments is, to my mind, not clear-cut, and institutional choices can also be determined by practical considerations pertaining to the historical tradition and the institutional environment. In practice, what matters in this context is that all three approaches can (if properly implemented) achieve satisfactory results, just as all (if ill-designed or badly implemented) may fail.

The need to enhance the monitoring of risks to financial stability stemming from securities activities is also present at the international level, given the internationalisation of major financial institutions and the increased integration of financial markets. This entails a strengthening of cooperation between all relevant authorities on a cross-border and cross-sector basis. International securities markets indeed have been affected by major disturbances in recent years. Incidents such as the Mexican and Asian financial crises, the Russian default, the Brazilian and Argentine crises, have drawn attention and caused concern in particular because there was a risk of spreading market tensions across countries and markets. Among the various policy responses, one should stress the importance of the Financial Stability Forum, set up in 1999 with the aim of strengthening cross-sector cooperation on a global basis.

With regard to Europe, the relevance of cross-border cooperation between micro- and macro-prudential supervision has been fully recognised by policy-makers. First, the Economic and Financial Committee of the European Union acknowledged the need to foster the exchange of information on major financial institutions and market trends between supervisory authorities and central banks. Second, the Committee of Wise Men proposed a more effective and responsive decision-making process for the EU regulation in the securities field and also recommended establishing cooperation mechanisms between micro- and macro-prudential supervisors to tackle the systemic risk issues arising from the increasing integration of securities markets. One possible way of implementing these recommendations would be to develop cooperation between the Banking Supervision Committee of the ESCB and EU securities regulators, given that the Banking Supervision Committee is already involved in fairly extensive activities in the macro-prudential analysis of the EU banking system.

5.5 Walls, Windows

The aim of this essay has been to examine the relationship between banking and securities activities in the light of a number of market developments. Examination was carried out with particular regard to the EU financial system, where the importance of securities markets has significantly increased. The emergence of several strong bridges between banking and securities activities has produced a number of positive consequences, but also the possibility of new and increased risks to individual financial institutions and the financial system as a whole. I took the view that such risks should not lead to the conclusion that non-bank financial firms have become sources of systemic risk in their own right, as long as the banking system itself is not disrupted. Indeed, the special role of banks in the liquidity provision remains a basic distinction between banking and securities businesses.

A notable development is the concurrent transplanting of prudential requirements of the banking regulation into the securities field, and the transplanting of transparency requirements into the banking sector from the securities regulation. This cross-fertilisation is mutually beneficial. Although I do regard the present regulatory framework for securities activities to be on the whole adequate from the stability perspective, there is a need to monitor the continued effectiveness of the framework.

Stepping up the micro- and macro-prudential monitoring of risks emerging from securities activities should be a clear priority. This entails strengthening cooperation among sectoral supervisors in the micro-prudential field, and between them and central banks in the macro-prudential field. The strengthening of cooperation should take place both at the national level and on a cross-border basis.

On the euro banknotes there are images of bridges and windows, representing the connection and openness between countries and peoples. The image chosen for the relationship between banking and securities activities in this essay was that of bridges and walls. As demonstrated, there are increasingly strong bridges between banking and securities activities, previously separated by walls. As some of these walls continue to remain in place, I needed to be more cautious and could not borrow the image in full from the euro banknotes.

Notes

1. I acknowledge the assistance of Inês Cabral and Jukka Vesala in the preparation of this lecture.
2. See also Essay 8, Section 8.4.
3. See also Essay 8, Section 8.5.
4. See also Essay 4, Section 4.5.
5. See also Essay 8, Section 8.7.

6

Alternative Regulators

6.1 Three Questions

As already frequently commented on in this volume, public interests in the financial sector revolve around the notions of stability and efficiency. This essay will again stick to the aspects pertaining primarily to financial regulation and supervision while, of course, public interests also include competition policy and monetary policy aspects. Here, the subject is the organisational structure of the regulatory and supervisory functions, rather than their content (i.e. the 'why' and 'how' questions discussed in the previous essays).

The essay is organised in the following way. It will first briefly review relevant recent developments, in order to put the issue of organisational structure in a perspective. Then, it will deal with the three main questions arising from the issue of what the optimal institutional setup for supervisory activities should be: (*a*) 'One supervisor or many?'; (*b*) 'Inside or outside the central banks?'; and (*c*) 'National or European?'.

In the context of the last question, a European perspective is not a straightforward concept: do we mean the European Union or the Euroland, or do we mean the future European Union with new members? This essay will mainly focus on the Euroland, because it is the most advanced area in European integration, and it will itself embark on a process of enlargement, possibly leading to its coincidence with the European Union. Furthermore, the process leading to an increasing coincidence between the European Union and Europe is also under way.

6.2 New World for Regulators

Challenges for supervisors due to recent market developments mainly arise from two sources. One is technology. The other is the euro, although one could also say the EU internal market process, or even the internationalisation process. These two forces, namely technology and internationalisation-driven changes, are interrelated, but not identical, nor extensively overlapping. Sometimes, however, it is difficult to trace a particular development to one or the other of the two.

Many, or the majority, of the characteristics of the traditional regulatory and supervisory universe were derived from three basic features of what was called in Essay 3 the 'old world'.[1] These were: (*a*) sharp distinction between different financial institutions in terms of their products and services; (*b*) nationally closed financial and regulatory systems; and (*c*) crucial importance of proximity in financial transactions.

All that—or most of it—is gone. Products are frequently mixed, containing features of two or all three of the original contracts (banking, securities, and insurance contracts). Financial institutions are less and less easily identifiable as belonging to one of the three sectors into which the industry was previously divided. The notion of proximity is fading away, as the scope for marketing products has widened immensely; moreover a number of products that were intrinsically non-marketable are now increasingly traded on organised markets. The very notion of a 'market' has changed. This may be the most profound of all changes under way, the one that may eventually lead to an earthquake in the part of the regulatory structure which concerns securities. A large part of securities regulation is related to the old notion of a market as a quasi-physical entity, with its own members, premises, etc. where companies or issuers are listed. But, one can now well imagine a world in which those features have become evanescent and the market has become an entity which has no address, no management bodies, no membership. This is already the case for today's largest market, the foreign exchange market. Imagine that this model is extended to all other asset markets: what will then be the future of the traditional regulatory structure in the field of securities? This issue is difficult and new.

With the euro, the last major factor of segmentation among national markets has disappeared. Only now that the euro has arrived do people fully understand how powerful currency specificity is as a factor identifying a market, a financial system, and a financial industry. Those who deal with the problems of the euro and Euroland are dealing with the forefront of the process of change.

Supervisors rarely lead—normally they follow. The problems they periodically encounter arise when they follow from too great a distance. Awareness of the risk of being too far removed from the rapid changes in the financial system is now triggering a reconsideration of what the supervisory structure should be.

At least three aspects are being reconsidered. One is what the 'philosophical approach' to regulation and supervision should be. Another is what instruments should be used, and the third is what the institutions should be. By philosophical approach, it is meant here, for instance, the reversal over a period of ten, maybe fifteen years from an approach based on restricting competition to one favouring competition in the financial field. By reconsideration of the instruments, it is meant the change from a regulatory and supervisory approach based on commands and prohibitions, for example, authorisation of operations, to one relying on more indirect instruments, such as capital requirements and, furthermore, capital requirements based on internal models rather than externally imposed methods.

The remainder of this essay will focus on the institutional framework which is, however, just one element in the rethinking of the supervisory structure. In discussing institutional issues, a reference is made to both regulation and supervision. Regulation can be defined as rule-making, supervision as rule enforcing, but the borderline between the two is not drawn in the same manner in every system. Therefore, regulation and supervision can be broadly interpreted as including the totality of public policy instruments lying below the level of primary legislation. In the reconsideration of institutional arrangements, the three questions stated at the beginning are the most debated in Europe, at the national and at the subnational level, but also at the European level.

6.3   One Supervisor or Many?

The first question in this debate is 'One supervisor or many?' When the United Kingdom moved to the single supervisor approach, it was not the first country to do so. Sweden and Denmark within the European Union and Canada outside had preceded the UK move. But, as the London market has been regarded for many generations and still is regarded as a model, the attention drawn by the single agency approach has grown immensely as a consequence of the UK reform establishing the Financial Services Authority (FSA). Following in the footsteps of the United Kingdom, other countries also have taken that approach, such as Japan and Korea.

There are clear advantages to a single agency approach, particularly in light of the recent developments (as frequently supported by Clive Briault). If the tripartition of the financial system is increasingly being overcome, it may be preferable to have a single supervisor. This goes without saying. The task of a single supervisor, however, now has become immense. The problems related to the creation and effective management of a universal agency are highly complex, and not necessarily less complex than the problems of coordination and interaction between different agencies. Furthermore, some key problems caused by the existence of different public interests in financial activity remain even with a single supervisor. I will be more specific in a while. Incidentally, we have to remember that the decision of the British Government to create the FSA was suggested by a number of considerations not exclusively related to the optimal design of supervisory agencies. The discussion on the implications of granting independence to the central bank played a major role, as well as the negative experience in the city of London during the years preceding the change. Time will tell whether the single agency approach is successful.

The variety of approaches observed includes, in addition to the old 'specialised agencies', at least two others, which in my view are worth mentioning. The first is the Italian example, which I know very well. In the Italian system the agencies are specialised by objectives. One agency is entrusted with the goal of stability, while another is assigned transparency and investor protection. Ideally, each agency should have jurisdiction over all institutions, whether banks or non-banks, although in Italy this approach has been applied only partially, since insurance companies still have a separate supervisor. In Italy, securities houses and banks are subject to the same authority—the central bank—for capital requirements and other stability-related instruments, and to a single supervisor—the securities commission—for transparency and consumer protection purposes. The rationale for this allocation of responsibilities is that the two objectives, both instrumental in achieving efficiency and financial stability, may sometimes come into conflict. Traditionally, full disclosure to the market of information on a bank's condition was not part of the tools or instruments of a banking supervisor. The second example of 'supervision by objective' is the Dutch supervisory system, which assigns to an *ad hoc* commission the task of coordinating the specialised agencies.

So the question 'One supervisor or many?' can have several answers. The traditional answer of relying on fully specialised agencies clearly needs some changes, but the changes can be made in several alternative ways.

6.4 Inside or Outside the Central Bank?

The second question is 'Inside or outside the central bank?' This question of course particularly applies to banking supervision. There are, here too, arguments in favour of and against entrusting banking supervision to the central bank. For many years, Germany has been regarded by outsiders as the homeland of separate supervision and central banking. Taking a closer look at the actual organisation of prudential supervision in this country, however, one realises that this is only half of the truth.

The Deutsche Bundesbank is actually heavily involved in supervisory activities: it invests relevant resources in gathering information on banks, processing the data, and being on the spot and heading the first and most direct assessment of a bank's condition. On the basis of this activity and experience, the Deutsche Bundesbank is now arguing that its involvement in banking supervision should increase, rather than decrease. And understandably so, because the arguments leading towards separation were fundamentally based on the possible conflicts, or moral hazard, implied by combining the responsibilities in the field of monetary policy with those related to banking supervision. Now that monetary policy is the responsibility of the European Central Bank and the Eurosystem, this argument no longer holds. It is quite natural, then, to look at the situation from a new perspective.

I come from a country where banking supervision has been entrusted to the central bank for decades, and I was brought up to believe that this is a very good arrangement. I still see the great benefits in entrusting supervisory responsibilities to a central bank. Being bankers—namely people who deal with the banks, who have daily market contacts and frequent talks with the banks, who have the opportunity to watch directly how banks behave in performing a number of functions, for example, in the payment system and the money market—provides those at the central bank with a comparative advantage in assessing the soundness of other banks. As a bank, not necessarily as a supervisor, the central bank is the recipient of a wide range of information which banks provide not only to comply with regulatory requirements, but in the course of normal banking business. If the banking supervisor is an administrative body, rather than the central bank, that is, if it is not a mixed entity which is half bureaucracy and half bank, commercial bankers may be reluctant to discuss issues in the way they would with fellow bankers at the central bank.

But, of course, there are also arguments against the supervisor being the central bank. A prominent argument points to the conflict of interest between monetary policy and banking supervision. In my experience such conflicts can be dealt with— they have to be dealt with. Separation is one way, but there are others. For instance, in Italy the law forbids the lending of last resort at a rate below market levels. The central bank can only offer special conditions when a bank is being liquidated, through procedures strictly defined by law. When a bank files for bankruptcy, public money may be involved and so the relevant decisions cannot be left exclusively to the banking supervisor: the Treasury or *ad hoc* governmental bodies have a major role to play. If the supervisory authority is the central bank, which needs to be independent in performing its monetary policy functions, the problem of reconciling the two tasks certainly arises. However, the issue can be dealt with without necessarily separating supervisory and central banking responsibilities. In Italy, the decree stating that a bank should be liquidated is signed by the Treasury Minister. The central bank knows that if taxpayers' money is involved, the final decision can only be taken by the authority responsible for the budget. But the same problem would arise for a separate agency, which would not be able to decide on the use of taxpayers' money without explicit approval from the Government.

This shows that it is not possible to be dogmatic on this issue. I am convinced that both solutions can work and, both solutions can fail. From my standpoint, it is important to highlight that today the national central banks which form part of the Eurosystem no longer experience the typical conflicts and the potential complications of combining responsibility for monetary policy and supervision.

6.5   National or European?

The third question is 'National or European?' The current situation is such that the jurisdiction of the currency—with the conduct of monetary policy and other relevant policy functions—extends to the euro-area, whereas the jurisdiction of banking supervision and, more generally, of financial regulation is national. Where does the financial industry lie? At the national, or at the European level? I believe that the industry is moving from a nationally based structure to a euro-area-wide structure much more rapidly than people generally think.

When financial industry developments are assessed, attention is normally focused on the most visible aspects, which happen to be those showing the slowest pace of change. The first aspect relates to the relatively limited extent of cross-border mergers or takeovers in the banking and financial field. The second is the predominantly domestic reach of retail banking activities. If these two dimensions were taken as a benchmark for assessing the relevant boundaries for banking and financial market activities, we would be forced to conclude that the industry is moving only very slowly from a domestic to a euro-area structure. But the same conclusion would apply to the United States as well. The United States removed restrictions on inter-state banking more or less when the European Union lifted those within the Single Market. Even there the provision of retail services remains largely local, because physical proximity still plays a role in this market segment. Furthermore, in the United States cross-state mergers involving major banks are still a fairly recent phenomenon and tend to be regional rather than nationwide.

In every other field of activity the financial system has already assumed a definitely euro-area-wide or EU-wide dimension. If we look at wholesale activities, that is, the business in which the two sides of the transaction are not end-users but banks or, more broadly, components of the financial system, the market shows a high degree of integration. The key feature of the wholesale market is the transmission and diffusion of liquidity among banks, mainly through unsecured inter-bank transactions. In this market spreads became virtually identical in all euro-area countries within a few days of the launch of the euro, signalling that arbitrage was effectively taking place on an area-wide basis. Cross-border transactions account for more than 50 per cent of all unsecured and repo transactions, and the infrastructure for wholesale payments is already strongly unified.

In capital market activities the 'league' in which European players compete is also clearly not a domestic one. International bond issues—targeted at non-domestic investors—by large- and medium-sized enterprises are growing much faster than domestic issues, reflecting the fact that 'international bonds' can now be denominated in the issuer's own currency, the euro. The leading underwriters of bonds issued by European corporations, as well as the leading arrangers of syndicated loans to those companies, include all the largest European banks together with major US institutions. In the provision of asset management services, only the distribution of products to individual investors takes place predominantly at the national level. The actual business of managing the assets and the trading activity tend to be concentrated and subject to international diversification, as there are important economies of scale and benefits to be derived from spreading the risks.

All in all, there are clear signs that a single Euroland financial industry is emerging.

6.6 Four Conditions

In a situation in which the jurisdiction of the currency and the financial industry are euro-area-wide, the burden of the proof that competences can remain purely national lies on those who want to preserve them, because such an arrangement never has been adopted for prolonged periods anywhere. In Germany it was adopted, then quickly abandoned in the early 1950s. However, it would be a mistake to claim that a change in present institutional arrangements is urgent and indispensable. For the time being we have to strive to ensure that this system functions well. Without elaborating here in detail, I would argue that in order to do so, four basic conditions have to be met.

First, the common regulatory platform provided by the EU directives has to be strengthened. Second, this platform must be made more readily adaptable: today any change in the directives takes about three years, an unacceptably slow speed for keeping up with the pace of change in the financial markets. Third, cooperation among national agencies has to be significantly stepped up. Finally, and this is an aspect that deserves more than just a mention, there is a substantial need to step up competition policy. The risk we face is that neither private nor public agents allow the competitive game to develop fully, thereby preventing progress towards further integration in the EU financial industry.

If these four conditions are met, it may well be that the European Union, which has piloted so many new institutional arrangements, will prove successful in making this original setup work smoothly. This may occur despite that the size of the market and the currency area do not coincide with the jurisdiction of the regulatory agencies. If this is not the case, changes to the institutional framework will have to be considered.

Note

1. See also Essay 8, Section 8.4.

7

Supervision in Euroland

7.1 After the Euro

The establishment of a single currency and a single central bank for a group of European countries was one of the most remarkable events in the history of monetary systems. These countries still retain their sovereignty in other key fields where the state exerts its power. However, to mint coins or print the currency, to manage it, and to secure the public's confidence in it has been, from the earliest times, a key prerogative of the sovereign. 'Sovereign' is indeed the name that was given in the past to one currency. Not so long ago British Prime Minister Thatcher explained her opposition to the idea of the single currency with the desire to preserve the image of the Queen on the banknotes.

For centuries money has had two anchors: a commodity, usually gold; and the sovereign, that is, the political power. Less than thirty years after the last bond to gold was severed (August 1971), the second anchor has also now been abandoned. Although I personally think that political union in Europe is desirable, I am aware that the present situation, in which the area of the single currency is not a politically united one, is likely to persist for a number of years. This means that we have created an entirely new type of monetary order. For the people, the success of this move will ultimately depend on the ability of governments and political forces to build a political union. For the central banker and for the users of the new currency, the success will be measured by the quality of the currency itself, as judged by its ability to secure price stability. Not only is this a requirement explicitly set by the Treaty of Maastricht, it is also, in the opinion of most, the 'new anchor' that purely fiduciary currencies need after the gold anchor is abandoned.

This essay will focus on another, less fundamental but still important novelty of the euro-area's monetary constitution. It will discuss the novelty of abandoning the coincidence between the jurisdiction of monetary policy and the jurisdiction of banking supervision. Monetary policy embraces the twelve countries that have adopted the euro, whereas banking supervision remains national. Just as there is no precedent of any comparable size of money disconnected from states, there is no precedent for a lack of coincidence between the two public functions of managing the currency and controlling the banks. In the run-up to the euro this feature of the system was explored, and some expressed doubts about its effectiveness.

The plan of the essay is the following. It will first review the existing institutional framework for the prudential control of banks in EMU. Next, it will examine the likely scenario for the European banking industry in the coming years. Against this institutional and industry background, it will then discuss the functioning of, and the challenges for, banking supervision and central banking in the euro-area, both in normal circumstances and when a crisis occurs.

7.2 Double Separation

The origin and developments of modern central banks are closely linked to key changes undergone by monetary systems over the past two centuries. Such changes could, very sketchily, be summarised as follows. Initially, paper currency established itself as a more convenient means of payment than commodity currencies. Later, commercial bank money (bank deposits) spread as a convenient substitute for bank-notes and coins. Eventually, the quantity of money was disconnected from the quantity of gold. Thus, a double revolution in the technology of the payment system, the advent of banknotes and that of cheques or giros, has shaped the functions most central banks have performed over this century: monetary policy and prudential supervision. Man-made money made monetary policy possible. The fact that a large, now a predominant, component of the money stock was in the form of commercial bank money made banking supervision necessary.

Ensuring confidence in the paper currency and, later, in the stability of the relationship, one could say the exchange rate, between central bank and commercial bank money, were twin public functions; in general, they were entrusted to the same institution. Just as money has three well-known economic functions—means of payment, unit of account, and store of value—there are three public functions related to each of them. Operating and supervising the payment system refers to money as a means of payment; ensuring price stability relates to money as a unit of account and a store of value; and pursuing the stability of banks relates to money as a means of payment and a store of value. In each of the three functions commercial banks have played, and still largely play, a crucial role.

In an increasing number of countries the original triadic task entrusted to the central bank has now been abandoned in favour of a 'separation approach', assigning banking supervision to a separate institution. Following the recent adoption by the United Kingdom and Luxembourg of the separation approach, only two of the twelve countries represented in the Basel Committee on Banking Supervision (Italy and the Netherlands) have the central bank as the only authority responsible for banking supervision. In all systems, however, whether it has the task of supervising the banks, the central bank is deeply involved with the banking system precisely because the banks are primary creators of money, providers of payment services, managers of the stock of savings, and counterparties of central bank operations. No central bank can ignore the need to have a concrete and direct knowledge of 'its' banking system that operates in its monetary jurisdiction.

Personally, I have an intellectual attachment to, as well as a professional inclination for, the central bank approach to banking supervision. Yet I can see, the arguments that have led a growing number of industrialised countries to prefer the separation approach. Such arguments basically point to the potential conflict between controlling money creation for the purpose of price stability and for the purpose of bank stability. On the whole, I do not think that one model is right and the other wrong. Both can function, and do function, effectively; however, if inappropriately managed, both may fail to satisfy the public interest for which banks are supervised.

Against this background, the institutional framework currently adopted by the Treaty can be described as follows. As the description will refer to the area in which both the single market and the single currency are established, it will not specially focus on the problems of the so-called 'pre-in' countries, including the United Kingdom.

The current institutional framework of EMU (i.e. the single market plus the single currency) is a construct composed of two building blocks: national competence and cooperation.

First, comes national competence. In a market based on the minimum harmonisation and the mutual recognition of national regulatory standards and practices, the principle of 'home country control' applies. According to this principle every bank has the right to do business in the whole area using a single licence, under the supervision, and following the rules, of the authority that has issued the licence. The full supervisory responsibility, thus, belongs to the 'home country'. This allows, *inter alia*, the certain identification of the supervisor responsible for each institution acting as a counterparty to the monetary policy operations of the Eurosystem. The only exception to this principle—the 'host country' competence for the supervision of liquidity of foreign branches—is no longer justified now that the euro is in place; hence, it should soon be removed.

Second, is cooperation. In a highly regulated industry such as banking, a single market that retains a plurality of 'local' (national) supervisors requires close cooperation among supervisors to safeguard the public good: openness, competition, safety, and soundness of the banking industry. EU Directives (the first and second Banking Directives and the so-called BCCI Directive) lay the foundations for such cooperation, but they do not contain specific provisions or institutional arrangements to this end. They limit themselves to stating the principle of cooperation among national authorities and to removing obstacles to the exchange of information among them.

How does the Eurosystem relate to this construction? Essentially in two ways. First, the Treaty assigns to the Eurosystem the task to 'contribute to the smooth conduct of policies pursued by competent authorities relating to the prudential supervision of credit institutions and the stability of the financial system' (Article 105 (5)). Given the separation between monetary and supervisory jurisdictions, this provision is clearly intended to ensure a smooth interplay between the two. Second, the Treaty gives the Eurosystem a twofold (consultative and advisory) role in the rule-making process. According to Article 105 (4), the ECB must be consulted on any draft Community and national legislation in the fields of banking supervision and financial stability; according to Article 25 (1) of its Statute, the ECB can provide, on its own initiative, advice on the scope and implementation of the Community legislation in these fields. It should be borne in mind that central banks are normally involved in the process of drawing up legislation relating to, for example, regulatory standards, safety net arrangements and supervision because this legislation contributes crucially to the attainment of financial stability.

Some observations should be made about the institutional framework just described. For one, such an arrangement establishes a double separation between central banking and banking supervision: not only a geographical, but also a functional one. This is the case because for the euro-area as a whole banking supervision is now entrusted to institutions that have no independent monetary policy functions. The separation approach that was chosen for EMU has effectively been applied not only to the euro-area as a whole, but to its components as well. Indeed, even in countries where the competent authority for banking supervision is the central bank, by definition this authority is, functionally speaking, no longer a central bank, as it lacks the key central banking task of autonomously controlling money creation.

Another observation is that the Treaty itself establishes (in Article 105 (6)) a simplified procedure that makes it possible, without amending the Treaty, to entrust specific supervisory tasks to the ECB. If this provision were to be activated, both the geographical and the functional separation would be abandoned at once. The fact that the Maastricht Treaty allows the present institutional framework to be reconsidered without recourse to the very heavy amendment procedure (remember that such procedure requires an intergovernmental conference, ratification by national parliaments, sometimes even a national referendum) is a highly significant indication that the drafters of the Treaty clearly understood the anomaly of the double separation and saw the potential difficulties arising from it. The simplified procedure they established could be interpreted as a 'last resort clause', which might become necessary if the interaction between the Eurosystem and national supervisory authorities turned out not to work effectively.

7.3   From National to Euroland Markets

When evaluating the functioning of, and the challenges to, banking supervision in the current institutional framework, two aspects should be borne in mind. First, the advent of the euro increases the likelihood of the propagation of financial stability problems across national borders. For this reason a coordinated supervisory response is important at an early stage. Second, the sources of banks' risks and stability problems depend on ongoing trends that are not necessarily caused by the euro, but may be significantly accelerated by it. On the whole, one is interested not so much in the effects of EMU or the euro *per se*, as in the foreseeable developments due to all factors influencing banking in the years to come.

It should be noted at the outset that most banking activity, particularly in retail banking, remains confined to national markets. In many Member States the number, and the market share, of banks that operate in a truly nationwide fashion is rather small. Although banks' international operations have increased, credit risks are still predominantly related to domestic clients, and the repercussions of bank failures would be predominantly felt by domestic borrowers and depositors.

Assessing the internationalisation of euro-area banks is a complex task because internationalisation can take a number of forms. One is via cross-border branches and subsidiaries. Although large-scale entry into foreign banking markets in Europe is still scarce via branching, reflecting pesistent legal, cultural, and conduct-of-business barriers (less than 6 per cent on average in terms of banking assets in the euro-area; Table 7.1), there are significant exceptions. The assets of the foreign branches of German and Dutch French banks account for a significant share of the assets of their respective domestic banking systems, however (Table 7.2).

Another way to spread banking activity beyond national borders is consolidation. Cross-border mergers or acquisitions still seem to be the exception, although things have started to change. The recent wave of 'offensive' and 'defensive' banking consolidation has mainly developed within national industries, thus significantly increasing concentration, particularly in the smaller countries (Table 7.3); it may be related not so much to the direct impact of EMU as to globally intensified competition and the need to increase efficiency.

In the coming years internationalisation is likely to increase because, with the euro, foreign entrants can now fund lending from their domestic retail deposit base or from euro-denominated money and capital markets. The relatively large number

Table 7.1. *Market Share of Branches of Foreign Credit Institutions as % of Total Domestic Assets*[2]

Host country	1997	2000
Austria	0.7	0.8
Belgium	*8.5*	*5.7*
Finland	0	*7.3*
France	*2.6*	*3.3*
Germany	1.0	1.3
Greece	9.0	6.4
Ireland	N.A.	*13.5*
Italy	3.4	3.5
Luxembourg	*17.9*	*16.6*
Netherlands	*2.1*	*2.7*
Portugal	*4.0*	*4.2*
Spain	4.7	3.4
Euro-area average	4.9	5.7

Source: Eurostat and ECB. Data in italics refer to branches from EEA countries and were calculated based on comparable figures from the 'Structural analysis of the EU banking sector: Year 2001', (2002), ECB.

Table 7.2. *Assets of Branches of Domestic Credit Institutions in Foreign Countries as % of Total Domestic Assets*[2]

Home country	1997	2000
Austria	0.2	3.5
Belgium	0.6	5.0
Finland	0.4	0
France	2.6	7.4
Germany	0.2	15.1
Greece	0.2	9.9
Ireland	0.9	9.0
Italy	1.0	5.6
Luxembourg	0.1	0.0
Netherlands	2.9	16.6
Portugal	0.9	3.0
Spain	1.9	4.3
Euro-area average	1.0	6.6

Source: Eurostat and ECB. Eurostat data concerning host countries available.

Table 7.3. *Concentration: Assets of the Five Biggest Credit Institutions as % of Total Assets*[2]

	1990	1995	1999	2000	2001
Belgium	48	54	76	75	78
Germany	14	17	19	20	20
Greece	83	76	67	65	66
Spain	35	46	52	54	53
France	42	41	43	47	47
Ireland	44	44	41	41	43
Italy	19	26	26	23	29
Luxembourg	N.A.	21	26	26	28
The Netherlands	73	76	82	81	82
Austria	35	39	41	43	45
Portugal	58	74	44	59	60
Finland	53	69	86	87	80
Euro-area average	46	49	50	52	53
Denmark	76	74	71	60	68
Sweden	70	86	88	88	N.A.
The United Kingdom	N.A.	27	29	30	30
EU average	50	51	53	53	52

Source: 1990, 1995 figures from the Possible effects of EMU on the EU banking systems in the medium, to long term (1999), ECB; 1999 to 2001 figures from the 'Structural analysis of the EU banking sector: Year 2001', (2002), ECB. Averages are unweighted and ignore missing values. CR5 is reported on a non-consolidated basis from 1999 onwards.

of foreign branches already established could be a sufficient base for an expansion of international banking activity (Table 7.4). A single branch, or a small number of branches, may be sufficient to attract customers, especially when they are served through direct banking techniques, such as telephone and Internet banking. Also, the cross-border supply of services on a remote basis is likely to spread as direct banking techniques develop. Cross-border mergers and acquisitions, on the other hand, are likely to remain scarce. Such aims at achieving a 'critical mass' for wholesale financial markets, or at rapidly acquiring local expertise and customers in the retail sector will suffer because the cost savings from eliminating overlaps in the retail network are likely to be limited. Moreover, the managerial costs of integrating different structures and corporate cultures are substantial.

However, banks' internationalisation does not provide the full picture of the interconnections of banking systems. As 'multi-product' firms, banks operate simultaneously in many markets which have different dimensions: local, national, continental (or European), and global. The advent of the euro is likely to enlarge the market for many banking products and services to the continental dimension; this will 'internationalise' even those banks that remain 'national' in their branch networks and organisation.

The formation of the single money market in the euro-area has largely taken place. The dispersion in the euro overnight rate across countries, as reported by fifty-seven so-called EONIA banks, fell in January 1999 from around fifteen to five basis points. The variation between banks has been significantly greater than between countries.

Table 7.4. *Number of Branches of Foreign Credit Institutions*[2]

Host country	EU		Third countries	
	1997	2000	1997	2000
Austria	6	15	0	1
Belgium	25	34	15	13
Finland	9	0	0	0
France	52	93	41	31
Germany	118	145	31	28
Greece	14	13	9	9
Ireland	N.A.	28	2	2
Italy	34	41	19	16
Luxembourg	55	62	7	8
Netherlands	0	9	11	10
Portugal	15	22	3	3
Spain	34	41	18	10
Euro-area average	42	34	13	11

Source: Eurostat and ECB. Data in italics refer to branches from EEA countries and were calculated based on comparable figures from the 'Structural analysis of the EU banking sector: Year 2001', (2002), ECB.

The TARGET system has rapidly reached the dimension of Fedwire, with a daily average value of payments of EUR 1,000 billion, of which between EUR 300 and 400 billion are cross-border. The ever-stronger inter-bank and payment system links clearly increase the possibility of financial instability spreading from one country to another. Through these links the failure of a major bank could affect the standing of its counterparties in the entire euro-area. On the other hand, the deeper money market could absorb any specific problem more easily than before.

As regards the capital markets, the effects of the euro will take more time to manifest themselves, but are likely to be substantial. The single currency offers substantial opportunities for both debt and equity issuers and investors. The increase in the number of market participants operating in the same currency increases the liquidity of the capital markets and reduces the cost of capital. The low level of inflation and nominal interest rates and diminishing public sector deficits are additional supporting factors of capital market activity, especially private bond market activity which was traditionally limited. Indeed, the introduction of the euro spurred a large increase in the private capital market activity in the euro-area (Table 7.5). Banks will, thus, operate in increasingly integrated capital markets and will be exposed to shocks originating beyond their national borders.

As for corporations, they may concentrate their operations (treasury, capital market, and payment management) in a single or few 'euro banks', while the disappearance of national currencies may break links between firms and their home country 'house bank'. This dissociation would make the domestic economy indirectly sensitive to foreign banks' soundness, thus creating another propagation channel of banking problems across countries.

When considering the industry scenario for the coming years, the viewpoint has to be broadened beyond the impact of the euro. Rather than the exclusive, or even primary, force for change, the euro is expected to be a catalyst for pre-existing trends driven by other forces. Such trends can be summarised as follows.[1]

Table 7.5. *Transactions in Euro (or Euro Legacy Currencies) Involving Euro-area Resident Firms, Value in EUR Billions and Number of Transactions*[2]

	Bonds		Equity	
	Value	Transactions	Value	Transactions
1995	5.3	53	20.6	56
1998	18.8	109	51.5	219
1999	37.0	123	76.1	301
2000	56.4	134	111.4	347
2001	83.5	161	44.7	119

Source: Bondware and Loanware.

Concerning, regulation, the industry has yet to feel the full impact of such fundamental, but relatively recent, regulatory changes as those related to the single market legislation.

Concerning disintermediation: other financial intermediaries and institutional investors will grow relative to banks, pushed by demographic and social changes, as well as by the increasing depth and liquidity of the emerging euro-area-wide capital market. Disintermediation is expected to take the form of increasing recourse to capital market instruments relative to bank loans by firms, and diminishing investment in deposits by households relative to mutual funds and related products.

Finally, concerning information technology; bank products, operations, and processes are changing rapidly, while technology offers increasing possibilities for dissociating the supply of a large number of services from branches and face-to-face contact with customers. The current tendency in the EU banking systems to reduce over-branching and over-staffing will grow stronger.

These factors will increase competition, exert pressure on profitability, and oblige banks to reconsider their strategies. Such effects are already visible throughout the European Union. They produce changes in organisation, new products and services, mergers, strategic alliances, cooperation agreements, etc. They also involve strategic risks, because the pressure for profitability and some losses of revenue due to the euro, for example, from foreign exchange, may push some banks to seek more revenue from unfamiliar business or highly risky geographical areas. Inadequate implementation of new technologies or failure to reduce excess capacity may also affect banks' long-term viability.

7.4 Regulation and Supervision

The following will now turn to the functioning of banking regulation and supervision in the euro-area against the background of the institutional framework and the industry scenario outlined above. Two preliminary observations are in order. First, the objective of financial stability pursued by banking supervisors is only one in a range of public interests, which also includes competition policy and depositor and investor protection policy. Second, current supervision and crisis management involve different situations and procedures and therefore will be examined in sequence.

As observed earlier, the regulatory platform for the euro-area banking industry combines harmonised rules with country-specific (non-harmonised, but mutually recognised, and hence potentially competing) rules.

The harmonised part of the platform includes most of the key prudential provisions that have been developed in national systems over the years. More than twenty years ago (1977), the first Banking Coordination Directive adopted a definition of a credit institution and prescribed objective criteria for the granting of a banking licence. In 1983, the first Directive on carrying out supervision on a consolidated basis was approved, and in 1986 the rules relating to the preparation of the annual accounts and the consolidated accounts of banks were harmonised. In 1989, the second Banking

Coordination Directive (which became effective on 1 January 1993) marked the transition from piecemeal to comprehensive legislation, introducing, *inter alia*, the principle of 'home country control'. A number of other specific directives have subsequently addressed the main aspects of the regulatory framework—notably, own funds, solvency ratios, and large exposures. A Directive imposing deposit guarantee schemes supplemented the legislation in support of financial stability. All in all, the European Union, including the euro-area, now has a rather comprehensive 'banking law' consistent with the Basel Committee's rules and with the 1997 Core Principles of Banking Supervision.

The country-specific, non-harmonised, part of the platform is also quite relevant and very diversified. It includes, among other things: the different organisational arrangements for the conduct of banking supervision (central bank, separate agency, or a mixed arrangement); the tools used by banking supervisors (e.g. supervisory reporting, on-site inspections); provisions for the liquidation and restructuring of banks; and the definition and legal protection of financial instruments and contracts. Even the key notion of a regulated market is harmonised only to a limited extent.

Such 'neutrality' and 'incompleteness' on the part of the EU legislator with respect to key aspects normally incorporated in the regulatory framework is a unique feature of EU banking regulations. Moreover, it is likely to trigger a deregulatory process, pushed by competition among the national systems and the different financial centres in the euro-area, and beyond that in the European Union. Against the background of the increasing competition and other changes in the banking industry, one can expect that the regulatory platform will evolve in the years to come. Additional EU legislation may prove necessary to complete and strengthen the harmonised part. One important part of common legislation, namely the draft Directive on liquidation and reorganisation measures for credit institutions, has not yet been adopted and, indeed, has been stalled for years. This Directive is needed to bring legal certainty to the framework for banking crisis management. In this regard, it would be useful for the Eurosystem, if necessary, to be able to exclude counterparties from the single monetary policy on prudential grounds. Also, the non-harmonised part of the platform will come under pressure to converge, as just mentioned, through the process of 'regulatory competition'. Like any other rapidly changing industry, the banking sector will require careful attention by regulators. As indicated earlier, the ECB will have the possibility of contributing to the rule-making process through its advisory tasks under Article 105 (4) of the Treaty and Article 25.1 of the Statute of the ESCB.

On the whole, and taking a euro-area perspective, the legislative-cum-regulatory platform of the banking industry, although rather unusual and diversified in comparison with those of most currency jurisdictions—does not seem to present loopholes or inconsistencies that may hamper the pursuit of systemic stability. Seen from the point of view of the regulatory burden, it is a light system. It will become even more so if competition among national banking systems and financial centres encourages national regulators to free their banks from regulatory burdens not required by the EU Directives.

Conversely, seen from the point of view of its flexibility, that is, how quickly it can adapt to new situations, it is, on the contrary, a heavy system. This is the case both because the EU legislative process is slow (three years or even longer may be needed to pass Directives) and, perhaps more importantly, because many provisions are embodied in the Community primary legislation (i.e. Directives) rather than in Community secondary legislation (amendable through simpler comitology procedures). The December 2002 decisions of the EU ECOFIN Council to adopt the so-called Lamfalussy framework in all fields of financial regulation represent a major step towards less rigid and consistent rule-making procedures in the European Union.

The establishment of EMU does not seem to determine a need for revising the pillars of the current legal framework. What seems to be necessary, however, is a more flexible legislative procedure which allows for a faster and more effective revision of Community legislation, whenever needed in relation to market developments.

It should immediately be recalled that supervision, contrary to regulation, is a national task, exercised by what the jargon of the Directives calls the 'competent authority'. Because the euro-area has adopted a separation approach between supervisory and central banking functions, it is natural to examine first the functioning of the 'euro area supervisor' (i.e. the cooperative system of national supervisors) and then turn to the tasks and needs of the 'euro-area central banker' (i.e. the Eurosystem).

The 'euro-area supervisor' can be regarded as a rather peculiar entity composed of national agencies working in three modes: stand-alone, bilateral, and multilateral. These modes are addressed below in turn.

The stand-alone mode is the one in which the supervisor exclusively operates in the national (or even local) context. Today, it is by far the most predominant mode. In most cases, this approach is sufficient to achieve the objectives of banking supervision because most banks in Europe are operating in a context that does not even reach the nationwide market of the country of origin. Such a decentralised model is even more effective because it allows the efficient use of information that may not be available far from the market in which the bank operates. That is why it is applied even within countries. In Italy, for example, over 600 of the 900 licensed credit institutions at end-1998 were entirely supervised by the Banca d'Italia branch of the town in which the bank is licensed.

The bilateral mode involves cooperation between two supervisory agencies. It is used for cross-border supervision of the same type of financial institutions, such as credit institutions, or the supervision of different types of financial institutions operating in the same market, such as credit institutions and securities firms. The instrument devised to organise bilateral cooperation between banking supervisors is the Memorandum of Understanding (MoU). With the implementation of the second Banking Co-ordination Directive, the Member States began to negotiate extensively MoUs in order to establish the necessary cooperation between 'home' and 'host country' authorities. These MoUs are used to supervise efficiently institutions that have cross-border activities or foreign country establishments.

A large number of bilateral MoUs have been signed between the EEA banking supervisory authorities. The key aims of MoUs are to establish a regular exchange of information between national supervisory authorities. Whereas the 'gateways' for the exchange of information have been laid down in Community legislation, MoUs provide a practical framework for communication to be carried out between supervisors. Moreover, MoUs define procedures and reciprocal commitments between pairs of EU supervisors related to the various parts of the supervisory process, such as establishment procedures and on-site examinations.

Finally, the multilateral mode is the one in which a group of supervisors works collectively as, say, a single consolidated supervisor. Such a mode is required when the problems involved are area-wide. They may be area-wide for a number of reasons with regard to the institutions, or groups, involved: their dimension, their linkages with a number of different markets in various countries, their role in the payment system or in other 'systemic' components of the market, etc. Multilateral cooperation can also enhance the quality of supervision by examining common macroeconomic influences on the banking system and common trends in the financial system that may not be revealed from the national perspective only.

The Banking Supervision Committee is the key forum for multilateral cooperation. It is composed of representatives of the banking supervisory authorities of the EU countries, either forming part of the respective NCB or separate bodies. The Banking Supervision Committee's main functions are the promotion of a smooth exchange of information between the Eurosystem and national supervisory authorities as well as cooperation among EU supervisory authorities. Another forum for dealing with the requirements of the multilateral mode is the Groupe de Contact. The Groupe is a group of EU banking supervisory authorities which, for many years, has discussed individual banking cases in a multilateral way, but at a lower organisational level than the high-level Banking Supervision Committee. The establishment of the 'Lamfalussy' committees will bring about new forums for multilateral cooperation in the European Union.

Before the euro, the need to develop the multilateral mode was relatively limited, as the emergence of a single banking market in the European Union was slow. Thus, the fact that the multilateral mode has not gone beyond periodic discussions among supervisors and joint industry-wide analyses should not be a cause for concern.

I am convinced, however, that in the future the needs will change and the multilateral mode will have to deepen substantially. Over time such a mode will have to be structured to the point of providing the banking industry with a true and effective collective 'euro-area supervisor'. It will have to be enhanced to the full extent required for banking supervision in the euro-area to be as prompt and effective as it is within a single nation.

There are no legal impediments to further cooperation. The existing legislation, whether Community or national, permits all the necessary steps to be made. Information can be pooled; reporting requirements and examination practices can be developed and standardised; common databases can be created; joint teams can be formed; and analyses of developments across the whole banking system can be conducted. The Community legislation providing for the unconstrained exchange of confidential information between supervisors does not distinguish between bilateral and multilateral cooperation, but the common interpretation is that it covers both modes. It will be the task of the Banking Supervision Committee, for its part, to develop the multilateral mode among EU banking supervisors.

If the above concerns primarily the euro-area supervisor, what about the euro-area central banker, that is, the Eurosystem? The euro-area central banker has neither direct responsibility for supervising banks nor for bank stability. Central bankers are however, no strangers in this land. The Eurosystem has a vital interest in a stable and efficient banking industry; it is, therefore, keen to see its action complemented with an effective conduct of the supervisory functions by the competent authorities. It needs a clear and precise knowledge of the state of the euro-area's banking industry as a whole and of its major individual players. One day the Eurosystem may have a role to play, as we shall see, in the management of crises.

For the Eurosystem, natural reference models are provided by the central banks of countries that apply the separation approach, for example: Germany before the euro; the United Kingdom after the creation of the Financial Services Authority; or Japan. In all these cases, the central bank has a well-developed expertise in the micro- and macro-prudential field; each distinctively plays a role in the macro-prudential field by addressing threats to the stability of the banking system and analysing the soundness of the structural features of the system. For their own purposes, these central banks also have precise and comprehensive information about the banks in their respective countries. This information is obtained from (*a*) performing practical supervisory duties, as in the case of the Bank of Japan or the Bundesbank; (*b*) from the national supervisory authority; (*c*) through direct contacts with the banking industry, as in the case of the Bank of England.

The Banking Supervision Committee is in a good position to cooperate with the Eurosystem in the collection of information. Indeed, the so-called BCCI Directive has removed the legal obstacles to the transmission of confidential information from competent supervisory authorities to 'central banks and other bodies with a similar function in their capacity as monetary authorities'. This includes national central banks and the ECB. Of course, the provision of supervisory information is voluntary and its development will have to be based on an agreed view of the central banking requirements the Eurosystem will have in this field.

7.5 Crisis Management

In normal circumstances central banking and prudential supervision have an arm's length distance between them. In crisis situations, however, they need to act closely together, often in cooperation with other authorities as well. Charles Goodhart and Dirk Schoenmaker have made a valuable contribution to analysing the handling of major banking problems in the history of industrial countries. One of their conclusions is that, in most instances, central banks indeed have been involved. Banking problems are so close to monetary stability, payment system integrity, and liquidity management that this finding hardly comes as a surprise. The advent of the euro will not, by itself, change this state of affairs.

When discussing crisis management, it should not be forgotten that, although central banks have a direct and unique role to play when the creation of central bank money is involved, this represents just one category of emergency action. Another category refers to the injection—by politically liable Finance Ministries—of taxpayers' money into ailing or insolvent credit institutions. There is also a third, market-based category, consisting of the injection of private money by banks or other market participants. All these three typologies of emergency action require the involvement of policy-makers, but they must not be mixed up when evaluating the existing arrangements. Therefore, before discussing the much-debated question of the lender-of-last-resort, let me briefly comment on the two, probably less controversial cases where central bankers are not the providers of extra funds.

First, the 'private money solution'. This market-based approach is clearly the preferable option, not just to save public funds and avoid imbalances in public finances, but also to reduce the moral hazard problem generated by public assistance to ailing institutions. Indeed, policy-makers are increasingly aware that the expectations of a helping hand can increase financial institutions' risk appetite in the first place. However, even when a market-based solution is possible, on the grounds of private interest, private parties may not be able to reach a solution for lack of information or coordination. Public authorities have, therefore, an active role to play for the market solution to materialise. The recent rescue package coordinated by the Federal Reserve Bank of New York to prevent the LTCM hedge fund from collapsing is a good example of public intervention being used to achieve a private solution.

Acting as a 'midwife' in brokering a private sector deal is not the only example of managing crises without injecting public funds. Banking supervisors have at their disposal a number of tools to intervene at the national level to limit losses and prevent insolvency when a bank faces difficulties. These tools include special audits, business restrictions, and various reorganisation measures.

In the euro-area, national supervisors and central banks will continue to be the key actors in the pursuit of market-based solutions to crises. The Eurosystem, or the Banking Supervision Committee, would become naturally involved whenever the relevance of the crisis required it.

Second, the 'taxpayers' money solution'. Taxpayers have been forced to shoulder banks' losses in the past, when public authorities felt that otherwise the failure of a large portion of a country's banking system or of a single significant institution would have disrupted financial stability and caused negative macroeconomic consequences. In such instances, banks have been taken over by the state, or their bad assets have been transferred to a separate public entity to attract new private investment in the sound part of the otherwise failed banks. The US savings and loans crisis of the 1980s, the banking crises in Scandinavia in the early 1990s and the current banking crises in Japan and some East-Asian countries are examples of system-wide insolvency problems that have triggered taxpayers' support. Crédit Lyonnais and Banco di Napoli are recent examples of public support to individual insolvency problems.

The introduction of the euro leaves crisis management actions involving taxpayers' money practically unaffected. The option of injecting equity or other funds remains available for the Member States, because these operations are not forbidden by the Treaty. Nevertheless, the European Commission will be directly involved in scrutinising and authorising such actions, as any state aid must be compatible with the Community's competition legislation; this happened, for example, in the cases of Banco di Napoli and Crédit Lyonnais.

The handling of solvency crises is not within the competence of the national central banks, nor that of the ECB, although national central banks are likely to be consulted, as they have been in the past.

Third, is the 'central bank money solution'. This is the Lender-of-Last-Resort issue that has brought the Eurosystem under vigorous criticism by distinguished academics and by the IMF's Capital Markets Division of the Research Department. Critics have alleged that the absence of a clear and transparent mechanism to act in an emergency raises doubts in the markets about the ability of the Eurosystem to handle crisis situations. It is said that the uncertainty generated by the present arrangements would entail new risks, including the possibility of investors requiring an additional risk premium at times of financial market volatility and, ultimately, damaging the credibility of EMU. Two examples of these concerns deserve an explicit mention. The IMF 'Report on Capital Markets' (September 1998) stated that 'it is unclear how a bank crisis would be handled under the current institutional framework...which is not likely to be sustainable'. Similarly, the first report of the Centre for Economic Policy Research (CEPR) on monitoring the ECB entitled 'The ECB: Safe at Any Speed?' expressly suggested that the Eurosystem lacks crisis management capacity and is too rigid to pass the 'A-Class test' to keep the vehicle on the road at the first steep turn in financial market conditions in Europe.

My response to this criticism is threefold: The criticism reflects a notion of lender-of-last-resort operations that is largely outdated; it underestimates the Eurosystem's capacity to act; and, finally, it represents too mechanistic a view of how a crisis is, and should be, managed in practice.

The notion of a central bank's Lender-of-Last-Resort function dates back more than 120 years, to the time of Bagehot. This notion refers to emergency lending to institutions that, although solvent, suffer a rapid liquidity outflow due to a sudden collapse in depositors' confidence, that is, a classic bank run. A bank could be exposed to depositors' panic even if solvent because of the limited amount of bank liquidity and an information asymmetry between the depositors and the bank concerning the quality of bank's assets that do not have a secondary market value.

Nowadays and in our industrial economies, runs may occur mainly in textbooks. They have little relevance in reality because, since Bagehot, many antidotes have been adopted: deposit insurance, the regulation of capital adequacy and large exposures, improved licensing, and supervisory standards. These safeguards all contribute to the preservation of depositors' confidence and minimise the threat of a contagion from insolvent to solvent institutions.

A more likely case is a rapid outflow of uninsured inter-bank liabilities. However, because inter-bank counterparties are much better informed than depositors, this event would typically require the market to have a strong suspicion that the bank is actually insolvent. If such a suspicion were to be unfounded and not generalised, the breadth and depth of today's inter-bank market is such that other institutions would probably replace (possibly with the encouragement of the public authorities as described above) those which withdraw their funds. It should be noted, in this respect, that the emergence of the single euro money market lowers banks' liquidity risk, because the number of possible sources of funds is now considerably larger than in the past.

Given all of these contingencies, the probability that a modern bank is solvent, but illiquid, and at the same time lacks sufficient collateral to obtain regular central bank funding is quite small. The textbook case for emergency liquidity assistance to individual solvent institutions, as a matter of fact, has been a most rare event in industrial countries over the past decades.

What if this rare event were, nevertheless, to occur and cause a systemic threat? The clear answer is that the euro-area authorities would have the necessary capacity to act. This is not only my judgement, but also that of the Eurosystem, whose decision-making bodies have, as you can imagine, carefully discussed the matter. We are, or shall be, naturally not infallible; no one can claim such a divine quality. But there are neither legal-cum-institutional, nor organisational, nor intellectual impediments to acting when needed. We are aware that central banks may be the only source of immediate and adequate funds when a crisis requires swift action, while solvency remains an issue and failure to act could threaten the stability of the financial system.

In these circumstances the various national arrangements would continue to apply, including those concerning the access of central banks to supervisors' confidential information. As is well known, such arrangements differ somewhat from country to country.

The criticism also underestimates the Eurosystem's capacity to act. To the extent that there would be an overall liquidity effect that is relevant for monetary policy or a financial stability implication for the euro-area, the Eurosystem itself would be actively involved.

The Eurosystem is, of course, well equipped for its two collective decision-making bodies (the Board and the Council) to take decisions quickly whenever needed, whether for financial stability or for other reasons. This readiness is needed for a variety of typical central bank decisions, such as the execution of concerted interventions or the handling of payment system problems. Indeed, it has already been put to work during the changeover weekend and in the first few weeks thereafter.

A clear reassurance about the capacity to act when really needed should be sufficient for the markets. Indeed, it may even be advisable not to spell out beforehand the procedural and practical details of emergency actions. As Gerry Corrigan once put it, maintaining '*constructive ambiguity*' in these matters may help to reduce the moral hazard associated with a safety net.

The question of who acts within the Eurosystem should also be irrelevant for the markets, given that any supervised institution has an unambiguously identified supervisor and national central bank. As to the access to supervisory information, the lack of direct access by the Eurosystem should not be regarded as a specific flaw of the euro-area's institutional framework, as has been frequently argued. After all, this situation also exists at the national level wherever a central bank does not carry out day-to-day supervision.

Finally, the criticism reflects an overly mechanistic view of how a crisis should be managed in practice. Arguing in favour of fully disclosed, rule-based policies in order to manage crises successfully and, hence, maintain market confidence, is almost self-contradictory. Emergency situations always contain unforeseen events and novel features, and emergency, by its very nature, is something that allows and even requires a departure from the rules and procedures adopted for normal times or even during the previous crisis. Who cares so much about the red light when there is 2 meters of snow on the road? As for transparency and accountability, these two sacrosanct requirements should not be pushed to the point of being detrimental to the very objective for which a policy instrument is created. Full explanations of the actions taken and procedures followed may be appropriate *ex post*, but unnecessary and undesirable *ex ante*.

The provision of emergency liquidity to a bank is not the only case in which central bank money may have to be created to avoid a systemic crisis. A general liquidity 'dry-up' may reflect, for example, a gridlock in the payment system or a sudden drop in stock market prices. The actions of the Federal Reserve in response to the stock market crash of 1987 is an often cited example of a successful central bank operation used to prevent a dangerous market-wide liquidity shortfall. This kind of action is close to the monetary policy function and has been called the 'market operations approach' to lending of last resort. In such cases, liquidity shortfalls could be covered through collateralised intra-day or overnight credit, or auctioning extra liquidity to the market. The Eurosystem is prepared to handle this kind of market disturbance.

7.6 A Collective Supervisor

This essay has looked at the euro-area as one that has a central bank which does not carry out banking supervision. This is normal, because in many countries banking supervision is not a task of the central bank. What is unique is that the areas of jurisdiction of monetary policy and of banking supervision do not coincide. This situation requires, first of all, the establishment of smooth cooperation between the Eurosystem and the national banking supervisors, as is the case at the national level where the two functions are separated. The most prominent reason for this is, of course, the scenario where the provision of liquidity from the central bank has to be made in a situation that is generated by problems of interest to the supervisor. But beyond that, all central banks are very closely interested in the state of health of the banking system, irrespective of its supervisory responsibilities.

In my view, we should move as rapidly as possible to a model in which the present division of the geographical and functional jurisdiction between monetary policy and banking supervision plays no significant role. I do not mean necessarily a single authority or a single set of prudential rules. Rather, the system of national supervisors needs to operate as effectively as a single authority when needed. Whereas the causes of banking problems are often local or national, the propagation of problems may be area-wide. The banking industry is much more of a system than other financial institutions.

We are far from having a common supervisory system. But since the euro has just been launched and will last, we have to look in prospective terms at what needs to be set in place. There is no expectation that the division of responsibility in the euro-area between the central bank and the banking supervisory functions should be abandoned. Although the Treaty has a provision that permits the assignment of supervisory tasks to the ECB, I personally do not rely on the assumption that this clause will be activated. What I perceive as absolutely necessary, however, is that co-operation among banking supervisors, largely voluntary but without obstacles in the existing Directives or in the Treaty, will allow a sort of euro-area collective supervisor to emerge that can act as effectively as if there were a single supervisor. This is desirable in the first instance to render the supervisory action more effective against the background of current and future challenges and, second, to assist the Eurosystem in the performance of its basic tasks.

Notes

1. See the ECB report prepared by the Banking Supervision Committee entitled 'Possible effects of EMU on the EU banking systems in the medium to long term', Feb. 1999.
2. Tables are updated with new information for the benefit of the reader.

8

Central Banks and Financial Stability

8.1 The Unbundled Composite[1]

Over the short span of my service as a central banker (little more than a third of a century) the art of central banking and the position of the institutions practising that art have changed profoundly. A third of a century ago, when currencies were still linked to gold, most central banks' monetary policies were aimed at balancing low inflation and high employment: they were often ready to sacrifice the former to have more of the latter. With few exceptions, central banks were controlled by the Treasury, which was the de facto monetary policy-maker. Most of them were in charge of banking supervision. Banking crises were virtually non-existent. However, the principle that the central bank would provide liquidity (and even capital) to support an ailing bank was an integral part of the good central banker's hallmark. Deposit insurance was rare. The notion of moral hazard was confined to the jargon of private insurers.

In that world, it was taken for granted that financial stability was a major responsibility of the central bank. Indeed, monetary policy, financial stability, and banking supervision formed a single composite, whose parts were difficult to disentangle. That world was, perhaps, not fundamentally different from what central banking had been one or one and a half centuries earlier. At that time, central banks had emerged as one of the pivotal institutions of a modern economy based on division of labour and exchange.

Much bigger are the changes that have occurred over the last three decades or so. Currencies are no longer anchored to gold. Central banks are assigned the overriding mission of preserving price stability. They have been granted independence, albeit in various degrees depending on the location. Economic theory re-established the long-term neutrality of money on a firm basis. More recently, the task of supervising banks has been taken away from the central bank in a number of countries.

These developments have unbundled the old composite to the point that one may wonder whether financial stability—a 'land in between' monetary policy and prudential supervision—still ranks among the tasks of a contemporary central bank. Indeed, both in academia and in government, there are supporters of the view that a central bank should regard financial stability as a good for which it simply takes no responsibility whatsoever. Yet, one needs only read the financial chronicles of 2002 to find resounding evidence for the contrary.[2]

This essay argues that the involvement in financial stability does, and should, remain, even today, an important component of central banking. Such involvement is rooted in the role of central banks as issuers of money. As all soundly managed financial institutions, central banks need to monitor the quality of their counterparties, whose realm spans over the whole banking system. This 'ordinary banking' concern adds to the role of providing emergency liquidity, from which no central bank can abdicate. Moreover, they exert an overall surveillance of the financial sector health, and strive to prevent the propagation of crises through financial markets and payments and settlement systems. They have a crucial interest in increasing the resilience of the financial system and minimising the recourse to emergency liquidity facilities. All these functions follow from the nature of the central banking business, not from the assignment of supervisory functions.

Central bank involvement has recently gained additional dimensions. Notably, the transformation of the financial system, both in European and in other countries, has engendered a new type of financial crisis and posed new challenges. These take the form of greater exposure of banks to markets, greater importance of non-financial institutions, emergence of large value payment systems outside the central bank, and renewed concerns about liquidity. Central banks are uniquely positioned to provide a positive contribution to meeting these challenges.

The role of central banks in the pursuit of financial stability occupies a 'land in between' monetary policy and prudential supervision. The difficulty in accurately defining this role results from the lack of a clearly established analytical and operational framework for financial stability. This essay is conceived as a contribution to filling this gap. Its primary aim is not to be prescriptive or to make definite policy recommendations, but rather to further the debate on these issues.

In the following sections, the focus will be on a central bank that does not have direct responsibility for prudential supervision. This assumption contributes to the clarity of the analysis. It also fits with an important feature of the Eurosystem[3]— the central bank system of the euro-area—and of several other national central banks. The issue of whether or not banking supervision should be inside or outside the central bank and of what is the most suitable supervisory structure at the national level is not addressed here.[4]

This essay is organised as follows. Section 8.2 will deal with the question of why central banks are involved in financial stability. To this end it reviews the relevant historical and theoretical underpinnings. Section 8.3 will look at recent challenges to the traditional paradigm presented in Section 8.2. Section 8.4 will discuss the recent transformation of the financial system and its implications for the nature of financial crises. The ensuing three sections will then present a framework to map 'the land in between' (Section 8.5), that is, to define the position and tools of the financial stability function in relation, respectively, to monetary policy (Section 8.6) and prudential supervision (Section 8.7). Sections 8.8 and 8.9 will discuss the specific context of the Eurosystem as an example, which is relevant for identifying the tools available to a non-supervisory central bank.

8.2 History and Theory

Central banks began to be involved in financial stability when they undertook the issuance of paper currency (i.e. banknotes), which replaced previous metallic currencies. They became even more involved when bank deposits grew into a substantial share of the money stock. In Europe, the model of a public central bank acting as the sole issuer of legal tender was adopted in the nineteenth century.[5] In the United States, this process took longer and was concluded in 1913 with the establishment of the Federal Reserve System. Around the first quarter of the twentieth century the total money supply had become a mixture of largely fungible central bank and commercial bank monies, the former risk-free and the latter potentially risky.

The establishment of a public monopoly for the issuance of legal tender (terms such as 'final', 'outside', or 'high-powered' money that were used as the jargon became more varied over time) was related to stability and efficiency needs.

The stability issue arose because, before the public monopoly, the issuers of banknotes were profit-maximising commercial banks, who had incentives to print more notes than they could back with holdings of gold or silver, or with deposits of government bonds. This led to 'wildcat' banks that heavily engaged in over-issuance.[6] The public's confidence was frequently abused and crises periodically rocked the financial system.

The efficiency issue was due to prohibitive transaction and information costs entailed by the coexistence of many different private monies. There was no single currency that could be used everywhere. More importantly, the price mechanism was severely impaired, as competing monies of equal nominal but different real value resulted in several price-quotations for the same goods. Such a system of multiple prices was very costly and complex for vendors to manage and for consumers to compare.[7]

The US experience with a system of competing private monies is exemplary of the above situation because it lasted for so long before the creation of a central bank. Hundreds of different banknotes were issued by commercial banks and circulated throughout the nineteenth century. The notes had different values depending on the creditworthiness of the issuer; consequently, there were publicly quoted 'exchange rates' between them. In the United States, the establishment of the Federal Reserve System was also a response to concerns about the anticompetitive nature of private-sector clearing-house arrangements that had existed before.[8] Such arrangements were private-sector solutions to accommodate some of the shortcomings of the private issuance of banknotes. They have been regarded as substitutes for public intervention as they established de facto prudential requirements on participating banks. However, they also tended to support an oligopolistic banking system, reducing competition and restricting entry.[9]

The stability need—that is, the need of a public institution to establish 'public' confidence in a currency that has no intrinsic value—remains an uncontested argument in favour of the central bank solution. Indeed no credible private sector alternative has emerged.

In contrast, it has been recently questioned whether the advances in computing technology could invalidate the efficiency rationale for a public central bank. For instance, King (1999) noted that if computing power substantially increased 'there is no conceptual obstacle to the idea that two individuals engaged in a transaction could settle by a transfer of wealth from one electronic account to another... There would be no unique role for [central bank] base money'. King, however, recognises that 'the choice of a unit of account would still be a matter for public regulation, [and] only if the unit of account was managed would there be a role for a body such as a central bank'.

However, as long as the singleness of the currency exists, technological progress will not abolish the economic need for overdrafts in the banking system and ultimately in central bank money balances to provide liquidity on demand to those in need of it.[10] As argued by Hicks (1974), this is the superior efficiency of an 'overdraft' economy, which needs to be supported by central bank money issuance, compared with a 'pure exchange economy', resembling the electronic exchange economy discussed by King and some others such as Friedman (1999).[11] Thus, while I am sceptical about the premise of the above argumentation, I would also stress much further the second aspect mentioned by King: singleness of the unit of account implies singleness of the medium of exchange and the latter cannot hold unless central bank money is there to act as the standard with which all other money-like liabilities must be fungible. In other words, central bank money is needed in the function of an ultimate and final means of payment it is also needed to effectively establish the unit of account.

A radical criticism of the single currency and single central bank was advanced by Hayek (1976). The origin of Hayek's critique was the historical experience of central banks failing to maintain a stable value of their currencies, partly due to the financing of government deficits. As the appropriate remedy he advocated a return to unregulated banking with competing private issuers of banknotes. However, Hayek's solution suffers from the same problem of 'free banking' related to the inefficiency of multiple units of account discussed above. Moreover, as Klein (1974) argued, some inherently liquid and solvent entity would have to guarantee convertibility into some other liquid asset when information about the solvency of the issuing private bank is costly to obtain.[12] A central bank is just such an entity. In fact, instead of Hayek's approach, an alternative remedy was followed, that consisted of increasing the independence of the central bank from treasuries. This set a clear mandate for monetary policy, while it also strengthened central bank accountability.

The combination of central bank monopoly on issuing 'final' money and commercial banks participating in the process of money-creation enhanced the involvement of central banks in financial stability. Two main reasons accounted for this.

First, central banks became the bankers' bank. Central banks lent to commercial banks by rediscounting commercial bank assets and held reserves of liquidity in the form of deposits. Central banks were the bankers' banks also in the sense that, to avoid conflicts of interest, they gradually ceased serving non-banks. In Europe this configuration emerged spontaneously; however, in the United States it was instituted by the law, which required the Fed to provide liquidity and settlement services to commercial banks. As a matter of prudent management of their activities, central banks needed to evaluate the soundness of counterparties, the commercial banks. Irrespective of the attribution of formal supervisory tasks, this puts central banks in a natural position to address financial stability concerns.

Second, central banks became the guarantors of the singleness of the currency in an environment in which commercial bank money progressively developed into a large share of the total money stock. As the value of money was more and more dependent on the creditworthiness of commercial banks, the concern of central banks for the orderly functioning and stability of the banking system became an integral part of their task to maintain the public's confidence in the national currency.

This included, although it did not coincide with, lending-of-last-resort when a solvent commercial bank suffered liquidity strains. By the end of the nineteenth century, most European central banks had acted as lenders-of-last-resort, for example, the Banque de France in 1882 following the collapse of Union Generale.[13]

As for the United States, the endemic financial instability of the free banking era showed the limits of private sector solutions in coping with major liquidity needs in times of stress.[14] Effective liquidity support measures proved ineffective without ultimate access to central bank liquidity even after private clearinghouse arrangements developed. After the establishment of the Federal Reserve, the frequency of banking panics substantially decreased, in part due to the provision of occasional liquidity assistance by the new institution.[15]

The provision of final liquidity remains the most powerful rationale for the role of central banks in promoting and providing financial stability. Indeed, central bank money has proven to be the most valuable settlement medium in times of crisis, when confidence in the ability of commercial banks to meet their liabilities has faded away. Central banks are the only public institutions that can provide large amounts of liquidity and act fast when needed.

Thus, the role of central banks in financial stability is part of their genetic code. It was—and, I would say, still is—an inseparable component of their role as the bankers' banks and of their monopoly on ultimate liquidity.

The way central banks developed a concern for banking as a 'system' is worth some further comment. Indeed, why do we dub banking as a 'system', whereas we do not use this notion for the steel or chemical industries, or even for the insurance or securities industries? First, banks are interconnected through the payment system, whose essential feature is currency-specificity. It refers to the circulation of one and the same money, which is completely fungible throughout the economy. Fungibility is an essential condition for the acceptance of a currency and one of the key public goods to be preserved in a monetary system. At the same time, however, the payment circuit links participants in a network that provides a channel for the propagation of risks. Second, banks collectively have the function of channelling liquidity to the rest of the financial sector and into the economy as a whole. In doing so they are critically dependent on access to central bank liquidity. Third, confidence in the currency and in the central bank is a good that exists only if shared by virtually all participants in a single currency area.

A financial system may, and usually does, remain segmented to some extent. However, if a liquidity need emerges in a specific segment of it, it is always the central bank that bears ultimate responsibility. Hence, all the answers to why banking is a 'system' have to do with the singleness of the currency and the central bank. This also shows that—with or without formal supervisory functions—the central bank is a key part of the financial system and responsible for its smooth functioning.

In Europe, prudential supervision was not formally inscribed in the charter of central banks.[16] These activities evolved naturally during the nineteenth and early twentieth centuries before they were explicitly recognised in law.[17] In contrast, a formal mandate to establish effective banking regulation and supervision was attributed to the Federal Reserve System from the outset.

In the early 1930s, banking regulation was considerably tightened after the banking crises shaking the United States and Europe. This included strict constraints on the composition of banks' assets and liabilities, rationing of licences, limits on maturity transformation, separation of commercial and investment banking, and geographical segmentation of activities. Later on, in the vast process of liberalisation and deregulation that started in the 1970s and progressed thereafter, such restrictions were relaxed throughout the world. Subsequently, supervisory tools and practices have evolved towards a more market-friendly approach. Administrative restrictions have been increasingly replaced by less intrusive, indirect prudential standards, such as capital requirements.

Deposit insurance schemes also became a key component of the arrangement put in place to foster financial stability. In the United States deposit insurance was introduced after the Great Depression, whereas in Europe such systems were mostly established in the 1980s or later.[18] This additional safety net was created to support bank stability by removing incentives for depositors to join a bank run, but there was also a social concern to protect 'unsophisticated' or 'small' depositors.

8.3   Recent Challenges

In the last thirty or so years, the role of central bank in the pursuit of financial stability was confronted with new intellectual and institutional challenges. These challenges called into question the validity of the paradigm shaped by the experiences of the nineteenth century and the first half of the twentieth century; a paradigm based on the combination of central banks serving as the Lender of Last Resort role while also maintaining regulatory and supervisory tasks. This same recent period, however, has also seen the emergence of an institutional architecture combining new elements in the arrangements of most countries. These elements consisted of a clear mandate for monetary policy to have price stability as its primary objective, the statutory independence of the central bank, and the assignment of banking supervisory tasks to an agency separate from the central bank.

A first challenge came from the heightened academic debate on whether banks are special or, in other words, whether any public intervention in the banking sector is justified on theoretical grounds. Recent academic research has found this justification in the inherent instability of the banking industry and the consequent threat to the stability of the financial system. The origin of this threat lies in the very nature of banks, and is now well understood: the transformation of short-term liabilities into illiquid long-term credits. As originally shown by Diamond and Dybvig (1983), banks provide liquidity insurance to depositors, but the maturity mismatch between deposits and loans makes them vulnerable to runs.[19]

It is important to stress that the evil to be avoided is not the failure of just a single bank. On the contrary—in the banking sector like in any other sector—occasional failures and exits from the industry are, and should be, part of a healthy market mechanism.[20] The supervisory community clearly recognises this point (e.g. in the Basel Committee's Core Principles on Banking Supervision of 1997) as a matter of principle. A different situation, however, arises if a bank risks failing as a result of a purely speculative and irrational behaviour of its depositors, or if a single failure risks degenerating into a panic. In the latter case, as other financial institutions may be simultaneously affected, essential functions of the banking system may be endangered, such as the provision of liquidity and payment services. Contagion is indeed recognised as a key component in the development of many financial crises (see Section 8.5).[21]

A second challenge came from increased and sometimes extreme concerns over the moral hazard consequences of deposit insurance and lending-of-last-resort by central banks (the so-called public safety net). 'Moral hazard' was originally an insurance term adopted to refer to a tendency of the insured to reduce the care taken to avoid insured losses.[22] In banking, the term refers to the tendency to take on extra risk—such as increasing leverage or investing in riskier assets—at the expense of the public safety net. Those (e.g. Benston and Kaufman) who push the argument against moral hazard to the extreme tend to emphasise its high cost relative to the benefits of the safety net.

Obviously, the very existence of a safety net makes complete elimination of moral hazard impossible. Moral hazard, however, can be substantially limited through specific design features. For example, discipline can be exercised on risk-taking by bank managers if deposit insurance is circumscribed, leaving uninsured some categories of depositors.[23] The same effect can be obtained through risk-based premia and co-insurance. As regards lending-of-last-resort, central banks have strengthened a cautious stance by adopting the policy of case-by-case discretion. They decline to specify in advance which financial institutions would be granted emergency liquidity and under which conditions, an attitude dubbed by Gerry Corrigan as 'constructive ambiguity'. Finally, it is crucially important that deposit insurance and lending-of-last-resort be complemented by effective prudential supervision. In fact, the element of insurance brought about by the lending-of-last-resort function was the major reason for developing the supervisory function in the nineteenth century.

In the academic debate, and at times in practice, alternative solutions to the safety net have been considered in order to remove the moral hazard. One consists of introducing new restrictions on banking to eradicate the very source of risk by separating the maturity transformation and the liquidity provision functions.

An early formulation of this idea was the suggestion, put forward by Friedman (1960), of '100 per cent reserve' banking, later supported by Tobin (1985).[24] A more recent proposal, by Merton and Bodie (1993), advocates a 'narrow banking' model based on obliging banks to hold only liquid and safe assets. As discussed in Essay 2, I share the view of those who argue that a renewed restriction of the banking business, one that would force it back to the 'narrowness' from which it started, would damage the economy by depriving it of the fundamental benefits obtained from modern banking. A risk of runs would be removed, but at the cost of substantial efficiency losses.[25] Without cars, the risk of car accidents would fall to zero, but is that what we want?

Another idea, which has received some intellectual support, is to suspend the convertibility of bank deposits into cash in periods of crisis. Seen as a practical solution to the fragility of the banking sector, suspension has been used by public authorities as a tool to 'buy time' only occasionally and with very negative results (most recently in Argentina).[26] Here again, I would share the views of those who think that suspending convertibility has more drawbacks than advantages. Not only are its legal foundations doubtful, but its effectiveness as a real solution has been shown to be limited.[27] Ultimately, confidence is unlikely to be supported by the statutory possibility, and the actual use, of the suspension of such a crucial obligation as the repayment of what is, for good reason, called a demand deposit.

A third challenge was the trend towards a separation of prudential supervision from central banks.[28] Various arguments have been advanced in favour of separation. Conflicts of interest are argued to arise when the two responsibilities of monetary policy and supervision are combined. Moreover, some fear an excessive concentration of power in a central bank endowed with a highly independent status. Finally, conglomeration and the blurring of the boundaries between different financial products and institutions are said to call for close interplay between banking, insurance, and securities supervision. The last two arguments are interrelated as concentration of power in an independent institution would be a particular problem if, in addition to maintaining price stability, it were to be entrusted with the supervision not only of banks, but also of non-bank financial institutions.

In my view, there is no conclusive theoretical or empirical research to back the arguments in favour of separation, nor any pointing to a single optimal model for supervision. The issue of a possible conflict between price stability and financial stability is further addressed in Section 8.6. As regards power concentration, mechanisms of checks and balances and procedures to ensure accountability are in place for central banks, as for other public bodies. Indeed, central bank independence by no means implies a lack of accountability. Moreover, different accountability regimes can be devised, depending on the particular central banking functions.

Considering these recent developments, the question arises of whether there is still a special role for central banks in financial stability.

A factor supporting the preservation of such a role is the inadequacy of deposit insurance as a sufficient tool to maintain financial stability. Deposit insurance prevents 'small' depositors from losing faith in their bank, but today the bulk of bank liabilities are held by other banks and financial firms, who are uninsured creditors. In the euro-area, for example, inter-bank liabilities account, on average, for around one-third of total bank liabilities, and they consist of approximately 70 per cent of non-collateralised deposits.[29] If a bank defaults on its obligation, its failure could spread to other banks leading to other defaults. Experience has shown that, among uninsured counterparties, rumours may trigger fear, and fear may spread even in circumstances in which the bank is sound and solvent. Panic is not a disease contracted by small depositors only.

In certain circumstances, wholesale markets are susceptible to a liquidity crisis. In principle, unlike retail depositors, banks, and other corporate counterparties can monitor banks to avoid large and risky exposures ('peer monitoring'). This argument has been used to assert that solvent but illiquid institutions would always be able to obtain funding from the market and the central bank should only care about the overall liquidity situation.[30] Although the latter is undoubtedly the foremost case for central banks acting against a market disruption, the occasional need to provide liquidity to individual institutions cannot be excluded. The possibility of an inter-bank market failure would justify central bank intervention.[31]

A form of central bank involvement, which carries less moral hazard implications than the provision of liquidity, consists of the central bank acting as a coordinator to facilitate private sector solutions. Even when there is a clear private sector interest in avoiding a liquidity crisis or a gridlock situation, private parties may not be able to reach such a solution because of a lack of information or of coordination. The rescue package coordinated by the Federal Reserve Bank of New York to prevent the LTCM hedge fund from collapsing is a telling example of public intervention being used to achieve a private solution.

The rationale for, and effectiveness of, the role played by central banks also derive from the fact that they have the special expertise, information, and tools necessary to perform coordination and liquidity support functions. Central banks have been confronted for two centuries with the problem of distinguishing between illiquid and insolvent institutions. Moreover, to avoid destroying incentives for banks to monitor each other and to limit moral hazard, a consensus seems to exist that liquidity assistance should be given only to prevent financial instability and only to the smallest possible degree.

To sum up, there is clear empirical and theoretical evidence that, at times, public intervention may be required to ensure financial stability. Banking is a business plagued by an inherent instability, which cannot be removed if its economic benefits are to be realised. Moreover, the banking industry operates as a closely interlinked 'system', prone to contagion through the payment system and inter-bank markets. The involvement of central banks in financial stability is rooted in their role as issuers of money. Central banks—like any soundly managed financial institution—need to monitor the quality of their counterparties. This is in addition to their role as ultimate providers of a safe settlement medium and liquidity to ensure the orderly functioning of the financial system.[32] It should be noted once more that these two special reasons for their involvement in financial stability are independent of whether central banks have formal supervisory functions.

8.4   Crises: Old and New

So far, we have reviewed the historical and theoretical foundations of, as well as recent challenges for, the role of central banks in financial stability. Indeed, many central banks were established to serve as bulwarks against episodes of financial instability that had been the endemic disease of the 'free banking era'. However, the establishment of central banks has not made the financial system immune to instability, thus banking and financial crises have continued to occur. Crises have actually become more frequent once the highly restrictive and efficiency-absorbing regulations introduced after the Great Depression were dismantled. Moreover, the disease has taken new forms as a consequence of the ongoing transformation of the financial system. This in turn has consequences for the role of central banks and the policies best suited to preserve financial stability.

This and the next section will examine a number of crises, which occurred since the liberalisation process, grouping them into 'old' and 'new' with reference to the changes in the financial system. The labels 'old' and 'new' are used as an expositional device. They are not meant to say that the more traditional sources of financial instability (such as credit risks related to financial cycles) have become less relevant, but rather that the transformation of the financial system has brought about additional concerns. Although the transformation of the financial system can be seen as global, its speed has varied across the world. For this reason, the episodes of financial instability will be ordered by cause rather than chronologically.

For the sake of a stylised description, we can say that the 'old' financial system was characterised by separation in four respects.[33] First, there was separation between institutions and markets. Negotiable assets were a negligible part of the balance sheet of banks and insurance companies. Notably, the exposure of banks to market volatility was limited, as they largely focused on the transformation of deposits into illiquid loans. Second, there was separation between the three main categories of financial intermediaries (banks, insurance companies, and securities houses or broker-dealers), as well as between the products they managed. Non-negotiable bank loans, insurance policies, and negotiable securities provided distinct ways of allocating savings and risks, each of them related to a different basic financial contract. Third, there was separation in the regulatory and supervisory structure, to reflect the tripartition between both financial products and financial intermediaries. The oversight of markets was conducted by a separate entity from the one supervising financial institutions, and banks faced a different supervisor than insurance companies. Perhaps more importantly, supervisory instruments differed substantially across sectors even when risks were analogous. Finally, domestic financial systems tended to be insulated from one another. Normally, in the 'old' world of finance the different elements of financial transactions, the intermediary, the currency, the central bank, the legislation applied, the court that would be addressed in case of litigation, the language, all belonged to the same country. Links between financial systems were tenuous and most countries fenced their national system with various types of barriers, which were encouraged by the Bretton Woods institutions.

These features of the 'old' finance were consistent with, and made possible by, the technological environment. The basic technology used in the financial world was based on paper and mail, with telex and telephones used for fast communication. Such technology was put in place towards the end of the nineteenth century and remained dominant until the 1970s. It permitted a number of regulations and segmentations whose effectiveness was subsequently wiped out by the advent of modern information and communication technology (ICT).

The 'old' system was susceptible to a type of crisis, illustrated by a number of episodes that occurred in the last quarter century. Latin America (early 1980s), the US Savings & Loans (throughout 1980s), and the three Nordic banking crises of Finland, Norway and Sweden (early 1990s) are the most relevant ones.[34] Similar crises also took place in several emerging and developing countries in the 1990s, such as Brazil (1994), Thailand, Korea, and the Philippines (1997–98). In some cases, the crisis was confined to a few or to individual institutions. In Europe relevant episodes are Banesto (1993), Credit Lyonnais (1994), and the banks in southern Italy (mid to late 1990s).

In Latin America, a banking crisis followed the debt crisis of the early 1980s, which resulted from the previous rapid accumulation of credit granted by US banks. Argentina, Chile, and Mexico had full-blown crises in 1980–83. In Argentina 9 per cent of loans were non-performing in 1980 (30 per cent in 1985) and 168 banks were closed. In Chile, 19 per cent of loans were non-performing in 1983 and the authorities intervened in thirteen banks. In Mexico, the government had to take over the troubled banking sector in 1982.

The US Savings & Loans crisis had its origins in the rapid increase in nominal interest rates resulting from the monetary policy tightening in the late 1970s and early 1980s. These institutions were exposed to interest rate risk, because the majority of their assets were invested in fixed-rate, low-yielding mortgages. As interest rates rose to record levels, Savings & Loan institutions were confronted with sharply rising funding costs and diminishing profits. Many institutions lost their net worth and engaged in excessive risk-taking, investing heavily in risky commercial real estate projects ('gambling for resurrection'); this resulted in institutions' failures when the real estate boom came crashing down in certain parts of the country.

Finally, the Nordic banking crises were a consequence of rapid credit expansion, made possible by the deregulation of foreign capital inflows and restrictions on banks' assets; these factors dangerously propped-up asset prices and the indebtedness of the domestic non-financial sectors. Credit was often denominated in foreign currencies, resulting in unhedged foreign exchange risk positions. The level of non-performing loans was highest in Finland, reaching 13 per cent of total loans in 1992.

All in all, these crises followed a fairly consistent, although not always predictable pattern. Deregulation of banking restrictions and capital controls led to a lending boom. Asset prices rose, particularly in real estate. A turn in the business cycle and asset price shocks (mainly real estate price and exchange rate shocks) were then followed by large-scale thrift failures. It is noteworthy that these crises affected banks, not financial markets or non-bank financial institutions. Financial instability generally resulted from credit risks. In the new environment that emerged from deregulation and liberalisation, both the risk management techniques of banks and the supervisory practices of public agencies proved inadequate to cope with traditional banking risks.

The pattern of crisis resolution was also rather similar across countries, not least in that the role of central banks was relatively limited in comparison with the role of the government and its agencies.[35] Whereas in most cases some initial liquidity support or bridging loans was provided by central banks, it was often clear from the outset that the problem was insolvency rather than illiquidity. The success of the crisis-resolution varied. For instance, Argentina's crisis in the early 1980s resulted in high inflation and disintermediation, whereas in Chile it led to a strengthened financial system.

Although there should be no illusion that the 'old' type of financial distress will not recur in the future, one could argue that the 'new' financial system brings to prominence new sources of instability. Recent changes in the financial structure can be summarised by the breakdown of the separations that characterised the 'old' system.

The two first separations—between financial institutions and markets as well as between the three traditional sectors of finance—have been replaced by an increasing integration of markets with banks, and of banks with other financial institutions. Integration has been the outcome of a search for more flexible and effective ways to transform savings into investments. Securitisation and the development of credit risk transfer are important aspects of this development, as they allow the reallocation of credit risk to the agents best suited to bear it. Such developments may also be seen as a market response to the previous crises, aiming at better risk diversification. For instance, the Latin American crises boosted the development of the secondary markets for credit instruments.

Corresponding changes have occurred in the supervisory structures, breaking down the separation between sectors and some differences between supervisory instruments. Many countries have integrated the supervision of different financial institutions and have switched from strict 'command and control' to incentive-based supervision; this switch has supported the development of risk management practices. These goals are central, for instance, in the current revision of the capital adequacy rules. International cooperation among supervisors has also developed. The Basel Committee on Banking Supervision actually has been the forum where many of the new approaches to prudential supervision were first devised and adopted.

The move from 'old' to 'new' finance has been closely linked to breaking down of the fourth separation, the one between national financial systems. National markets are no longer isolated entities, rather they are embedded in a complex system of interlinkages, which calls for close international cooperation.

The key to all these developments has been the profound change in the technology underlying financial activity. The move from the 'paper-mail' technology to ICT that has marked the last quarter century has permitted the circumvention of many regulatory barriers to the point of eventually entailing their abolition. By spreading information worldwide in real time and by connecting markets, it has made possible the emergence of trading 'round-the-clock'. ICT has provided the instrument for constructing new financial products and for unbundling the old ones into different components that could be traded separately. By allowing a direct contact between the two sides of a financial transaction it has revolutionised and, to a certain extent, made superfluous, the services of financial intermediaries.

Four important new potential sources of disturbances closely related to this changed environment can be identified. First, a rapid increase in banks' financial market-related activities has heightened their exposure to the vagaries of markets, implying that bank stability may be increasingly vulnerable to market instability. Second, the greater prominence of markets has implied that financial instability may emanate also from non-bank financial institutions, should the banking system and the liquidity redistribution function be affected by an exposure to these institutions. Third, liquidity conditions and contagion risks may play an increasingly important role. Whereas the liquidity of markets may have increased and institutions' access to liquidity improved in tranquil times, during a crisis liquidity has a tendency to dry up more rapidly. Fourth, large value payments traffic has grown exponentially and clearing and settlement systems—operating under the principle of net settlement— have emerged outside central banks, which has increased payment system-related risks. The following paragraphs will examine in more detail these changes in the light of the crises we have already witnessed.

Exposure of banks to financial market developments—the first new potential source of instability—has grown as a result of several structural factors. Private capital markets and the associated derivatives markets have so substantially deepened over the years that banks have been stimulated to participate in the market. Meanwhile, the rise in household wealth has increased the propensity of individuals to invest in securities, while the development of supplementary pension schemes has also boosted the demand for marketable assets. This movement has been particularly pronounced in the euro-area where bank deposits, formerly comprising the dominant share in households' assets, have now declined considerably below the share of direct or indirect security investments (via collective investment schemes). These demand-side developments have opened up opportunities for firms to diversify funding sources, to reduce funding costs by issuing securities, and to finance corporate restructuring from capital markets.[36]

Banks have been able to exploit their extensive retail distribution networks to reach investors, particularly in Europe, offering a full range of mutual funds and brokerage services. European banks have also developed strong investment banking services, with some of them now acting as global investment banks in competition with US institutions. Banks have also undertaken significant trading activities of their own. Until the middle of 2000, as the market conditions were very favourable, the growth in securities-related activities has boosted non-interest income from fees and commissions.[37] In 2000, that is, before the stock market fall, consolidated non-interest income accounted for 57 per cent of the total net income of the fifty largest euro-area banks (in 1995 the share was below 30 per cent).

The other side of this coin is that the vulnerability of banks to financial market developments has increased, as witnessed by a number of episodes. Barings is a good illustration. Whereas inadequate internal controls can, of course, lead to problems also in the more traditional lending business, the speed at which one 'rogue trader' was able to take a huge position is only possible in modern securities and derivative markets. Barings also highlights the importance of taking a decision on the systemic nature of a bank failure in an extremely short lapse of time.[38] On the afternoon of Friday, 24 February 1995, the bank's senior management notified the Bank of England that its securities subsidiary in Singapore had made large losses in Japanese financial markets. Barings requested the Bank of England's support in winding down its activities. The decision on whether to support Barings had to be made by the time trading started in Japan on the Monday morning local time, because insolvent institutions are not allowed to trade. The decision not to start a rescue was founded on the assessment that a failure of Barings would not threaten stability in the United Kingdom or the global financial system. Parties with a potential interest in seeing Barings continue operation were, therefore, invited to bid for a takeover. Although no direct support was provided, the Bank of England announced a willingness to provide liquidity to the UK banking system as a whole in order to smooth out the repercussions of the failure.

The failures of two Japanese securities houses in 1997 illustrate the second source of risks, related to non-bank financial institutions. The first, Sanyo, failed in November 1997. Sanyo was a medium-sized securities house with client assets of JPY 2.7 trillion. Even though the Bank of Japan initially assessed the failure as having few systemic implications, when Sanyo defaulted on its unsecured money market obligations (although the amount was relatively small) there was a substantial negative impact on overall liquidity in the inter-bank market. The Bank of Japan was eventually forced to inject liquidity into banks via the purchase of eligible bills, repos, and bilateral lending against collateral. The second failure occurred three weeks later and was similar, albeit more serious. It involved Yamaichi Securities, the fourth largest securities house in Japan with client assets in excess of JPY 22 trillion. No doubt due to the lessons learnt in the Sanyo case, Yamaichi was allowed to continue in operation to settle its existing contracts. The authorities were also faced with the difficult question of whether the Bank of Japan would be permitted to provide direct emergency liquidity to the company, which it did in the end.[39]

Systemic concerns about non-bank financial institutions have been linked with concerns about the impact on the banking sector. Another issue is whether the failure of an independent securities firm could by itself be a source of risk to financial stability even if banks were not affected. Here, my conclusion would be negative. I would subscribe to the traditional view that financial stability could be at stake only in so far as shocks transmit to the banking sector. The episodes of turbulence over recent years suggest that difficulties assume systemic relevance only when the banking system and the liquidity redistribution mechanism are hit. When turbulence occurred outside the banking system, it could be managed as long as banks were in a position to support the liquidity needs of other intermediaries.

Liquidity conditions and contagion are the third source of instability related to the new developments in the financial system. Actually, in the two Japanese cases, financial distress spread through money markets. The inter-bank links were the source of concern also in the United Kingdom's 'small bank crisis' of 1991–92.[40] As foreign banks grew increasingly concerned about the UK property price decline, they reduced their exposure to UK banks. The Bank of England used its close ties to financial markets and to the large clearing banks to acquire quantitative and qualitative information about the affected banks and to assess the likelihood of a systemic impact. At first, some failures were tolerated, but soon it became apparent that many simultaneous failures of small banks could have systemic implications. Thus, when the National Mortgage Bank and some other banks ran into liquidity problems in late 1991, the Bank of England decided to provide emergency liquidity assistance.

Continental Illinois (the seventh largest US bank at the time of its failure in 1984) provides another early example of a liquidity crisis, due to an outflow of wholesale deposits.[41] A run by such depositors was caused by rumours that the bank would fail because of its Mexican exposures. In view of Continental's size and function as a money centre bank, public support operations, involving the central bank and the deposit insurance agency, were undertaken. As in the 'small bank crisis', the underlying problem was illiquidity rather than insolvency.[42]

Market liquidity outside inter-bank money markets is also important for financial stability. The failure of the Drexel Burnham Lambert Group and the collapse of the market for lower-grade bonds in the late 1980s, and the collapse of the market for perpetual floating rate notes in the mid-1980s are early examples.[43] The Russia/LTCM crisis of 1998 has shown that not only relatively specialised markets with a concentrated structure are subject to abrupt declines in liquidity, even though perhaps they are more likely to be so. All these crises resulted in a substantial decline in liquidity in global corporate and emerging country bond markets. Moreover, the LTCM incidence highlighted the risk that a disorderly failure of a major securities player could severely depress prices in illiquid markets and lead to contagion via market prices. Prices could fall to a point where other institutions holding important risk concentrations in the same markets would also incur major losses.[44]

All in all, these episodes point to three conclusions. First, whereas runs by retail depositors may have become a rare event and can be effectively prevented by deposit insurance, runs by wholesale depositors (other banks or firms) may have become more important. Second, financial market liquidity has gained substantially in importance. The deepening of the markets has improved the ability of banks to access funds in normal times, but liquidity may be more prone to dry up when it is most needed. Third, contagion risk via inter-bank money markets as well as other financial markets has become a substantial component of the overall risk environment surrounding a bank.

Payment system related risks are the fourth potential source of instability. Such risks are mainly related to the increases in the sheer volume of transactions, to structural changes in the systems, and to increased cross-border financial activity.

As financial market transactions have dramatically increased, payment volumes have increased correspondingly.[45] In order to cope with the increased volumes, private systems for the settlement of payments have emerged, such as CHIPS in the 1970s, a private US clearinghouse that settles on a multilateral netting basis.

In a multilateral netting system, commitments to transfer funds at settlement time usually accumulate during the day and each participant transfers only its net position vis-à-vis all the other participants at the end of the day. This implies, however, that each participating bank extends intra-day credit and thus runs settlement risks (with regard to both credit and liquidity risks) vis-à-vis other participants in the system, not necessarily only its trading counterparties. The standards developed by central banks (see Section 8.9) for large-value netting systems enable such systems to withstand the failure of the largest participant and to settle on the same day even in such circumstances. In addition, central banks all over the world have put into place gross settlement systems, providing real-time finality of payments, thus eliminating the risk associated to netting procedures.

Increased cross-border financial activity largely has taken the form of an expansion of exchange trading. The settlement of foreign exchange (FX) transactions typically involves a principal risk because one party might pay out the currency it has sold before receiving the currency it has bought. Indeed, the settlement of the two legs of FX transactions occurs in two different payment systems, often operating in different time zones. The potential systemic implications of FX settlement risk surfaced for the first time when a German bank, Bankhaus Herstatt, failed in 1974.[46] Although central banks have been concerned ever since about what came to be called Herstatt risk, it took twenty-eight years for this risk to be fundamentally addressed. In 2002, a new settlement arrangement (the CLS bank) became operational—at first in limited capacity. It ensures that the final transfer of one currency occurs if, and only if, the final transfer of the other currency occurs.

The vulnerability of the financial system may also be due to operational causes (the so-called operational risk), mainly the vulnerability originating from payment and settlement systems. In 1985, a pure software disruption at the Bank of New York caused a major payment system problem, which had to be addressed by the Federal Reserve Bank of New York. After the attack of 11 September 2001, the telephone system, the major communications tool in the transfer of payments, was severely disrupted in the lower Manhattan district. As a consequence, many banks were unable to execute payments to each other via Fedwire, and liquidity became extremely scarce.[47] At the same time, the Bank of New York, a dominant player in the settlement of US government bonds with several offices located in and around the World Trade Centre, was unable to continue operations. Because it was not sending out securities, liquidity accumulated in the accounts of the Bank of New York, causing further disruptions to the payment system. To avoid a major liquidity crisis, the Federal Reserve injected vast amounts of liquidity, first through discount window lending and later through market operations.

All the episodes reviewed in this section point to the active role played by central banks in safeguarding financial stability when a crisis occurs. This is largely due to concerns about liquidity, contagion, and payment system risks. Section 8.2 focused on the origin of central banks, showing that they were created to protect against the fragility and risks stemming from the banking and financial system of the nineteenth and early twentieth centuries. Instead, the episodes reviewed in this Section relate to the most recent history of banks and central banks. As a matter of fact, these new patterns seem to have reinforced, rather than weakened the original role of central banks as ultimate providers of liquidity to facilitate orderly market conditions and, if needed for financial stability, to neutralise threats of liquidity shortages.

8.5 The Land in Between

The preceding sections have surveyed the role played by central banks for the preservation of financial stability. This role has appeared to be rooted in the very origin of central banks, confirmed by their long history, and based on solid theoretical arguments. Despite the new challenges brought about by recent developments, most visible in the episodes of financial instability that have plagued the last quarter of the twentieth century, this active role has continued.[48]

The remaining task is to discuss how this role fits in today's central banking. In a world where—as has become more frequent—the central bank has the assigned objective of price stability while prudential supervision is entrusted to a separate agency, the three functions of monetary policy, financial stability, and prudential supervision no longer form a single composite. The composite has been unbundled. Thus, central bank involvement in financial stability constitutes 'a land in between', whose boundaries, morphology, and relationships with adjacent lands need to be considered anew.

The difficulty of the task results from the lack of a clearly established analytical and operational framework for financial stability. This is in contrast to the clear terms of reference available for both monetary policy and prudential supervision. In the case of monetary policy, we can rely on a large body of academic research and a clearly defined framework with measurable objectives and tools. Furthermore, we have established decision-making procedures and communication protocols. For prudential supervision—long neglected by academic research, left instead to practitioners and legal experts—important contributions over the last two decades have laid the foundation for a more rigorous understanding of its rationale and tools.

This and the following two sections represent an attempt to clarify the position and tools of the financial stability function of central banks in relation to monetary policy and prudential supervision. Without having the ambition to be comprehensive or to give precise policy prescriptions, it proposes some elements to draw a road map for exploring the subject further. After defining financial stability and outlining the related tools and actions, the interplay and overlap of such actions with monetary policy and prudential supervision will be discussed.

Let us start with a working definition of financial stability. It is striking that although a number of central banks regularly publish financial stability reports, they tend either to avoid the question of how to define financial stability entirely (e.g. the Bank of England) or to explicitly acknowledge the elusiveness of a consistent definition (e.g. the Austrian National Bank). In general, the core economic function of the financial system consists in channelling savings into investments and providing for an efficient and safe payment mechanism. Along these lines, I would suggest defining financial stability as a condition in which the financial system is able to withstand shocks without giving way to cumulative processes that impair the allocation of savings to investment opportunities and the processing of payments in the economy.

The definition immediately raises the related question of defining the financial system. In this essay, I adopt a broad definition, whereby the financial system consists of all financial intermediaries, organised as well as informal markets, payments and settlement circuits, technical infrastructures supporting financial activity, legal and regulatory provisions, and supervisory agencies. This definition permits a complete view of the ways in which savings are channelled towards investment opportunities, information is disseminated and processed, risk is shared among economic agents, and payments are facilitated across the economy.

This broad definition does not contradict the earlier contention that banks are special because their failure could lead to systemic instability, which also justifies the specific safety net. Nor does it imply disregarding the importance of non-financial sector imbalances (corporate and household sector leverage, for instance), problems of non-bank financial institutions, and asset prices for the robustness of the financial system. As previous experiences amply demonstrate, such financial imbalances or disturbances often have preceded and indeed caused bank failures and financial crises, although they did not always do so. A forward-looking assessment of financial stability should of course duly consider these aspects.

To clarify the tools available for the pursuit of financial stability in the 'land in between', it helps to start from a broad list of tools. Table 8.1 includes all the tools— irrespective of the institution to which they are assigned—potentially playing a role in this regard, relating them to the objectives of price stability and financial stability.[49] Table 8.1 further distinguishes between tools immediately affecting the stability of the system as a whole and tools aimed at the stability of individual financial institutions. In order to highlight a 'pure central bank perspective' of financial stability, it assumes that the agency in charge of prudential supervision is not the central bank, although the taxonomy of the policy instruments as such is independent of the specific institutional arrangements. Table 8.1 is intended to be descriptive, rather than normative, that is, it illustrates conceivable approaches, rather than making policy prescriptions.

Table 8.1 is an attempt to be as precise as possible on an issue where precision is elusive. It cannot avoid putting together such diverse and heterogeneous objects as institutions (central bank, supervisory authority), policy instruments (interest rates, market operations, etc.), operational arrangements (payment systems). Indeed, this very heterogeneity is indispensable to map the total territory where the land in between lies.

The first four lines (monetary policy strategy, short-term interest rates, money market operations, and standing facilities[50]), combined with commenting (either to

Table 8.1. *Tools for Maintaining Price and Financial Stability*

Tool	Price stability	Financial stability	
		System-wide	Individual institutions
Monetary policy strategy	××	×	
Short-term interest rates	××	×	
Money market operations	××	×	
Standing facilities	××	×	×
Payment systems		××	
Public and private comments	××	⊗	⊗
Emergency liquidity support		××	××
Crisis coordination		⊗	⊗⊗
Prudential regulation		○	○○
Prudential supervision		○	○○

Notes: Two symbols (×× or ○○) = primary use of the tool; one symbol (× or ○) = secondary use of the tool; × = tool of a central bank without supervisory powers; ○ = tool of an authority other than a central bank; ⊗ = tool available for both.

the public at large or, in private, to financial institutions or other authorities) primarily relate to central bank actions aimed at achieving price stability. At the same time, prudential supervision and regulation, while ultimately concerned with financial stability, influences the behaviour of individual institutions.[51] That leaves four tools in the 'land in between': payment systems (operation and standards); the crisis management measures of emergency liquidity support and coordination of private sector solutions; and, again, public and private comments. These entries represent the 'dedicated' tools available to a central bank without explicit supervisory duties to contribute to financial stability. Thus, these tools facilitate the role of central banks in financial stability fundamentally rooted in the two aspects previously highlighted of being the bankers' bank and the ultimate provider of liquidity.

It should be noted that the term emergency liquidity support includes actions to support liquidity in the financial system as a whole (through market operations) as well as emergency liquidity assistance to individual banks (Lending-of Last Resort). Finally, Table 8.1 reflects the fact that financial stability considerations are taken into account when designing the monetary policy strategy, the payment system, as well as the regulatory, supervisory, and crisis management frameworks.

The fact that price stability and financial stability need to be reconciled is immediately obvious from Table 8.1, which shows the potential for conflict arising from the overlap in tools. For example, short-term interest rates and market operations can conceivably be used to accomplish both price stability and financial stability. Equally obvious is the need for close cooperation between the central bank and the supervisory agency in financial stability activities, given that they ultimately pursue the same objective, albeit generally with different tools.

The rest of this essay will be devoted to further defining the boundaries of the financial stability function in relation, first, to price stability and, second, to the actions addressing the stability of individual financial institutions. The specific features of the different tools will be discussed in Section 8.9, focusing on the euro-area context.

8.6 Monetary Policy

Consider the potential conflict between price stability and financial stability. Such a conflict would emerge if there were circumstances in which the monetary policy stance required to maintain price stability (as reflected in short-term interest rates and market operations) were to harm the stability of the financial system.

A forceful argument supporting the view that such a conflict is unlikely to exist is that the absence of stable prices—in the form of either inflation or deflation—is a major threat to financial stability. For example, when price inflation develops, misperceptions about the current state of the economy and the level of future returns are likely to spread among economic agents; unproductive lending will increase, because inflation makes it more difficult for lenders to discern the quality of borrowers and projects. Deflation, on the other hand, tends to trigger a vicious circle in which an increasing real value of debt leads to further defaults. Some observers have further suggested that financial crises may have been caused by deflationary pressures not sufficiently combated by central banks through the supply of liquidity.[52]

Overall, there is little doubt that price stability supports sound investment and sustainable growth, which in turn is conducive to financial stability.[53] The suggestion that large price movements can cause financial instability is supported by evidence from major financial crises. All in all, because the fragility of banks and their counterparties tend to be more frequent when prices are unstable, the pursuit of price stability can be seen as a crucial contribution to financial stability.

Some day-to-day monetary policy tools, in fact, are to a significant extent associated with financial stability considerations. In the case of the Eurosystem, for example, the lending and deposit facilities at the central bank (i.e. standing facilities) provide upper and lower bounds for money market rate fluctuations and give individual institutions a means to deal with end-of-day liquidity imbalances. Also, fine-tuning money market operations, which take place at a higher frequency than interest rate decisions, are intended to reduce the volatility of short-term interest rates and to ensure smooth provision of liquidity. These operations are primarily aimed at providing sufficient liquidity to the money market and at facilitating an orderly liquidity management by individual banks. In the jargon of the past, this was generally referred to as maintaining 'orderly market conditions'.

Having said this, it would be simplistic to close the issue here and to rely, without any further reflection, on the reassuring proposition that price and financial stability cannot and do not ever conflict. A few considerations make me unsatisfied with this perfunctory conclusion.

First, it is a fact that significant episodes of financial crises—or situations that could have easily led to crises—took place in the last two or three decades in a context of overall price stability. For example, the Japanese banking problems started to emerge in the early 1990s, resulting from a lending-asset price cycle that took place despite low inflation. Important individual failures (e.g. BCCI, Barings, Credit Lyonnais, and Yamaichi) have occurred in the presence of price stability. The example of Japan suggests a further reflection. Even though it is always easier to comment on policy *ex post* than making it on the spot, one could consider that in the late 1980s monetary policy underestimated the risk of domestic inflation. In 1988, the short-term inflation forecast looked very benign, but a more forward-looking approach would have highlighted the risks of inflation stemming from the strong growth in the money supply. Double-digit money supply growth rates and booming real estate and equity prices helped to fuel the bubble. A tighter monetary policy, thereby accepting for a short period a lower inflation rate than normally desirable, would (most likely) have been an appropriate response.

Might the last six to seven years of US monetary history eventually turn out to be another example? The final verdict is still outstanding. Should the Fed have raised the federal funds rate more aggressively between early 1999 and May 2000 in order to increase the likelihood of bursting what later appeared to have been a bubble?[54] In that case, the Fed would have had to accept a lower inflation rate than originally targeted until the bubble had burst. Would the US economy, and thus the world economy, have been in better shape in 2001 and 2002? Honestly, no one knows for sure, but no central banker can avoid contemplating the possibility.

Recently, some authors have pushed the critique of the 'no conflict view' to the point of arguing that the regime of low and stable inflation could even create a 'false sense of security' and generate myopic short-sighted expectations, which lead to financial instability.[55] I would downplay the importance of this danger. What I would conclude, instead, is that the historical evidence does not support the belief that an environment of stable prices relegates financial instability to such a low order of importance as to be ignored by the central bank. Although both inflation and deflation are detrimental to financial stability, price stability is certainly not a sufficient condition for financial stability.

Second, even a central bank having price stability as its explicit primary objective is likely to be, in the short-term, above or below its inflation target. It adjusts its policy rate on the basis of an assessment of future price developments, which is inevitably subject to uncertainty. If, for example, the central bank assigns a relatively high probability to financial instability and presumes that such instability is associated with deflationary tendencies, it may accept higher inflation in the short term. Policy dilemmas lurk precisely in the shadows between the short-, medium- and long-term; not to mention, of course, Keynes' aphorism about death before the long-term. The point is that a clear mandate and a clear strategy for monetary policy are not sufficient to determine what the central bank should decide when a particular situation arises, and indeed allow for genuine discussions, diverse views, and disagreements on the best decision to take in any given circumstance. Moreover, they are insufficient to determine the exact weighting of financial stability considerations against other considerations. Ultimately, the substantive issue is, in the analysis, the relationship between financial and price stability and, in the decision, the weight to be given to financial stability considerations.

A closely related issue is the argument that a smooth path of interest rates is propitious to financial stability.[56] This argument is based on the maturity transformation function of banks, whereby they convert variable rate liabilities into fixed-rate assets. Of course, if the central bank were to interpret its responsibility for financial stability as implying that it must smooth interest rates, a trade-off with the objective of price stability would easily arise. To the extent various monetary policy frameworks entail different volatility of central bank rates, the choice of the monetary policy framework has, per se, implications for financial stability.[57]

Third, in a context of general price stability there may be sectors or regions of the economy subject to a price shock, which in turn may cause a financial crisis of sufficient proportions to entail systemic risk. The overall price index considered by monetary policy may not signal a significant deviation from price stability, but a more circumscribed observation may reveal a situation in which both price and financial stability are seriously threatened. At this *local* level the positive correlation between price stability and financial stability may not be violated, but it runs in the opposite direction from the one prevailing at the *general* level. Such asymmetric shocks are, of course, fully contemplated in a properly designed monetary policy framework, but this may not be of much help when they arise and decisions are needed.

Fourth and final, even if it is true that an environment of stable prices is more propitious to financial stability than either inflation or deflation, the question remains whether conflicts may arise when the economy is *moving* towards price stability. Particularly in the transition towards a regime of low inflation, the potentially high real interest rates associated with such a disinflationary process may impose a great burden on financial institutions. Some evidence suggests that a number of financial crises were caused by a sharp increase in short-term interest rates necessitated by price stability considerations. The increase in interest rates impinged on banks in the money market by suddenly increasing their funding cost. Although in the longer term, this effect could vanish as banks can pass on the increased funding cost to their borrowers, upon impact this has led in the past to disruptions in the banking system.[58]

Hence, situations where the objective of maintaining, or perhaps restoring, price stability demands a policy response which is not compatible with financial stability, do have fairly robust theoretical underpinnings.[59] However, empirically, these occasions appear to be quite rare, mainly due to the strong link between recessions and financial crises.

A special reflection needs to be devoted to the relationship between asset prices, financial stability, and monetary policy. On the one hand, there is the issue of choosing the appropriate price index for monetary policy. On the other hand, it cannot be ignored that large asset price movements often have been a trigger for financial crises.[60] Taking these two considerations to their ultimate conclusion, it may be argued that the chosen measure for inflation should include prices of financial asset.

If this approach were to be implemented, central banks would directly adjust policy rates to combat asset price inflation.

However, I would concur with the view that such a direct link should be avoided, due to its serious drawbacks.[61] If directly linked to asset prices, monetary policy would end up being dominated and manipulated by financial markets, thus becoming volatile and unpredictable.[62] Moreover, it is likely that financial market participants would increase risk-taking in anticipation of the central bank providing a floor for asset prices, possibly resulting in less rather than more financial stability.[63] Not only asset prices, but also the policy tool would strongly depend on market expectations, and the outcome for inflation could become largely arbitrary.[64] Furthermore, it would become exceedingly difficult—in the case of assets—to make a clear distinction between price increases and price inflation, a distinction of crucial importance for any monetary policy oriented to price stability. Indeed, it does not seem that the major difficulties in estimating the fundamental value of financial assets could be easily overcome, at least at present.[65] In view of these arguments, I would conclude that including asset prices in the policy-relevant price index would most likely lead to problems with the pursuit of price stability. In point of fact, most central banks do not include asset prices in the concept of price stability used for their monetary policy decisions.

This being understood, the issue remains how a central bank should position itself with respect to changes in asset prices? Indeed, the question is currently much debated, partly because of the recent extraordinary vagaries of stock prices in the United States and in other parts of the world. What should a central bank do in the face of asset price changes?

The first and foremost part of the answer is straightforward. Given a price stability-oriented and forward-looking monetary policy, a central bank would be well advised to evaluate all the implications of large asset price change for future inflation. It should look at such implications both in relation to demand effects and in relation to financial stability considerations. A central bank should adjust the policy rate in order to maintain price stability over the relevant horizon.[66]

The answer, however, has also a more problematic part, which concerns the occurrence of extreme movements in asset prices, combined with the proven ability of central banks to 'influence' markets by commenting on and analysing current events in the economy. When an asset price—be it the exchange rate, house prices, or stock prices—grossly deviates from any plausible 'normal' level, should the central bank speak up or keep silent? Should the famous expression 'irrational exuberance' (Greenspan, December 1996) never have been used? Should subsequent Fed analyses, providing explanations for the extraordinary and unexpectedly prolonged 'boom without inflation', not have been made for fear they might encourage a bubble? Should the ECB never have stated that 'the present level of the euro does not reflect the strong fundamentals of the euro area' (April 2000)? When does reticence pass the limits of neutrality? On the one hand, of course, the central bank should avoid driving the market as well as taking responsibility for developments it cannot really influence. On the other, the central bank is aware that asset markets can sometimes lose their sense of direction, and that either overshooting or undershooting are recurrent and potentially damaging even if the equilibrium value of assets cannot be precisely determined. Undoubtedly, the central bank should be well aware of what is the rule and what is the exception, but there are circumstances in which non-interference or neutrality may be impossible and even silence speaks.

8.7 Prudential Supervision

After discussing the relationship of the financial stability function with monetary policy, another boundary remains to be addressed: public actions concerned with individual bank stability. As noted earlier, this boundary is most visible when the central bank does not have explicit supervisory tasks.

Here, a distinction is commonly drawn between micro-prudential and macro-prudential concerns. The distinction focuses on the activities and the analytical approaches to measure risks, rather than questioning the commonality of their ultimate common objective of financial stability (see Table 8.1). The macro-prudential dimension is usually associated with the central bank, the micro-prudential one with the supervisory authority.

The macro-prudential dimension looks at the financial system as a whole. Accordingly, it encompasses assessment and monitoring of potential threats to financial stability arising from macroeconomic or financial market developments (common shocks) and exposures to systemic risk (contagion). This is in line with the definition of financial stability introduced earlier, as the analysis focuses on evaluating the risk of financial distress, which would be costly for the economy. The macro-prudential risk measurement approach focuses on common (possibly multiple) sources of risk for financial institutions and on the risk of correlated failures. If it looks at individual institutions, it pays attention to characteristics that may determine their significance for the financial system as a whole, such as size and links with other institutions.

In this area, the central analytical issue is to identify how much the financial system is exposed to certain risks (such as a stock market decline) and how robust the system is likely to be in absorbing shocks. Robustness depends on the availability of financial buffers (profits, reserves, and capital) in financial institutions.

A second issue, where less progress has been made, is to establish whether financial imbalances have reached an unsustainable level. Although authorities cannot precisely predict the incidence of shocks, it is nevertheless important to assess potential downside risks. For instance, unambiguous evidence that an asset price bubble is emerging before it actually bursts remains controversial. Many indicators are available and can be compared against historical norms,[67] but it is not easy to distinguish between sound earnings expectations and unwarranted and euphoric risk-taking.[68] Other types of financial imbalance are also difficult to assess. For example, when does lending growth, corporate and household sector leverage or the external debt position of a country reach a level which is likely to generate financial instability? Again, the active use of indicators and the comparisons with norms derived from the past are helpful but inconclusive instruments to assess new specific cases.

Turning to the micro-prudential dimension, it focuses on the financial conditions and risks of individual institutions, and compares it with similar institutions ('peer group analysis').[69] Traditionally, it has regarded developments in macroeconomic and financial market conditions as given for an individual entity. The approaches followed by supervisory authorities have not been well suited to measuring risks which are correlated or concentrated in a larger number of institutions, or which could lead to system-wide vulnerabilities. They have often disregarded the feedback effects on overall developments caused by the behaviour of individual institutions. Nowadays, supervisory authorities spend considerable resources on assessing the risks run by individual institutions from the micro-prudential perspective. There is no standardised approach, although a recent survey of supervisory risk measurement practices indicates that supervisors tend to emphasise relative, or cross-sector, risk assessment rather than system-wide assessment or time (or cyclical) variation in risk.[70]

The 'macro–micro' distinction is common in our days. However, whereas the distinction has some undeniable ground, strict separation of the macro-prudential and micro-prudential dimensions would be conceptually inappropriate and could even be detrimental in practice. The distinction should not be regarded as a hard and fast concept. Fundamentally, macro- and micro-prudential analyses and controls are as inseparable as two sides of the same coin. After all, both activities are concerned with the stability of the financial system as a whole, rather than the stability of individual institutions. Actually, an increasing number of supervisory authorities feel quite comfortable with the task of limiting systemic risk and preserving financial stability, rather than preserving the integrity of individual institutions. The danger of a hard separation is that it risks leading to a situation in which neither central banks nor supervisory agencies would be able to perform their functions satisfactorily.[71]

First, to assess the safety of payment systems and other market infrastructures, as well as to be sure that their counterparties are sound and prudent institutions, central banks need micro information. If, to this purpose, they had no reliable information from supervisory sources, or if they were not fully sure that indirect information is adequate, central banks would have to put in place alternative means. Like any other bank, they could always ask their counterparties to provide them with direct information. When selecting the institutions eligible to participate in monetary policy operations or in credit and payment facilities, central banks undoubtedly have both the obligation and the power to exclude institutions for whose soundness they lack sufficient assurance.

Second, supervisory input is important for the conduct of macro-prudential analysis and surveillance. The best results are achieved by combining information coming from supervisory, central bank, and market sources. Moreover, macro-prudential analysis could be misleading if it was only focused on aggregated data and average behaviour, because averages conceal individual situations that can trigger a crisis. Indeed, significant exposure of a single major institution or across institutions can be important sources of financial instability and result in the propagation of risks throughout the financial system.

Third, central bank macro-analyses of the overall economy and of the banking and financial sectors can be valuable for supervisory agencies. These analyses are partly based on information—for example, concerning payment systems and monetary policy operations—available to the central bank only. Past system-wide crises, such as the Scandinavian and Japanese ones, clearly indicate the relevance of the macro-dimension of financial stability, and hence the importance of macro-prudential analysis also for supervisory authorities. Indeed, as Crockett (2000b); pointed out, 'actions that may seem desirable or reasonable from the perspective of individual institutions may result in unwelcome system outcomes'. For instance, a single bank finds it only natural to relax lending standards in an upturn, but if all banks do so an unsustainable lending boom will follow, sowing the seeds of subsequent financial instability. Only effective macro-prudential analysis can highlight overall exposures, relevant for the soundness of individual institutions and merit further investigation by supervisory authorities. This view has not yet been fully incorporated into the traditional micro-prudential paradigm, which tends to consider financial stability to be ensured as long as individual institutions are sound.

As regards their key tools, such as capital charges, provisioning policies, and risk limits, supervisory authorities still feel more comfortable with the micro-prudential perspective, and hence tend not to use prudential tools to respond to financial system-wide or macroeconomic concerns. Whether this attitude should be partially corrected, thus using such tools also to limit financial and economic cycles, is currently an important policy question. A strong counter-argument, made by many supervisory authorities, is that the efforts already under way to upgrade prudential safeguards should be sufficient for maintaining financial stability.[72] Progress in this respect certainly has been important, but it remains that potential credit and asset price cycles, as well as increased exposure by banks to financial market fluctuations, might leave scope for considering more forward-looking supervisory measures. Such measures would strengthen defences during good times by establishing reserves to be drawn upon during bad times.[73]

The issue of increased vulnerability of banks to economic and financial cycles recently has been addressed by many central banks, including the ECB, in the context of the Basel Accord revision.[74] Consensus now exists on the need to avoid strongly pro-cyclical supervisory requirements.

Summing up the discussion of this and the previous two sections, the 'land in between' does exist. The objectives and tools identified for cultivating it are significant and can be effective, albeit less clearly than for monetary policy and prudential supervision. The boundaries and synergies with adjacent lands can be outlined. The financial stability area cannot be ignored by central banks; moreover, it should be the focus of further debate and research.

For a central bank concerned with financial stability, I do not see a fundamental or likely conflict with preserving price stability. In the long-term, price stability is a powerful facilitator of financial stability, and is, in turn, hardly sustainable without financial stability. A successful and long-lasting price stability-oriented monetary policy is most suitable for minimising the risk of a potential conflict between price and financial stability. However, it is not by itself sufficient to ensure financial stability. A successful pursuit of price stability over the medium term might imply accepting, in some instances, a deviation from the price stability objective in the short term for reasons of financial stability. Although maintaining price stability is often the primary objective of a central bank, the relationship between price and financial stability is such that, in the medium term, price stability might even be impaired if measures were not taken to address financial stability concerns in the short term. However, since the synergy between price stability and financial stability is generally strong, situations of conflict would be rare events.

As for the relationship with prudential supervision, the frequent distinction between micro- and macro-prudential tasks should not lead us to forget that the tasks are two sides of the same coin; neither of the two can be effective without the other. Important synergies point to the strong desirability of maintaining close links and information exchange between supervisory authorities and central banks when the two functions are separated.

8.8   The Eurosystem

While the previous sections discussed central banks and financial stability in general terms, referring to different countries and periods depending on the argument, this and the following section focus on the Eurosystem. It serves as a paradigmatic case to explore more concretely the policy tools and actions available to a non-supervisory central bank. To this end it refers to the list of tools in Table 8.1, which, albeit sufficiently complete to support the discussion of a general case, was drawn with the Eurosystem in mind.

Because of its unique legal and geographical features, the Eurosystem is a special central bank. Its single monetary jurisdiction, that is, the single currency area, spans many supervisory jurisdictions, due to the fact that national supervisors have largely retained their responsibility. Meanwhile, the Eurosystem operates within a regulatory framework designed at the EU level. The resulting framework is composed of three distinct legal and geographical entities: the national authorities, responsible for the ongoing supervisory function; the ECB (geographically the euro-area), responsible for monetary policy; and the European Union (geographically the euro-area plus three countries), responsible for regulation. This special structure raises a number of considerations.

First, recalling the arguments of Section 8.2—that is, what makes the banking and financial industry a 'system' is the singleness of the currency and the central bank— the euro-area is, and should be considered as, a single financial system, rather than the sum of many national systems. This holds irrespective of the empirical evidence suggesting differing degrees of integration in the markets for various financial activities.[75] Such a system encompasses a single currency, a central bank system (the Eurosystem), and a payment system linking the participants in a network. In channelling funds across the financial sector as well as to the real economy, banks rely on a common payment system and a single source of central bank liquidity.[76] This per se implies that the stability of the financial system (using the definitions of stability and financial system adopted in Section 8.5), as well as the micro- and macro-prudential functions safeguarding it, has in effect become a euro-area-wide concern.

Second, as argued in Section 8.4, one important source of financial instability may arise from the exposure of banks to financial markets and the tendency of market liquidity to suddenly dry-up in times of crisis. Due to its size and diversified nature, the euro-area has a higher capacity to absorb economic shocks than the financial systems in individual countries used to have before the euro.[77] For example, the integrated euro-area-wide money market has given banks a source of funding which is wider and deeper (and thus more liquid) than the previous national markets.[78] However, this high integration has also increased the risk of cross-border contagion. In particular, major banks operating in the common wholesale system now form a fully integrated network. Furthermore, given the 'tiered structure' of the inter-bank market, a significant problem at a large institution acting as 'money centre bank', can now be easily and immediately transmitted to other countries. The combined effect of a deeper market and an easier cross-border contagion has yet to be ascertained.

Third, while conceptually and economically (not only geographically) distinct from the EU Single Market, the euro-area has, nevertheless, inherited the regulatory and supervisory framework designed for the Single Market. It is based on the general principle that rule-making is European and rule-enforcement is national, or 'European regulation with national supervision (narrowly defined, ref. note 15)'. Four aspects characterise this framework: (*a*) minimum harmonisation of the EU-wide regulation; (*b*) mutual recognition of non-harmonised national rules; (*c*) national competence for ongoing supervision; and (*d*) close cooperation between national authorities.[79] Within this framework, some cooperation has developed in both bilateral and multilateral terms.

For the regulatory and supervisory framework to be effective, both the rules and their implementation should be uniform or at least consistent across the area. This is not the case today. As far as the rules are concerned, banks and other financial intermediaries operate under national rulebooks that, although meant to transpose the common EU legislation, de facto differ widely. As to implementation and enforcement, the supervisor should obviously 'see' the whole system, but this is impossible unless close cooperation and information sharing between central banks and supervisory authorities goes well beyond present practices.[80] To address financial stability concerns from an area-wide perspective, bilateral and especially multilateral cooperation needs to be significantly enhanced. Of course, it must also extend to crisis management, despite the absence of clear references to crisis management in Community legislation. If a crisis occurred at a subsidiary (rather than a branch) of a banking group, the licensing authority of the host country would be expected to address the problem in close cooperation with the home authority of the 'mother' bank.

Finally, an appropriate supervisory framework should not only be effective in addressing financial stability concerns, it should also imply a minimum supervisory burden for the industry, thus supporting efficiency in the financial system. The European Union and the euro-area are now far from this standard. Supervisory reporting requirements and rulebooks still differ markedly between countries. These differences represent major obstacles to cost-efficiency for financial groups active in different countries and/or sectors as pointed out in recent reports from the industry (e.g. the report of the 'Forum Group').

After the introduction of the single currency, European policy-makers have repeatedly addressed the appropriateness of the framework for the purposes of the euro-area and the Single Market. The current approach is to fundamentally stick to the framework based on 'European regulation with national supervision' while trying to improve its functioning. Improving the functioning should mean moving forcefully in the direction indicated in the previous two points. The December 2002 decisions of the EU ECOFIN Council represent a step towards greater consistency and lower burden for financial groups operating in several countries, as well as towards more flexible rule-making.[81]

The Eurosystem relates to this whole construction in three principal ways, spelled out by the Treaty. It has the task of contributing 'to the smooth conduct of policies pursued by competent authorities relating to the prudential supervision of credit institutions and the stability of the financial system' (Article 105(5)). It is entrusted with an advisory role in the rule-making process.[82] Additionally, it has the obligation to 'promote the smooth operation of payment systems' (Article 105(2)). The Eurosystem fulfils each of these tasks by way of decisions made by the ECB and executed by the ECB and the national central banks.

8.9   Tools for Action

Embedded in this unique institutional framework, the involvement of the Eurosystem, like that of any central bank without supervisory duties, is directly linked to the central bank instruments as identified in Table 8.1.

These tools include the central bank's role in payment systems, public and private commenting in the area of financial stability, emergency liquidity support operations and, finally, crisis coordination. In this context, one should distinguish between tools aimed at crisis prevention, such as central bank involvement in payment systems, and tools aimed at crisis resolution, such as emergency liquidity support and crisis coordination. An appropriate communication serves both crisis prevention and crisis containment. As discussed earlier in Sections 8.5 and 8.6, monetary policy tools may also serve the purpose of preventing or tackling financial instability. However, the powerful arguments against a mechanical monetary policy reaction to emerging financial instability should not be forgotten.

Payment and settlement systems are the first tool I consider in this review. As indicated earlier in the essay, they are at the nexus of the financial system. Potential risks related to a disruption of the payment circuit—due either to a failing participant or to an operational breakdown—are extremely serious. In addition, credit positions across banks in netting systems can constitute a source of contagion risk.

Central banks have considerably developed mechanisms to limit the potential increase of these various risks. Specifically, in the field of large value payments they have promoted enhanced safety arrangements in net settlement systems,[83] supported the introduction of real-time gross settlement systems (RTGS),[84] and developed the payment and settlement system oversight function.[85] As operators of payment systems, they have unique expertise to identify potential risks and to handle stability problems. In particular, more efforts seem warranted to better use the data from payment systems for identifying liquidity risks.

The Treaty directly implies the ability of the Eurosystem to operate payment systems and set payment system standards. These functions are generally aimed at minimising the danger of system breakdowns and contagion, should an institution fail or a financial market distress occur.

In the euro-area, a single RTGS system, TARGET, has been established, which links together the national RTGS systems of the EU countries.[86] The system was instrumental in the creation of the integrated euro-area money market, in turn a prerequisite for the single monetary policy and more generally for the creation of a single payment area. National netting systems, operating in parallel with TARGET, all meet a same level of safety.[87] Oversight is a direct Eurosystem competence, with national central banks responsible for the systems located in their respective countries. The ECB has been allocated the responsibility for the oversight of certain international systems such as EURO1 and CLS.

Financial stability concerns increasingly also relate to securities clearing and settlement. The tendency towards consolidation in this area, including across borders, although improving efficiency, results in a concentration of transactions in a few systems. The ESCB and the Committee of European Securities Regulators are currently designing safety standards for security settlement systems, including clearing systems.[88] Further risks may arise from the fact that most cross-border transactions are still conducted via custodian banks, rather than through links between national security settlement systems. The growing volume of cross-border transactions has increased the importance of these banks. It is a concern that such entities are currently insufficiently regulated or supervised with respect to their settlement capacity.

Public and private comments, the second tool I consider, can be a powerful additional way to influence market behaviour in a manner, conducive to financial stability. Technically, comments are usually disseminated through financial stability reviews, official statistics, and public statements.[89] Bilateral and private communication with market players, banks, and policy-makers is also quite important. For instance, bilateral consultations with banks always carry an influence, and even include an element of 'moral suasion' when deemed necessary.

There is a view that because central banks are unlikely to possess an information advantage, efficient markets are not influenced by their communication and are perfectly able to deal with irrational expectations on their own. In particular, if central banks were able to assess the development of a destabilising 'herd' or a 'bubble' correctly, they would do so on the basis of information available to other agents as well, so that such a development would be unlikely in the first place.[90] I do not share this view, and I am pleased that some recent academic literature seems to support me.[91] For instance, private market analysts may lack incentives to move against the 'herd', because market participants tend to be evaluated against a benchmark of their peers. It is clear that in such a system, risk adverse agents prefer the safety of being wrong along with everyone else to the slim chance of being right alone.

In reality, the judgement of a central bank has an impact even if its communication does not contain new information. The reason lies, first, in the authority deriving from its high expertise. It also depends on the fact that a central bank does not aim at maximising profits—and therefore faces different incentives from market participants—giving its views a different and greater weight in the marketplace than private sector commentators. In this sense public 'comments' by a central bank may be useful in preventing and containing financial instability. Sometimes public availability of credible information is enough to shift perceptions of investors, and thus prevent detrimental herds or bubbles from developing.[92] Furthermore, given that they speak much less frequently than other market participants, the mere fact that central banks (or other policy-makers) reveal their views may have a stabilising impact on financial markets.[93]

Naturally, the tool of public commenting needs to be used prudently and sparingly to maintain its effectiveness. Just as in monetary policy-making, an essential ingredient of communication in financial stability to be effective is credibility and reputation. Of course, comments could be extremely counterproductive if information is released at the wrong time or turns out to be incorrect.[94] Finding the right words at the right time, with respect to monetary policy as well as financial stability, remains at the core of the art of central banking.

In addition to their judgement on situations and events, central banks can bring to the public helpful information on risk exposures (e.g. lending levels to particular sectors and countries) and other vulnerabilities. When addressing system-wide vulnerabilities, cooperation between central banks and supervisory authorities is valuable to combine the view of macroeconomic and financial risks with information on the exposures of individual financial institutions.[95] Effective communication should include exchange of information between central banks and supervisory authorities (e.g. as regards emergency liquidity assistance to individual institutions), macro-prudential analysis, and surveillance of risks to financial system stability.

The ECB, in cooperation with the national authorities on the Banking Supervision Committee, has established a framework for macro-prudential analyses focusing on the stability of the EU banking sector. As noted in Section 8.7, such analyses are also needed for the effective use of policy tools in the financial stability area by supervisory authorities. Regular internal macro-prudential reports are produced twice a year,[96] as well as ad hoc reports on relevant issues, five of which have been published (e.g. on asset prices and banking stability). As for financial markets, relevant analyses are carried out in cooperation with national central banks, and also benefit from contacts with market participants. For instance, regular monitoring of money markets, as well as of other important financial markets and financial infrastructures is undertaken within the ESCB.

Liquidity injections into the market as a whole (market operations) or into individual institutions (Lending of Last Resort or emergency liquidity assistance, that is, ELA) are the third and most traditional tool available to a central bank for dealing with financial instability.

It is important to recognise that not all liquidity injections aimed at preventing the spreading of a liquidity problem relate to a crisis. As discussed in Section 8.5, central banks routinely offer the lubricant of adequate liquidity against specified collateral requirements in order to support the orderly functioning of markets. For the ECB, this crucial function is not only embedded in the ordinary assessment of the amount to be allotted in the weekly tender. It is also specifically assured by the two standing facilities that regularly and automatically prevent the emergence of liquidity tensions that would otherwise call for discretionary counteractions.[97]

Yet, the eye-catching events are those associated with the rare occasions in which liquidity injections occur once a crisis has already erupted. Such rare events epitomise the image of a central bank's role in financial stability, much more than the ordinary actions aimed at preventing crises, like ordinary liquidity provisions, or setting payment systems standards or, even more, communication. The various recent episodes, reviewed in Section 8.4, have shown how much timely provisions of liquidity can stabilise markets and mitigate the repercussions of shocks.

Also the academic community has focused its attention on liquidity assistance and public bailouts of banks. Early criticism of the ECB, for example, doubted its capability to act (e.g. CEPR 1998) should a liquidity crisis occur. I regard these doubts as not warranted.[98] The arrangements concerning ELA have been revised in conjunction with the launch of the euro in order to adapt to the new institutional and operational framework created by the euro. Generalised liquidity operations via market operations are in the Eurosystem's area of competence, whereas ELA to individual institutions remains, according to an agreement reached in 1999, a national competence and outside the direct scope of Eurosystem policies. Accordingly, the associated costs and risks are to be incurred by the national central banks concerned.[99] However, in the Eurosystem, the normal communication channels have to be activated to address the potential cross-border effects in liquidity crises, and the ECB would become involved, if required by the scope of the crisis.

The evidence reviewed in Section 8.4 suggests that the transformation of the financial system has increased the potential for liquidity shortages in a crisis. While, in the presence of deposit insurance, bank runs by retail depositors have become less likely, losses of liquidity from wholesale markets have become more important. This suggests that market operations especially aimed at preserving adequate liquidity conditions continue to be central among central bank tools.

The ability shown in responding effectively to the implications of 11 September 2001 has demonstrated the Eurosystem's capacity to deal with liquidity problems. In the days following the attack, many euro-area banks hoarded their liquidity and were unwilling to lend to the market, as reflected in high overnight rates and bid–ask spreads. The Eurosystem reacted by injecting additional funds through fine-tuning operations. Although the Federal Reserve System provided ample liquidity through its discount window and market operations, euro-area banks without a US banking licence were not able to get US dollars through direct access to the discount window. To channel the necessary US dollar funds to euro-area banks, the ECB and the Federal Reserve Bank of New York concluded a USD/EUR swap agreement, followed by corresponding agreements between the ECB and the NCBs and between the NCBs and market counterparties.

It should be noted here that the injection of liquidity required for resolving a crisis does not necessarily take the form of a provision of central bank money. Coordinated private sector solutions without the injection of public funds are also frequent and, as such, they are formally unaffected by the advent of the euro. However, the potential area-wide nature of the issues can call for cross-border cooperation and for an involvement of the Eurosystem to facilitate such solutions.

It is outside the scope of this essay to deal with the issues of solvency support and the interplay between monetary and fiscal authorities and deposit insurance agencies. Some have expressed a concern that there is no EU or euro-area-wide system to authorise or fund solvency support to banks that operate in several countries and whose failure would impinge on many countries (because we do not have a European supervisory and fiscal authority). Hence, it has been argued, support decisions made by national Ministries might be suboptimal in specific cases, as they might ignore the effects in other countries. Also, as has been further observed, home countries might lack the resources needed to rescue a major international bank.[100] It could of course be noted that, in a way, the implied reduction in the supply of solvency support could have a positive aspect, since it could reduce the expectation of public bailouts, and thus reduce moral hazard. This, however, is a partial answer. Undoubtedly, to orderly wind-down and restructure a large failed institution with substantial cross-border operations would constitute a major challenge for cooperation among national authorities. Yet, the current institutional arrangements for handling a solvency crisis are still adequate and can function provided there is increasing cooperation among all relevant authorities from different countries.[101]

Crisis coordination is the fourth and final tool available for dealing with financial instability. For the Eurosystem, as for any central bank, the effectiveness of such a tool can, of course, only be tested in a crisis. Just as a peaceful country should have an effective army even in peacetime because, once an attack comes, it is too late, so the central bank should prepare itself for crises in periods of financial stability. As part of these preparations, the adequate capability of financial institutions to produce relevant information for authorities in a swift manner (contingency plans) has been recently addressed in a number of European and international forums.

In a crisis, there is no alternative to close cooperation and exchange of information between central banks and supervisory authorities. The Banking Supervision Committee has done extensive work to prepare central banks and supervisory agencies to such a contingency. Obviously, the practical issues in crisis coordination, which are always difficult, become especially thorny in the international context.

For example, differences in opinion may arise when assessing the systemic relevance of a problem or when selecting the policy tools to activate. National authorities have a natural inclination to emphasise domestic considerations and may undervalue the legitimate rights of foreign stakeholders.

In concluding this section, it should be stressed that the Eurosystem (like any central bank, irrespective of whether it is the formal supervisor or not) has a strong interest in individual institutions. Indeed, as outlined in Section 8.2, the role of a central bank as the bankers' bank implies a need to be concerned with the soundness of its individual counterparties. This adds to the maintenance of what I have earlier referred to as general conditions of financial stability, or also orderly market conditions.

For the Eurosystem, such interest is reflected in the statutes, which impose upon it the general obligation to operate under the principles of an 'open market economy with free competition' (Treaty Article 105(1)). Moreover, the System has a specific obligation to manage its own exposures prudently. For instance, all credit operations of the Eurosystem must be collateralised.[102] When, in the second half of 1998, the decisions on how to select counterparties were taken, it was decided to delegate the selection to some extent to the supervisory agencies. Indeed, almost without exception, access to Eurosystem monetary operations and the TARGET system is provided to all credit institutions (i.e. banks as defined by the European Union) which meet the requirement of being licensed and supervised by competent national authorities.[103] Of course, such an arrangement can deliver a satisfactory outcome, provided that the regulatory and supervisory arrangements are deemed adequate. Nothing, however, could have prevented the Eurosystem from deciding to check counterparties itself. Moreover, should the eligible institutions encounter severe problems, or should the delegation for any reason be felt as an insufficient guarantee, the Eurosystem would have not only a legitimate right, but also a duty to assure itself of the soundness of its counterparties.

In this context, it should be noted that the Eurosystem already sets to some extent its own standards. This is visible, for example, in the field of settlement systems. In this field the Eurosystem has developed standards that must be met by all EU securities settlement systems as a condition to be eligible for Eurosystem credit operations.[104] In particular, the Eurosystem must be assured that central bank refinancing is granted through procedures, which will prevent central banks from assuming inappropriate risks in conducting monetary policy and intra-day credit operations and which will ensure the same level of safety, regardless of the settlement method. As a consequence, these standards have effectively become supervisory standards and a guide for the industry's development; as such they apply not only to operations related to central bank credit, but also to all kinds of operations.

8.10   Interplay at the Borders

The key points emerging from this essay can be recapitulated as follows. Central banks are bound, by construction, to be involved in financial stability: they are themselves banks with business operations; they must control the soundness of their counterparties; and they are entrusted with the exclusive task of creating ultimate liquidity. No other public or private institution has been invented which is equally capable of avoiding and mitigating the 'indiscriminate public terror' (Bagehot 1873) of a financial crisis. Thus, central banks do play and should play an important role in maintaining financial stability, regardless of the institutional structure for supervision that happens to be adopted in their jurisdiction.

The profound transformation that both financial systems and central banks have undergone over the last quarter century provide impetus for carefully re-examining our approach to financial stability and the role central banks play. The transformation has influenced the kind of financial crises we might face. In particular, because the importance of liquidity and contagion risks is increasing, we should expect an increase in the role of central banks in financial stability. Attention should be paid to the risks stemming from non-bank financial activities and financial market price developments. Given the improvements in risk management techniques and procedures, as well as in the conduct of prudential supervision and payment systems oversight, it is tempting to argue that the probability of a crisis has diminished. This conclusion, however, may be premature, as recent experience and the daily reading of the financial press suggests. At the same time, should a crisis occur, it would probably result in a situation where central bank expertise is in high demand.

This essay has addressed the issue of defining a central banks' function in the field of financial stability and its place among public policies. This function occupies a 'land in between' monetary policy and supervision, somewhat independent of, but also closely related to, both adjacent functions. Smooth interplay on both borders is, therefore, crucial. I do not see a fundamental or likely conflict between preserving price stability and being concerned with financial stability. In special circumstances, however, a central bank could enter a 'price stability versus financial stability' trade-off in the short run. Even though synergies between price stability and financial stability prevail in the longer term, a successful monetary policy (successful in keeping prices stable) will not always be sufficient to prevent financial instability. Hence, central banks cannot be indifferent to financial stability: benign neglect is not an option. The Eurosystem cannot be an exception to this.

Central bank involvement in financial stability is distinct from, and complementary to, supervisory functions. Nevertheless, the role of the central bank absolutely needs the underpinning of an appropriate overall supervisory regime, whether or not it is entrusted to the central bank. A successful conduct of supervisory and central bank functions requires close cooperation and information exchange, and central banks should continue to provide advice on supervisory rules and policies.

There are many unresolved issues on the way to designing successful policies to maintain financial stability. This essay was not intended to be prescriptive or to make strong policy recommendations on each and every issue. Rather, its intention was to provide a road map for discussing salient issues.

Central bank activities addressing financial stability are increasingly preventive. Overseeing payment systems, disseminating information to markets, and setting standards should further increase in importance and lessen the moral hazard arising from being the lender-of-last-resort to illiquid markets and institutions. Central banks are involved in financial stability because they implement monetary policy by managing the liquidity situation in the inter-bank money market. They also usually run the main wholesale payment systems, either settling in central bank money or developing safety standards for systems operating in commercial bank money. As experience has shown (e.g. by reacting to 11 September), central banks swiftly respond to situations of financial distress in a way that mitigates the impact of the event and protects the financial system from systemic risk.

Financial cycles could become stronger in the future because of the increased importance of financial markets for financial and non-financial sectors of the economy. Hence also the risk of disruptive economic booms and busts is likely to remain relevant or even to grow. This could endanger financial stability, even if a sound supervisory framework reduces the risk. The way forward is to enhance cooperation among central banks and supervisory authorities in addressing financial instabilities, and to combine more system-wide and counter-cyclical supervisory policies with the readiness of central banks to address financial stability concerns.

Finally, and turning to the Eurosystem, all the above considerations apply to it as much as to any central bank. In particular, the Eurosystem has very limited supervisory duties, yet has all the typical tools for financial stability that non-supervisory central banks have. Unlike other central banks, financial stability is explicitly mentioned in the Treaty as one of its obligations. Furthermore, the Eurosystem has an obligation to deal only with sound counterparties. Therefore the Eurosystem has a precise interest in strong and far-reaching European supervisory cooperation, as well as in global cooperation under the auspices of the Basel Committee on Banking Supervision. Unnecessary firewalls should not be created between central banks and supervisory bodies.

A euro-area financial system has been created by the very fact of adopting a single currency. Since the euro was introduced, the internal integration of this system is proceeding apace, thus financial stability concerns effectively have become a euro-area-wide issue. This strengthens the case for a further deepening of the area-wide perspective. The euro-area has inherited the supervisory framework established for the needs of the EU Single Market. However, the unique challenge faced by the ECB lies in the threefold separation between the regulatory body (the European Union), the single currency area (the euro-area), and supervisory jurisdictions (each euro-area country). This threefold separation requires special forms of cooperation between public bodies.

Notes

1. The author gratefully acknowledges the assistance and support from Reint Gropp and Jukka Vesala in the preparation of this paper. Valuable input particularly in reading through literature and collecting evidence was also provided by Ivan Alves, Inês Cabral, Carsten Detken, Cornelia Holthausen, Cyril Monnet, and Simone Manganelli. The paper

has greatly benefited from extensive discussions with Vítor Gaspar, Mauro Grande, Philipp Hartmann, and Pierre Petit.

2. The Bank of Japan recently decided to purchase corporate equities held by Japanese banks in order to reduce the market risk within the banking system and to support financial stability. In the United States, a debate has developed on what the Fed did, or did not do, or should have done, to prevent or burst a stock price alleged bubble. In the European Union, a wide debate on how to best organise financial supervision, and on what role central banks should have in it, has occupied officials, academics and the media for years and it is not finished yet.

3. The Eurosystem consists of the European Central Bank (ECB) and the national central banks (NCBs) of the countries that have adopted the single currency. Several Eurosystem NCBs conduct supervisory responsibilities as their national tasks (i.e. outside their tasks within the Eurosystem), while some others do not have such responsibilities.

4. See also Padoa-Schioppa (2002a) and Goodhart and Shoenmaker (1995) for discussion of these issues.

5. In some countries this function was assigned to a commercial bank (e.g. in the United Kingdom), which was no longer permitted to compete with other banks in exchange for this privilege. In others, this function was originally assigned to a private bank (e.g. in Sweden and Denmark) or to a new institution (e.g. in Belgium, France, Germany, Switzerland, and Italy). See Capie et al. (1994) and Goodhart (1991).

6. See, for example, Rockoff (1974). The term 'wildcat' banks refers to banks that issued notes far in excess of what they planned to redeem, located redemption offices in remote areas (hence the association with wildcats), and then disappeared, leaving the public with notes worth considerably less than their original value.

7. See Padoa-Schioppa (1994).

8. See, for example, Gorton (1999), Rolnick et al. (1998), and Calomiris and Kahn (1996).

9. See, for example, Hirch (1977) and Rolnick et al. (1998).

10. See Padoa-Schioppa (2000).

11. See related discussion also in, for example, Kareken and Wallace (1981) and Monnet (2002).

12. Recent analysis has confirmed that the core presumption needed to support free banking is perfect and costless information. See Cavalcanti and Wallace (1999) and Williamson (1999).

13. See Capie et al. (1994), and Goodhart (1991).

14. See, for example, Calomiris and Kahn (1996) and Rolnick et al. (1998).

15. See Miron (1986).

16. To clarify, the term supervision is used here to cover both rule-making (regulation) and rule implementation and enforcement (supervision narrowly defined). The former consists in establishing the rules which financial institutions are required to follow, whereas the latter is concerned with enforcing compliance with the regulations and examining the risk exposures and management of institutions.

17. See Revell (1975) and Goodhart (1991).

18. In some countries this occurred in conjunction with the implementation of Directive 94/19/EC, which requires the existence of a deposit insurance scheme and harmonises the minimum level of protection (at EUR 20 000).

19. Diamond and Dybvig showed that standard deposit contracts in combination with investment in illiquid assets always create the possibility of bank runs, even if the bank in question is solvent (a 'speculative bank run').

20. In the literature this is referred to as 'information induced' bank runs. See Postlewaite and Vives (1987), Chari and Jagannathan (1988). Saunders and Wilson (1996) argue that most US bank runs have been of this type.

21. See, for example, Freixas and Parigi (1996) and Allen and Gale (2000a). Humphrey (1986), using data from the private US clearing house CHIPS, found that roughly a third of participants would default after the failure of one major participant. Less dramatic results were found by Angelini et al. (1996) for an Italian netting system.

22. The pioneering work on moral hazard was carried out by Ross (1973). The first formal analysis of this problem was by Mirrlees (1974).

23. See Gropp and Vesala (2001).

24. This idea is certainly not new and it can even be traced back to Fisher and Simons' writings in the 1930s.

25. According to Wallace (1996), narrow banking limits the ability of the banking sector to transform savings into investments. Kashyap et al. (1999) argue that the benefits of a bank intermediation would disappear, because narrow banking would break the synergies between providing liquidity on both sides of the balance sheet.

26. Wallace (1990) and Diamond and Dybvig (1983) argue that in a bank run situation, a bank should announce a suspension of convertibility. In this way, a solvent bank protects its assets from undesirable runs and ensures that it can fulfil its liabilities later on.

27. See Engineer (1989) or Qi (1994) for theoretical arguments against the suspension of convertibility.

28. This development has occurred in Denmark, Sweden, and Canada and, more recently, in the United Kingdom, Australia, South Korea, and Japan.

29. See Santillán et al. (2000).

30. See, for example, Goodfriend and King (1988).

31. See Rochet and Tirole (1996) for an analysis showing the possibility of such a market failure. In addition, Flannery (1996) shows that high uncertainty associated with a crisis makes it more difficult for banks to estimate counterparty credit risk, and this may cause them to withdraw from the inter-bank market altogether.

32. There seems to be evidence that a properly implemented liquidity support function of a central bank, accompanied by sufficiently stringent supervision, has a positive effect on financial stability. See Miron (1986).

33. See Padoa-Schioppa (2002b).

34. See, for example, Goodhart et al. (1998), Drees and Parsabasioglu (1998) (Nordic crises), and White (1991) (US S&L crisis).

35. First, governments typically gave a blanket guarantee that all banks would meet their obligations. Second, insolvent banks were either temporarily nationalised or forcibly merged, with 'bad loans' being transferred to a state agency. See, for example, for Sweden, England (1999) and Ingves and Lind (1996).

36. Between 1995 and 2000, that is, before the recent market turmoil, capital market transactions by companies in the euro-area increased substantially. In this period bond

issuance grew at its fastest rate ever, resulting in issue volumes growing by a factor of 10 over the period, and the boom continued through 2001.

37. The ECB (2000*a*) highlights a longer-term trend towards an increased share of non-interest income for EU banks.

38. See Board of Banking Supervisors (1995).

39. See Nakaso (2001) for further details.

40. Although the main business of the affected banks was retail lending, most of the banks were heavily reliant on wholesale funding. Their capital ratios were exceedingly high; the median capital ratio of the banks that would subsequently fail was 26%. Nevertheless, the recession of the early 1990s and declining property prices resulted in high pressure on these banks. See Logan (2001).

41. One of the triggers of this crisis was the earlier failure of Penn Square in 1982. The authorities had adopted a 'pay-out' strategy, which implied that all creditors apart from insured depositors would lose their money. The heightened concerns of depositors resulting from this and Continental's aggressive growth increasingly led to funding problems from wholesale deposits, upon which it relied.

42. In fact, at the time of its closure, Continental Illinois' net worth was over $2 billion. See Wall and Peterson (1990), and Jayanti and Whyte (1996) for more information on the event.

43. As liquidity in the secondary market for low-grade bonds suddenly deteriorated following rumours about a change in regulations, which would have greatly reduced the attractiveness of the market, Drexel found it difficult to manage its liquidity through asset sales or collateralised loans. See Allen and Herring (2001).

44. In the LTCM case, financial stability concerns were perhaps related more to this type of contagion than to traditional credit exposures of banks to LTCM through money market instruments and other lending. This can be inferred from the statements made at the time by Fed Chairman Alan Greenspan and President McDonough.

45. In 2001, the combined average daily turnover of the two largest US systems, Fedwire and CHIPS, exceeded USD 2.8 trillion. The relatively new European system, TARGET, now processes around EUR 1.6 trillion per day, three times the amount that all large-value payment systems in the 12 euro-area countries processed together in 1990.

46. Herstatt was heavily involved in FX transactions. When the German authorities closed Herstatt, it had very large amounts of outstanding intra-day debt, especially vis-à-vis its US counterparties, who because of the time difference had already irrevocably paid Deutsche Mark to Herstatt, but had not yet received the corresponding US dollars. The liquidity losses in the American markets were so large that liquidity assistance became necessary.

47. See McAndrews and Potter (2002).

48. Indeed, many central banks—including the Eurosystem—have an explicit reference to financial stability inscribed in their statutes. Recent work by the BIS shows that even those central banks that do not have an explicit mandate consider the pursuit of systemic stability and the stability of the payment and settlement systems as one of their key duties. When there is no explicit mandate, the legal basis for central bank responsibility for financial stability is often found in interpretations of central bank law, or sometimes banking law.

49. The term 'tool' here refers broadly to the possible actions and procedures available to competent public authorities. I omit here discussion of any restructuring and government financial support measures in order to focus on the interplay of central banks' financial stability tools with monetary policy and supervisory measures.

50. The usual distinction is made between money market operations, undertaken at the initiative of the central bank, and standing facilities, used at the initiative of banks.

51. One has to be quite careful here: the stability of individual banks is not an objective of either central banks or supervisors, if a bank failure has no systemic implications. Nevertheless, the supervision of individual banks clearly serves the objective of the stability of the financial system as a whole, but at the same time, while necessary, is not sufficient to achieve the ultimate goal of overall financial stability.

52. See Schwartz (1998) and Bordo and Wheelock (1998).

53. See Schwartz (1998).

54. The Fed increased interest rates by 175 basis points from 4.75 percent to 6.50 percent during this period.

55. See Blinder (1999), Crockett (2000a), and Vinals (2001).

56. See, for example, Cukierman (1990).

57. High volatility of interest rates is a distinguishing feature of monetary policy frameworks characterised by exchange rate or monetary base targeting. Inflation targeting, on the other hand, seems to be more compatible with a high degree of interest rate smoothing.

58. See Mishkin (1997).

59. See Kent and Lowe (1997) and Brousseau and Detken (2001) for further related arguments.

60. See, for example, Allen and Gale (2000b) and Kaufman (1998).

61. Cecchetti, for instance, has advocated a different opinion.

62. See, for example, Cukiermann (1990).

63. See, for example, Goodhart and Huang (1999) and Miller et al. (2002).

64. See Bernanke and Woodford (1997).

65. See, for example, Issing (1998).

66. See the article 'The stock market and monetary policy' in the ECB Monthly Bulletin of February 2002.

67. Such as P/E ratios, equity risk premia, and probability distributions derived from options prices.

68. Fed Chairman Alan Greenspan (2002) recently addressed these issues, also suggesting some future avenues for identifying discrepancies between current asset prices and their fundamental values.

69. See Borio et al. (2001).

70. See Van den Bergh and Sahajwala (2000).

71. Crockett (2000b) and Lamfalussy (2002) recently echoed this view.

72. See, for example, the strategy formulated in the G10 and the core set of international standards available from the Financial Stability Forum (www.fsforum.org).

73. This could include adjusting capital buffers in boom periods (e.g. via stress testing), establishing forward-looking provisions against expected but yet not realised risks ('dynamic

provisions') and adopting counter-cyclical collateral valuation and loan-to-value ratios. See, for example, Borio and Lowe (2002) and Crockett (2000*b*).

74. See ECB (2001).

75. See Padoa-Schioppa (2001) for more detailed discussion of this issue.

76. This obviously does not preclude the existence of linkages and contagion between financial systems. A 'global' financial system would then be considered a network of financial systems.

77. See Duisenberg (2001).

78. See Santillán et al. (2000) for evidence of this rapid integration and ECB (2002) evaluation of banks' liquidity risk management.

79. The first two principles concerning regulation were adopted in Community legislation in the mid-1980s in order to accelerate the creation of the Single Market, including financial services. In 1999, as integration has remained incomplete, the European Commission identified a number of areas for action by 2005 (the Financial Services Action Plan). The principle of national supervision maintains that every financial institution operates throughout the Single Market under the authority of the home country who had issued its licence. This allows the supervisory authority responsible for each institution to be identified unambiguously.

80. The Economic and Financial Committee of the European Union (2000) recommended fostering the exchange of information on the major financial institutions and market trends among supervisory authorities and central banks ('Brouwer I report'). Another report of the Committee (2001) called for strengthened information exchange and coordination of policies across national authorities in crisis situations. The report also notes that central banks need to be involved at an early stage in a crisis ('Brouwer II report').

81. The decisions of the ECOFIN Council are in line with the proposals of the Committee of Wise Men (2001) concerning the securities industry, but now applied to all financial sectors and financial conglomerates. The system relies on the establishment of new regulatory ('level 2') and supervisory committees ('level 3'), for the functions of establishing common rules and ensuring their consistent implementation, respectively. To exploit the synergies between banking supervision and central banking, both national banking supervisory authorities and non-supervisory central banks, including the ECB, will attend the new 'level 3' banking committee. For details, see the press release on the 2471st ECOFIN Council meeting of 3 December 2002.

82. According to Article 105(4), the ECB must be consulted on any draft Community and national legislation on issues falling within its field of competence. According to Article 25(1) of its Statute, the ECB can provide, on its own initiative, advice on the scope and implementation of the Community legislation in these fields.

83. In 1990, the G10 *'Report on Inter-bank Netting Schemes'* (Lamfalussy Report) set minimum safety standards for net settlement systems. Following the report most systems in the world have amended their operational rules and procedures. The follow-up report in 2001, *'Core Principles for Systemically Important Payment Systems'*, complemented the standards and extended their applicability globally.

84. RTGSs became technically feasible and cost-efficient in the mid-1980s, when the development of ICT removed virtually all obstacles to increasing the velocity of money. RTGS ensures the immediate finality of each payment, thereby eliminating intraday counterparty risk positions between banks and thus substantially reducing contagion risks. The risk of a payment system gridlock and liquidity shortfall, however, remains in place.

85. The oversight function aims to ensure the soundness of the systems from the legal, credit, liquidity, and operational risk control and governance viewpoints. It ranges from setting standards to monitoring systems and assessing their compliance with the standards.

86. TARGET is an EU-wide system for euro payments. It is a real-time gross settlement (RTGS) system for the euro consisting of fifteen national RTGS systems and the ECB Payment Mechanism.

87. Such levels have to be at least equivalent to that required in the 'Lamfalussy Report'.

88. This work also relies on the global standard setting of the CPSS and IOSCO.

89. In the European Union, the Austrian, Belgian, Danish, Finnish, French, Spanish, Swedish, and the UK central banks issue financial stability reviews at the moment.

90. See, for example, Santos and Woodford (1997) for a recent formulation. However, see Tirole (1985) and Allen and Gale (2000*b*) for the possibility of bubbles even if all players are rational, but there is, nevertheless, no room for beneficial announcements by authorities.

91. Alternatively, a public announcement can help bring prices back in line with fundamentals. See Abreu and Brunnermeier (2001).

92. Technically, 'herding' is observed if there is a convergence of behaviour, that is, if agents ignore private information and follow the actions of others. A 'bubble' occurs if rational agents know that the price of an asset is too high relative to fundamentals, but they believe that they can unwind their positions at a higher price before the bubble bursts. See Brunnermeier (2001), Bikhchandani et al. (1992), Banerjee (1992), and Lee (1998).

93. In this spirit Bhattacharya and Weller (1997) argue that a central bank intervention can stabilise foreign exchange markets. In addition, Heinemann and Illing (2002) show that greater transparency on the part of the central bank can reduce the probability of speculative attacks.

94. It might also happen that agents overreact to imprecise information from central banks, thereby increasing volatility and decreasing welfare. See, for example, Morris and Shin (2002).

95. This was the objective in some of the publications of the Banking Supervision Committee. See in particular ECB (2000*b*).

96. The techniques for assessing banking sector stability involve a systematic and regular monitoring of developments on the basis of the interpretation of quantitative macro-prudential indicators (MPIs) together with the qualitative assessment carried out by the authorities with detailed information on the risks of individual banks. In addition, forward-looking information from public (e.g. financial market) sources on bank and non-financial sector health are used to complement the picture.

97. A significant demonstration of the usefulness of these facilities to prevent monetary and financial disruptions was given on the occasion of Y2K, when, contrary to other central banks in the world, the ECB did not need to put up special measures to handle the much feared shortages of central bank money.

98. See also Padoa-Schioppa (1999).
99. Nevertheless, the agreement includes measures to ensure management of the monetary consequences of the ELA operations to maintain an appropriate monetary policy stance and to ensure adequate information exchange about the potential cross-border effects. For these reasons, for large operations there has to be advance information to and consent from the Governing Council of the ECB. In the case of smaller operations, information exchange after the event has been deemed sufficient. See, for example, the ECB's Annual Report for 1999.
100. See Goodhart (2002) and Freixas (2002).
101. See the Economic and Financial Committee of the European Union (2001).
102. See Article 18(1) of the Statute. Collateralisation is, of course, not a perfect substitute for checking the soundness of the counterparties, because the market value of collateral can suffer in times of crisis.
103. See '*The Single Monetary Policy in the Euro Area: General Documentation on Eurosystem Monetary Policy Instruments and Procedures*', ECB, Apr. 2002 (update of the Nov. 2000 edition). See also '*TARGET—Update 2001*', ECB, Nov. 2001.
104. See '*Assessment of EU Securities Settlement Systems against the Standards for Their Use in ESCB Credit Operations*', ECB, Sept. 1998.

References

Abreu, D. and Brunnermeier, M. (2001). 'Bubbles and Crashes', Working Papers in Economic Theory, Princeton University, *Econometrica*, forthcoming.

Allen, F. and Gale, D. (2000*a*). 'Financial Contagion', *Journal of Political Economy*, 108(1): 1–33.

—— and —— (2000*b*). 'Bubbles and Crises', *Economic Journal*, 110: 236–55.

—— and Herring, R. (2001). 'Banking Regulation versus Security Markets Regulation', Working Paper Wharton Financial Institutions Center, July.

Angelini, P., Maresca, G., and Russo, D. (1996). 'Systemic Risk in the Netting Systems', *Journal of Banking and Finance*, 20: 853–68.

Bagehot, W. (1873). *Lombard Street: A Description of the Money Market* (London: H. S. King of London).

Banerjee, A. (1992). 'A Simple Model of Herd Behaviour', *The Quarterly Journal of Economics*, 107: 797–817.

Basel Committee on Banking Supervision (1997). *Core Principles for Effective Banking Supervision*, Basel.

Benink, H. and Bossaerts, P. (2001). 'An Exploration of Neo-Austrian Theory Applied to Financial Markets', *Journal of Finance*, 56(3): 1011–27.

Benston, G. and Kaufman, G. (1995). 'Is the Banking and Payments System Fragile?', *Journal of Financial Services Research*, 5: 209–40.

Bernanke, B. and Woodford, M. (1997). 'Inflation Forecasts and Monetary Policy', *Journal of Money Credit and Banking*, 29(4): 663–84.

Bhattacharya, U. and Weller, P. (1997). 'The Advantage of Hiding One's Hand: Speculation and Central Bank Intervention in the Foreign Exchange Market', *Journal of Monetary Economics*, 39(2): 251–77.

Black, F. (1970). 'Banking and Interest Rates in a World without Money', *Journal of Bank Research*, (1): 9–20.

Bikhchandani, S., Hirshleifer, D., and Welch, I. (1992). 'A Theory of Fads, Fashion, Custom, and Cultural Change as Informational Cascades', *Journal of Political Economy*, 100: 992–1026.

Blinder, A. (1999). 'General Discussion: Monetary Policy and Asset Price Volatility', *Federal Reserve Bank of Kansas City Economic Review*, 4: 139–140.

Briault, C. (1999). *The Rationale for a Single National Financial Services Regulator*, FSA Occasional Paper Series, 2.

Board of Banking Supervisors (1995). *Report of the Board of Banking Supervision Inquiry into the Circumstances of the Collapse of Barings*.

Bordo, M. and Wheelock, D. (1998). 'Price Stability and Financial Stability: The Historical Record', *Federal Reserve Bank of St. Louis Review*, Sept./Oct.: 41–62.

Borio, C. and Lowe, P. (2002). 'Asset Prices, Financial and Monetary Stability: Exploring the Nexus', BIS Working Papers, 114, July.

—— Furfine, C., and Lowe, P. (2001). 'Pro-cyclicality of the Financial System and Financial Stability: Issues and Policy Options', in *Marrying the Macro- and Micro-prudential dimensions of Financial Stability*, BIS Working Papers 1, Mar.

Brousseau, V. and Detken, C. (2001). 'Monetary Policy and Fears of Financial Instability', ECB Working Paper, 89, Nov.

Brunnermeier, M. (2001). *Asset Pricing under Asymmetric Information: Bubbles, Crashes, Technical Analysis, and Herding* (Oxford: Oxford University Press).

Brunsson, N. and Jacobsson, B. (2000). *A World of Standards* (Oxford: Oxford University Press).

Calomiris, C. and Kahn, C. (1996). 'The Efficiency of Self-Regulated Payment Systems: Learning from the Suffolk System', *Journal of Money, Credit, and Banking*, 28(4): 766–97.

Capie, F., Goodhart, C., Fischer, S., and Schnadt, N. (1994). *The Future of Central Banking* (Cambridge: Cambridge University Press).

Cavalcanti, R. and Wallace, N. (1999). 'A Model of Private Bank-Note Issue', *Review of Economic Dynamics*, 2(1): 104–36.

CEPR (Centre for Economic Policy Research) (1998). *The ECB: Safe at Any Speed?* (London).

Chari, V. and Jagannathan, R. (1988). 'Banking Panics, Information, and Rational Expectations Equilibrium', *Journal of Finance* XLIII (3): 749–61.

Committee of Wise Men (2001). *Report on the Regulation of European Securities Markets*, Feb.

Crockett, A. (2000*a*). *In Search of Anchors for Financial and Monetary Stability*, SUERF Colloquium, Vienna, Apr.

—— (2000*b*). *Marrying Micro and Macro-prudential Supervision*, Speech delivered at the Eleventh International Conference of Banking Supervisors, Basel, Sept.

Cukierman, A. (1990). 'Why Does the Fed Smooth Interest Rates?' in Michael Belongia (ed.), *Monetary Policy on the Fed's 75th Anniversary* (Amsterdam Kluwer Academic Publishers).

Diamond, D. and Dybvig, P. (1983). 'Bank Runs, Deposit Insurance, and Liquidity', *Journal of Political Economy*, 91(3): 401–19.

—— (1984). 'Financial Intermediation and Delegated Monitoring', *Review of Economic Studies*, 3, 393–414.

Dewatripont M. and Tirole, J. (1993). *The Prudential Regulation of Banks* (Lausanne: Editions Payot).

Drees, B. and Pazarbasioglu, C. (1998). *The Nordic Banking Crises: Pitfalls in Financial Liberalisation?* IMF Occasional Paper 161.

Duisenberg, W. (2001). *Contribution of the Euro to Financial Stability*, Apr.

ECB (1999). *The Effects of EMU on the EU Banking Systems*, Feb.

ECB (2000*a*). *EU Banks' Income Structure*, Apr.

ECB (2000*b*). *Asset Prices and Banking Sector Stability*, Apr.

ECB (2001). *The New Capital Adequacy Regime—the ECB Perspective*, Apr.

ECB (2002). *Developments in Banks' Liquidity Profile and Management*, July.

Economic and Financial Committee (2000). *Report on Financial Stability*, Apr.

Economic and Financial Committee (2001). *Report on Financial Crisis Management*, Apr.

Engineer, M. (1989). 'Bank Runs and the Suspension of Deposit Convertibility', *Journal of Monetary Economics*, 24(3): 443–54.

Englund, P. (1999). 'The Swedish Banking Crisis: Roots and Consequences', in Federal Deposit Insurance Corporation (ed.), *Managing the Crisis: The FDIC and RTC Experience 1980–1994*.

Ferguson, R. (2001). G-10 Study on consolidation, 2001, Co-ordinated by R. Ferguson, Vice-Chairman of the Board of Governors of the US Federal Reserve System, Jan.

Flannery, M. (1996). 'Financial Crises, Payment System Problems, and Discount Window Lending', *Journal of Money, Credit, and Banking*, 28(4): 804–24.

Freixas, X. (2002). 'The Role of the Lender of Last Resort in EMU', in Kremers, J., Schoenmaker, D., and Wierts, P. (eds.), *Financial Supervision in Europe* (Amsterdam: Edward Elgar).

Freixas, X. and Parigi, B. (1996). 'Contagion and Efficiency in Gross and Net Interbank Payment Systems', *Journal of Financial Intermediation*, 7(1): 3–31.

Friedman, M. (1960). *A Program for Monetary Stability* (New York: Fordham University Press).

Friedman, B. (1999). 'The Future of Monetary Policy: the Central Bank as an Army with only a Signal Corps?', Paper presented at the Conference on 'Social Science and the Future', Oxford, 7–8 July.

Goodfriend, M. and King, M. (1988). 'Financial Deregulation, Monetary Policy and Central Banking', *Federal Reserve Bank of Richmond Economic Review*, 74(3).

Goodhart, C. (1991). *The Evolution of Central Banks* (Cambridge: MIT Press).

—— (2002). '*The Political Economy of Financial Harmonisation in Europe*', in Kremers, J., Schoenmaker, D., and P. Wierts (eds.) *Financial Supervision in Europe* (Amsterdam: Edward Elgar).

—— Hartmann, P., Llewellyn, D., Rojas-Suarez, L., and Weisbrod, B. (1998). 'Financial Regulation, Why, How and Where Now?' (London and NY: Routledge, Bank of England).

—— and Huang, H. (1999). 'A Model of the Lender of Last Resort', IMF Working Paper 99/39.

—— and Shoenmaker, D. (1995). 'Should the Functions of Monetary Policy and Banking Supervision Be Separated?', *Oxford Economic Papers*, 47(4): 539–60.

Gorton, G. (1999). 'Pricing Free Bank Notes', *Journal of Monetary Economics*, 44: 33–64.

—— and Mullineux, D. (1987). 'The Joint Production of Confidence: Endogenous Regulation and the 19th Century Commercial Bank Clearinghouses', *Journal of Money Credit and Banking*, XiX(4): 457–68.

Greenspan, A. (1997). 'Regulating Electronic Money', in J. Dorn (ed.), *The Future of Money in the Information Age* (Washington DC: Cato Institute).

—— (2002). 'Economic Volatility', Remarks at a symposium organised by the Federal Reserve Bank of Kansas City, Jackson Hole, Wyoming, 27 Aug.

Gropp, R. and Vesala, J. (2001). 'Deposit Insurance and Moral Hazard: Does the Counterfactual Matter?', ECB Working Paper 47.

—— —— and Vulpes, G. (2001). 'Equity and Bond Market Signals as Leading Indicators of Bank Fragility', ECB Working Paper, 150.

Hayek, F. (1945). 'The Use of Knowledge in Society', *American Economic Review*, 35: 519–30.

—— (1948). *Individualism and Economic Order* (Chicago: University of Chicago Press).

—— (1976). *Denationalisation of Money*, (London: Institute of Economic Affairs).

Hicks, J. (1974). *The Crisis in Keynesian Economics* (Oxford: Basil Blackwell).

Hirsch, F. (1977). '*The Bagehot Problem*', The Manchester School of Economic and Social Studies, XLV.

Heinemann, F. and Illing, G. (2002). 'Speculative Attacks: Unique Sunspot Equilibrium and Transparency', *Journal of International Economics*, 58(2): 429–50.

Humphrey, D. (1986). 'Payments Finality and Risk of Settlement Failure', in A. Saunders and L. J. White (eds.), *Technology and the Regulation of Financial Markets: Securities, Futures and Banking* (Lexington Books), 97–120.

Ingves, S. and Lind, G. (1996). 'The Management of the Banking Crises in Retrospect', *Quarterly Review of the Swedish Central Bank*, I.

Issing, O. (1998). *Asset Prices and Monetary Policy: Four Views*, CEPR and BIS, 20–2.

Jayanti, S. and Whyte, A. (1996). 'Global Contagion Effects of the Continental Illinois Failure', *Journal of International Financial Markets, Institutions and Money*, 6: 87–99.

Kareken, J. and Wallace, N. (1981). 'On the Indeterminacy of Equilibrium Exchange Rates', *Quarterly Journal of Economics*, 96: 207–22.

Kashyap, A., Rajan, R., and Stein, J. (1999). 'Banks as Liquidity Providers: An Explanation for the Co-existence of Lending and Deposit-Taking', *Journal of Finance*, 57(1): 33–73.

Kaufman, G. (1998). 'Central Banks, Asset Bubbles, and Financial Stability', Working Paper Series, Federal Reserve Bank of Chicago WP-98-12.

Keeley, M. (1990). 'Deposit Insurance, Risk, and Market Power in Banking', *American Economic Review*, 80, 1183–1200.

Kent, C. and Lowe, P. (1997). 'Asset-Price Bubbles and Monetary Policy', Research Discussion Paper, Reserve Bank of Australia RDP 9709.

King, M. (1999). 'Challenges for Monetary Policy: New and Old', Paper presented at the Symposium on 'New Challenges for Monetary Policy' sponsored by the Federal Reserve Bank of Kansas City, Jackson Hole, Wyoming 27 Aug.

Klein, B. (1974). 'The Competitive Supply of Money', *Journal of Money Credit and Banking*, 6: 4.

Laffont, J.-J. and Tirole, J. (1993). *A Theory of Incentives in Procurement and Regulation* (Boston: MIT Press).

Lamfalussy, A. (2002). *Statement before the Economic and Financial Committee*, Copenhagen, 6 Sept. 2002.

Lee, I. (1998). 'Market Crashes and Informational Avalanches', *Review of Economic Studies*, 65: 741–59.

Logan, A. (2001). 'The United Kingdom's Small Banks' Crisis of the Early 1990s: What Were the Leading Indicators of Failure?', Bank of England Working Paper.

McAndrews, J. and Potter, S. (2002). 'Liquidity Effects of the Events of September 11, 2001', mimeo Federal Reserve Bank of New York.

Merton, R. and Bodie, Z. (1993). 'Deposit Insurance Reform: A Functional Approach', Carnegie Rochester Conference Series on Public Policy 38, North Holland, 1–34.

Miller, M., Weller, P., and Zhang, L. (2002). 'Moral Hazard and the US Stock Market: Analysing the "Greenspan Put"', *The Economic Journal*, 112(478): 171–86.

Mirlees, J. (1974). 'An Exploration in the Theory of Optimum Income Taxation', *Review of Economic Studies*, 38, 175–208.

Miron, J. (1986). 'Financial Panics, the Seasonality of the Nominal Interest Rate, and the Founding of the Fed', *American Economic Review*, 76(1): 125–40.

Mishkin, F. (1997). 'The Causes and Propagation of Financial System Instability: Lessons for Policy Makers', *Review of the Federal Reserve Bank of Kansas City*: 55–96, 1, August.

Monnet, C. (2002). 'Optimal Public Money', ECB Working Paper, 159.

Morris, S. and Shin, H. (1999). '*Risk Management with Interdependent Choice*', *Oxford Review of Economic Policy*, 15(3): 52–62.

—— —— (2002). 'Social Value of Public Information', mimeo London School of Economics, *American Economic Review*, 92(5): 1521–34.

Nakaso, H. (2001). 'The Financial Crisis in Japan during the 1990s', mimeo Bank of Japan.

Padoa-Schioppa, T. (1994). *The Road to Monetary Union in Europe* (Oxford: Oxford University Press).

—— (1999). 'EMU and Banking Supervision', *International Finance*, 2: 295–308.

—— (2000). *Licensing Banks: Still Necessary?* William Taylor Memorial Lecture 5, Group of Thirty, Washington.

—— (2001) 'Is a Euroland Banking System Already Emerging?', in B. Morten et. al. (eds.), *Adapting to Financial Globalisation* (London-New York: Routledge International Studies in Money and Banking 14), 46–58.

—— (2002*a*). 'Financial Supervision: Inside or Outside Central Banks', in Kremers, J., Schoenmaker, D., and Wierts, P. (eds.), *Financial Supervision in Europe* (Amsterdam: Edward Elgar).

Padoa-Schioppa, T. (2002*b*). 'Securities and Banking: Bridges and Walls', London School of Economics Special Paper, 136.

Postlewaite, A. and Vives, X. (1987). 'Bank Runs as an Equilibrium Phenomenon', *Journal of Political Economy* 95(3): 485–91.

Qi, J. (1994). 'Bank Liquidity and Stability in an Overlapping Generations Model', *Review of Financial Studies*, 7(2): 389–417.

Revell, J. (1975). 'Solvency and Regulation of Banks', Bangor Occasional Papers in Economics 5, University of Wales Press.

Rochet, J. -C. and Tirole, J. (1996). 'Interbank Lending and Systemic Risk', *Journal of Money, Credit, and Banking*, 28(4): 733–62.

Rockoff, H. (1974). 'The Free Banking Era: A Re-examination', *Journal of Money, Credit, and Banking*, 6: 141–67.

Rolnick, A. B., Smith, and Weber, W. (1998). 'Lessons from a Laissez-Faire Payment System: The Suffolk Banking System', *Federal Reserve Bank of Minneapolis Quarterly Review* 22(3): 11–21.

Ross, S. (1973). 'The Economic Theory of Agency: The Principal's Problem', *American Economic Review*, 63: 134–9.

Santillán, J., Bayle, M., and Thygesen, C. (2000). 'The Impact of the Euro on Money and Bond Markets', ECB Occasional Paper 1, July.

Santos, M. S. and Woodford, M. (1997). 'Rational Asset Price Bubbles', *Econometrica*, 65: 19–57.

Saunders, A. and Wilson, B. (1996). 'Contagious Bank Runs: Evidence from the 1929–1933 Period', *Journal of Financial Intermediation*, 5(4): 409–23.

Schwartz, A. (1986). 'Real and Pseudo Financial Crises', in Capie, F. and Wood, G. (eds.), *Financial Crises and the World Banking System* (London: Macmillan).

—— (1998). 'Why Financial Stability Depends on Price Stability?', in Wood, G. (ed.), *Money, Prices and the Real Economy* (Cheltenham: Edward Elgar).

Stigler, G. (1988). *The Theory of Economic Regulation* (Chicago: University of Chicago Press).

Spaventa, L. (2002). Introductory statement in the 2001 Annual Report of the CONSOB, Rome.

Tirole, J. (1985). 'Asset Bubbles and Overlapping Generations', *Econometrica*, 53: 1499–528.

Tobin, J. (1985). 'Financial Innovation and Deregulation in Perspective', *Bank of Japan Monetary and Economic Studies*, 3: 19–29.

Van den Bergh, P. and Sahajwala, R. (2000). 'Supervisory Risk Assessment and Early Warning Systems', Basel Committee on Banking Supervision Working Paper, 4.

Vinals, J. (2001). 'Monetary Policy Issues in a Low Inflation Environment', in Garcia Herrero, A. et al. (eds.), *Why price stability* (Frankfurt: European Central Bank).

Wall, L. and Peterson, D. (1990). 'The Effect of Continental Illinois' Failure on the Financial Performance of Other Banks', *Journal of Monetary Economics*, 26: 77–99.

Wallace, N. (1990). 'A Banking Model in Which Partial Suspension Is Best', *Federal Reserve Bank of Minneapolis Quarterly Review*, 14(4): 11–23.

—— (1996). 'Narrow Banking meets the Diamond-Dybvig Model', *Federal Reserve Bank of Minneapolis Quarterly Review*, 20(1): 3–13.

White, L. (1991). *The S&L Debacle*, (Oxford: Oxford University Press).

Williamson, S. (1999). 'Private Money', *Journal of Money, Credit, and Banking*, 31(3): 469–91.

Index

Note: Information in notes is indicated by n after the page number.